Along the Sandy
Our Nikkei Neighbors

by

Clarence Mershon

Clarence E. Mershon

A project by Clarence Mershon, Crown Point Country Historical Society, to recognize and honor our neighbors of Japanese ancestry, who farmed the land as our parents did and whose children were our classmates in East Multnomah County schools. Their sons fought alongside their school mates in World War II against a common enemy.

© 2006, Clarence Mershon. This book contains some information previously published in the following: Mershon, Clarence E., *Living East of the Sandy, Volume 1*, © 1999; Mershon, Clarence E., *Living East of the Sandy, Volume 2*, © 2003; and Mershon, Clarence E., *East of the Sandy, The Two World Wars*, © 2001. No part of this publication may be reproduced or distributed in any form or by any means, or stored in any database or retrieval system without the prior written permission of Clarence Mershon.

First Edition published in 2006.

Library of Congress Control Number: 2006902003

U.S. History - West Coast - Oregon
    East Multnomah County - An oral history of persons of Japanese Ancestry living in Oregon prior to World War II. Farming - Internment - Serving in the Armed Forces

Front Cover: The Uyetake Farm on Mershon Road has been in the family since 1918. Shio and Nobuko Uyetake now live there. The Mershon family farm bordered the Uyetake farm on the west, south and east.

Back Cover: Jack Asakawa, left, is among the some 3600 Nisei soldiers awarded the Purple Heart for war injuries. George Nishimura, right, received the Silver Star Medal after taking out a German machine gun emplacement, killing its crew, capturing three prisoners and holding off an enemy counterattack as his platoon withdrew.

Published by Guardian Peaks Enterprises
1220 N.E. 196th Avenue
Portland, Oregon 97230

Foreword

On February 19, 1942, President Franklin D. Roosevelt issued Executive Order No. 9066, which authorized and directed the Secretary of War "to prescribe military areas in such places and of such an extent as he or the appropriate Military Commander may determine, from which any and all persons may be excluded, and with respect to which the right of any persons to enter, remain in, or leave, shall be subject to whatever restrictions the Secretary of War or the appropriate Military Commander may impose at his discretion." President Roosevelt cited the successful prosecution of the war as requiring "every possible protection against espionage and against sabotage to national-defense materiel, national-defense premises, and national-defense utilities," as the rationale for the order.

In response, on May 7, 1942, Lieutenant General J.L. DeWitt, Military Commander, Western Defense Command, issued exclusion orders, a sample of which is found on page 121. U.S. Army military police nailed a notice on nearly every light pole in our community east of the Sandy River. The "persons of Japanese ancestry" had *five days* to prepare for and move to the assigned assembly area; *five days* to crate their furnishings for storage; *five days* to find a neighbor willing to store and care for their personal possessions, photographs and artifacts; *five days* to find someone to care for their home and farm; *five days* to sell their farm machinery and vehicles; *five days* to dispose of their livestock, including work horses; *five days* to prepare for an unknown future, taking only bedding and linens, toilet articles, clothing, dishes and personal effects.

After a decade of difficult times for farmers, economic conditions improved in 1940, largely due to the war-induced shortages of food and fibre. In 1940, potatoes, which had sold for one-half cent a pound a year earlier (if the crop could be sold at all) brought two cents a pound, a four-fold increase. Strawberries, which had sold for five cents a pound a year earlier also quadrupled in price. One of our neighbors, the Takeuchi family, did so well in 1940 that Hiro Takeuchi purchased a brand new 1941 Pontiac club coupe, the latest in stylish automobiles. After years of discouragement, low prices and difficult markets, the fortunes of local farmers seemed bright; the destruction in Europe foretold a thriving market for the produce of local farms.

The December 7, 1941, attack by the Empire of Japan at Pearl Harbor certainly created uncertainty and anxiety for our neighbors of Japanese ancestry. However, their youngsters continued to attend Springdale and Corbett schools without incident. They harvested the spring crop of spinach, which sold for a good price. Early potatoes were planted and the strawberry fields, weed-free and carefully tended, were in bloom, portending a bumper crop. The cabbage and cauliflower beds had been seeded, with sufficient plants emerging to plant acres of cabbage and cauliflower. Both will bring a good price; cauliflower, which sold for for twenty-five cents a crate during the depression years will bring $2.00 per crate in 1942; cabbage, which sold for fifty-cents per crate will bring $2.25. With strawberries and potatoes, the hard, painstaking work is done and the harvest near.

However, our neighbors, these very efficient and productive farm families, will not share in the prosperity engendered by the conflict that affects them so personally. Hiro Takeuchi sells his new 1941 Pontiac at a bargain price. Their farm equipment will be used by others. The farmers that rent the fields left by our neighbors on May 12, 1942, will prosper. Because of good prices and excellent markets, these farmers build up their wealth during the war years. This war-driven prosperity often provides the capital that allows them to purchase the land that our Nikkei neighbors formerly farmed. For many Nikkei families, after being torn in 1942 from a stable and secure life on the farm, their world suddenly shrinks to a confined, monotonous existence in a facility built for animals. The "assembly center" to which our neighbors reported was the Pacific International Livestock Exposition Center near Jantzen Beach in North Portland. There, stalls and other areas designed for livestock were hastily converted to living quarters for families. Horse-high plywood walls separated families, but did not provide privacy. And the center's restrooms were inadequate to accommodate the sudden influx of thousands of individuals, from the aged to the new-born. A crash program to build internment camps was underway, but most of our neighbors spent the summer months of 1942 at the center, lacking privacy, adequate toilet and bathing facilities and furnishings. To make matters worse, the hot summer days of 1942 brought innumerable flies, which added to the discomfort experienced. Our neighbors' loss of freedom, privacy and dignity there is only the beginning of an interlude unimaginable to most Americans. Because of their Japanese ancestry, our neighbors have become a prisoners-of-war in their own land. In the Sakurai family, seven of eight are American citizens (see "Internment," this volume). Our neighbors of German or Italian ancestry did not suffer a similar fate.

Terms

Issei - Persons of Japanese ancestry born in Japan, who immigrated to the U.S.

Nikkei - Persons of Japanese ancestry, all generations, including Issei, Nisei and Sansei.

Nisei - Persons born in the United States of Issei parents, literally, the 2nd generation.

Sansei - Persons born in the United States of Nisei parents, literally the 3rd generation.

Dedication

This book is dedicated to my neighbors, who were "evacuated" in 1942 because they were, in the Western Defense Command's words, "of Japanese ancestry, both alien and non-alien [U.S. citizens]."

Shio Uyetake

Shio Uyetake: The Uyetake family was the Mershon family's nearest neighbor until May 12, 1942. On that date, neighborhood youngsters, including the author and his sister, Isabelle, stood by Lucas Road to wave goodbye to our childhood friends and neighbors. During depression years, my brother, sister and I picked berries for Shio's father. All members of the Uyetake family worked in the fields. They knew the hard work required to bring a crop to harvest; their produce was clean and their berries, large. They too knew the disappointments of depression days when beautiful, unsold crops of cabbage and cauliflower were disked under. In 1945, the Uyetake family returned to the farm they owned. Shio Uyetake has been a member of the the Pioneer Association and the Crown Point Country Historical Society for years. He and the author are life-long friends. In 2002, Shio spoke to members of the Crown Point Country Historical Society (CPCHS) about his experiences during the war.

Lily (Sakurai) Kajiwara: Lily Sakurai grew up on a farm located off Wand Road on "cabbage hill" about one-half mile west of the Mershon farm. Scheduled to graduate from Columbian High School in 1942, the "evacuation" of people of Japanese ancestry kept her from participating in the ceremony with her classmates, though she received her diploma. When the Western Defense Command issued its exclusion order on May 7, 1942, forcing the Sakurai family from their farm, seven of the eight Sakurai family members affected were United States citizens. The family's final trip in their new automobile was to the Troutdale assembly point, where they turned it over to a buyer. The Sakurai family, with other Nikkei families, traveled to the Portland Assembly Center by bus. Lily spoke of her experiences at the CPCHS meeting mentioned above. The stories related by Lily, Leke Nakashimada and Shio Uyetake were a major factor in the author's decision to document how this momentous event affected our neighbors.

Lily (Sakurai) Kajiwara

Leke Nakashimada

Leke Nakashimada: Leke Nakashimada's family leased a farm on "cabbage hill" from Alma Bramhall. In 1942, after the family was forced from the farm by the Western Defense Command's order of May 7, 1942, the author (age 11) helped harvest the Nakashimada family's strawberry field. For several years he cultivated with a horse, Pack, left behind when the family reported as ordered to the Portland Assembly Center. Leke has been extremely helpful to the author in finding veterans of the 442nd Regimental Combat Team who lived "along the Sandy [River]." Leke also shared his wartime experiences with the members of the Crown Point Country Historical Society in 2002. He has assisted the author in obtaining information about Nisei who served in the Army during World War II. He has also been most helpful by introducing the author to Nikkei families who are often reticent about sharing information.

Two other veterans of the 442nd Regimental Combat Team have been particularly helpful to the author. They are recognized for their efforts of behalf of other Nisei who served their country during World War II and later. Both deserve recognition for what they have done to make the accomplishments of the "little iron men" known.

Kazuo "Kaz" Fujii

Kaz Fujii helped the author locate several veterans or a surviving member of a veteran's family, which enabled the author to complete this work. He has been active in the effort to fund the World War II memorial in Washington, D.C.

Art Iwasaki

Art Iwasaki, recipient of the Purple Heart with an Oak Leaf Cluster, grew up on a farm in Hillsboro. He has been active in the effort to gain recognition for all Nisei veterans, whether they served in the 442nd, the Military Intelligence Service or another branch.

Contents

Foreword iii

Dedication v

Farmers of Japanese Ancestry "East of the Sandy"

    Roy Ken/June Kondo 1

    Gisaburo/Takaye Kuge 7

    Shigeko/Kiyomi Matsubu 11

    Tatsuzo/Kisano Nakashimada 18

    Shintaro/Tatsu Okita 25

    Masaru/Chiyoko Sakurai 30

    Sakajiro/Yaye Takeuchi 36

    Kaguma/Yone Toya 45

    Juichi/Chise Uyetake 50

Farmers of Japanese Ancestry "West of the Sandy"

    Iomon/Kiku Asakawa 55

    Bukichi/Yoshino Fujii 63

    George/Tsugi Kumazawa 70

    Katumi/Sakae Mishima 77

    Hikosaku/Suga Murahashi 80

    Sakaju/Seki Naemura 83

    Josuke/Tsutano Nakata 89

    Etsuo/Shizuno Namba 93

    Ikasburo/Mizu Onchi 102

    Roy Rikizo/Asa Shiiki 108

    Minekishi/Sute Tamura 115

Internment 121

Nisei Veterans	141
Bob Minoru Ando	151
Jack Asakawa	155
Edward Fujii	157
James "Jim" Fujii	158
Kazuo Fujii	159
Menow M. Hara	165
Arthur Iwasaki	171
Ike Iwasaki	176
Yoshio Kinoshita	181
Toshiaki "Toshi" Kuge	184
Richard Mishima	188
Leke Nakashimada	190
Takey Nakashimada	192
Kennie and Tom Namba	195
George Nishimura	199
Frank Okita	205
Joe Masayuki Onchi	207
Jim Sadaki Onchi	212
Frances/John Ota	214
Ray Shiiki	217
Shigeru Takeuchi	220
Shiro Takeuchi	222
George and Fred Toya	224
Nisei "Gold Star" Veterans	228
Sources/Special Note	236
Index	237

The Kondo Family

Front, from left: Oscar and June (holding Helen). Rear: John, Roy, Roy Ken, Mary and Henry Kondo.
Photo courtesy of Helen (Kondo) Okai.

Roy Ken Kondo
June (Takashima) Kondo

Roy K. Kondo, born August 12, 1882, in Nagoya, Honshu Island, Japan, emigrated to the United States when he "was age 16 or 17," according to family members. Apparently, he soon migrated to Colorado, where he farmed. June Takashima, born in Fukuoka, Japan, on January 1, 1899, remained in Japan with her mother and siblings when her father emigrated to the United States in the early 1900s. In 1912, after becoming established, Takashima sent for his family, who joined him in the United States. June Takashima met Roy Ken Kondo, likely through the customary intermediary, and the couple married, probably in 1917 or early 1918. The couple lived on the Colorado farm where their first two children were born: Roy, in 1919; and Mary, in 1920. Shortly after Mary was born, Kondo moved his family to a farm in Laramie, Wyoming, and planted 300 acres of lettuce. According to his son, Roy, the lettuce "bolted rather than heading up," so Mr. Kondo decided to take up dairying. That farm venture also failed, which led Mr. Kondo to obtain work with the Union Pacific Railroad as a laborer. The family lived in company housing in Hanna,

1935 Graduates, Springdale Grade School

From left: John Kondo, Clarence Lucas, Elaine Collins, Fred Toya, Floyd Bates and Harold Shelley. Teacher: Mrs. Lillian Strachan.   *Photo, the author.*

Wyoming. Through hard work, diligence and a willingness to accept responsibility, Kondo advanced to the position of section foreman. During the years he worked for Union Pacific, three more children were born: John, in 1921; Henry, in 1922; and Oscar, in 1924. In 1927, Roy Kondo decided to try farming once again, and moved his family to Damascus, Oregon, where June's parents lived.

Roy Kondo's search for a suitable farm to rent took him to East Multnomah County where he found a 60-acre place near Springdale, Oregon, which had a two-story home for his family and a barn to shelter the horses he had acquired. Roy and June moved their family to the Farquahar place, which bordered Christensen Road and Northway Road. At the time, Northway Road, which fronted the home, was an unimproved wagon road, but it provided a short cut to Springdale for neighborhood kids walking to school. Less than one-half the acreage was tillable, the balance being timbered and sloping to a bluff above the Sandy River. The tillable land had previously been used for pasturing livestock, so Kondo experienced some difficulty in getting the ground plowed and worked so that he could plant. Since Kondo had horses, he hired an experienced local "teamster," Fred Kerslake, to plow the ground.

Similarly to other farmers in the area, he planted strawberries, which were picked for the fresh market or for the Gresham Farmers' Cooperative. He grew peas, lettuce, broccoli, cauliflower and cabbage, which were primarily marketed at the Eastside Farmers' Market. He also grew cucumbers, which were

Cabbage Planting Time, Kondo Farm ca 1937

From left: Henry Kondo (carried plants), Mary Kondo (sticker), Grace Kerslake (sticker), Charles Youngblood (shovel), Oscar Kondo (front - carried plants) and Roy Kondo (shovel).   *Photo courtesy of Grace Kerslake.*

contracted through Libby, McNeil and Libby's field man, Ron Burnett. The firm had a processing and pickling plant in S.E. Portland. The Kondos worked the land with horses, using a plow, a springtooth cultivator, a harrow and a plank (for leveling [floating] the ground). The latter smoothed the ground so that a seeder could be used. With five youngsters old enough to help on the farm, Roy Kondo did not have to hire much "outside" help. Similarly to other youngsters of that era, his children helped till the ground, plant the crops, weed, cultivate and hoe, and help with the harvest. The youngsters, with some "outside" help, planted acres of cabbage, cauliflower and broccoli by hand. This required a two-person team, one to man a shovel and a second to place the

Roy Kondo, U.S. Army

Roy Kondo's schooling as a dentist was interrupted by the war. After completing his training in Kansas, he served two years in the Army.

Photo courtesy of Roy Kondo.

plant. Rows were marked and the person with the shovel would scrape the ground to reveal moisture and plunge the shovel in to make a hole. The "sticker" would insert a plant into the hole, which the "shoveler" would pack in with his foot as he simultaneously withdrew the shovel. During the harvest, Roy Kondo loaded his truck with farm produce to sell at the early wholesale market, leaving the farm around 3:00 a.m. Each farmer rented a "stall," displayed his produce and hoped that the family's care in harvesting and packing the vegetables would attract a buyer. Sometimes a wholesale buyer would take an entire load; other times, just one crate. Produce not sold would be delivered to Pacific Fruit on consignment.

In 1931, during the period that the Kondos lived in Springdale, their sixth child, Helen, was born. The youngsters attended Springdale Grade School (SGS), a two-room schoolhouse located on the Columbia River Highway across from Art Groce's mercantile store. When Roy and Mary graduated from SGS in 1933, Mr. Kondo took the entire class and their teacher, Lillian Strachan, to the Oregon State Fair in Salem; kids and teacher transported in Mr. Kondo's farm truck. In 1936, Roy Kondo moved his family to a 40-acre farm at Orient, purchased in his oldest son's (Roy's), name. Because of the move, Roy, Mary, John and Henry graduated from Gresham High School, rather than Columbian High School (CHS) in Corbett. Though the Orient farm was smaller, nearly all the land was tillable, so Kondo actually had more land to farm. He decided to plant more berries, particularly blackberries, loganberries and boysenberries, in addition to his usual crops. He kept the Springdale farm for a time after the move to Orient, and also purchased more farm land in Gresham, again in his son's name.

On May 12, 1942, the Kondo family, together with other Nikkei families in the area, was forced from their home and land. Kondo family members quickly became disenchanted with living conditions at the Pacific Livestock Exposition Center. When representatives of the Army sought families willing to help prepare the Tule Lake Camp for the influx of Nikkei families to come, Roy Kondo volunteered. Consequently, the Army sent the Kondo family there to

The Kondo Siblings, 1993

Front, l to r: Henry Kondo and Helen Okai. Rear: Roy, John and Oscar Kondo. Mary (Kondo) Wakabayashi had passed away earlier.   Photo courtesy of Roy Kondo.

assist in the preparation of that facility for its "guests." Once that task was accomplished, a call for volunteers to help Idaho farmers harvest their crops was posted. Once again, Roy Kondo volunteered, and his family was soon dispatched to an Idaho farm. There, they picked prunes and helped with the potato harvest. In 1943, Henry and Oscar rented 60 acres of irrigated land near Boise, planting potatoes, onions and sugar beets. In 1944, the family purchased 160 acres of farm land near Jamieson, Oregon, by exchanging their holdings in the Gresham area. From that beginning, Henry and Oscar started buying and renting land and eventually farmed about 5000 acres, growing potatoes, onions, sugar beets, wheat and barley. They also grew peppermint, which they distilled in their family-owned still. One year, Henry and Oscar planted 4500 acres of potatoes in Idaho and near Hermiston, Oregon, most of which was not contracted. A poor potato market that year caused a horrendous loss for the two brothers, who had speculated that the market would hold.

Of the Kondo children, the eldest, Roy Kondo (Jr.), was studying to become a dentist at the Oregon Dental School when the war started. He had to complete his studies in Kansas. After graduating from dental school after the war, he served as a dentist with the U.S. Army, stationed principally at Fort Lewis. He married Midori Tamiyasu and the couple had two children, Dorinne and Jeffrey. His sister, Mary, who was studying nursing at the Good Samaritan Hospital when the war started, also had to complete her training elsewhere. She completed a nursing program in St. Louis, Missouri, married Fred Wakabayashi, and had 1 child. She became a nurse employed by the Veteran's Administration in California. The next son, John, worked on the farm with his family after the move to Idaho, then to Jamieson, Oregon. Drafted in 1944, he was soon transferred to an intelligence unit because of his ability to speak and understand Japanese. His unit was sent to Japan as part of the occupation army, where he served as an interpreter during the completion of his two-year obligation. When he returned to the States, he attended college on the GI Bill, earned a master's degree in economics, and worked for Varian Industries in California. He married Nori Kido, and the couple had three children. As mentioned earlier, the two younger Kondo brothers, Henry and Oscar, became partners, purchased land in Eastern Oregon and Idaho, and raised potatoes, onions and sugar beets. They were very successful until getting involved in the venture in Hermiston, which cost them a "fortune," according to family members. Henry married Alice Adachi and they had five children; Oscar married Lois Itano, and they had 3 daughters. The youngest sibling, Helen, married Thomas Okai, who farmed at Nyssa, Oregon. The Okais raised potatoes, onions, sugar beets and a specialty crop, flower seeds (zinnias, marigolds and blue flax). They had two children. Roy Ken Kondo died on September 25, 1959; June Kondo on December 30, 1981. Roy Kondo lives in Ontario, Oregon; Henry Kondo lives in Nampa, Idaho; and Helen (Kondo) Okai lives in Nyssa, Oregon (2003). Mary, John and Oscar Kondo are deceased. No member of the Kondo family returned to East Multnomah County after the war.

Scene in Occupied Japan

Japanese fishermen (and women) bring in their catch from the Sea of Japan, which lies to the west of the Islands of Japan.   *Photo courtesy of George Mershon.*

Gisaburo and Takaye Kuge Family

From left: Chosei, Takaye, Kiyoko, Tamotsu, Yutaka, Toshiaki and Gisaburo Kuge. At this time, the family lived in Vernonia, Oregon. Photo courtesy of Tom Kuge.

Gisaburo Kuge
Takaye Kuge

According to family members, Gisaburo Kuge emigrated to the United States from Japan because of difficulties he experienced as a result of the rise of militarism after the Russian-Japan war of 1904-05. The death of Emperor Meiji in 1912 hastened this political change. Hence, Gisaburo Kuge likely came to the United States with his wife, Takaye, during this period of unrest. The couple settled in Astoria where Kuge obtained employment as a mill worker. The couple's first two children, Yutaka and Toshiaki "Toshi," were born in the United States. During a visit to Japan to visit her parents, Takaye Kuge gave birth to the couple's third child, Kiyoko. In the early 1920s, Kuge moved his family to Bridal Veil, where he worked for the Bridal Veil Lumber Company. His job was to off-load the flume, which delivered rough-cut "cants" from the mill at Palmer to the Bridal Veil mill. Kiyoko remembers her mother removing slivers from her father's hands each evening after work. The company's Bridal Veil planing mill finished lumber to be shipped to its customers by rail. The couple had six more children, Tamotsu "Thomas," Mitsuru "Henry," Chosei, Seiji and Kingo. Henry accidentally drowned when, as a tot, he decided to go fishing without telling his family.

Second Grade, Vernonia Grade School, 1931

Thomas Kuge, who completed high school in 1942, is pictured here with his second grade class at Vernonia. Thomas is first left, 2nd row.   Photo courtesy of Tom Kuge.

When the Bridal Veil mill experienced a temporary shut down because of the depression, Kuge found employment at a lumber mill in Vernonia, Oregon. There the youngsters attended Vernonia public schools. When the "union movement" became an issue in the lumber business, the Vernonia mill closed. Kuge then took a job at a lumber mill in Linnton, though his family remained in Vernonia. Later, Yutaka Kuge, who had remained in Vernonia to work as a gardener, joined his father to work at the Linnton mill. While working in Linnton, Gisaburo Kuge suffered a heart attack, which forced him to find work in another field. He purchased a small store near N.W. 4th and Davis. There, he started making tofu and udon (a type of noodle) for customers that shopped in "Japan Town." The next son, Toshi, after graduating from Vernonia High School in 1937, enrolled at Oregon State College. There, he completed a pre-med program, after which, in 1940, the University of Oregon Medical School accepted him into its physician-training program. Toshi Kuge had nearly completed his second year at the medical school when he was forced from the program by events. Kiyoko completed her junior year at Vernonia before the family moved. She would have preferred to finish high school at Vernonia and might have stayed there with her brother. However, she moved with the family and graduated from Girls Polytechnic High School, Portland, in 1939.

The outbreak of hostilities between the United States and Japan led to the "evacuation" of the Kuge families at the Portland Assembly Center, where they

Farm Laborers Harvest Sugar Beets

Workers and overseers are identified from left, as follows: Mara Taraka, Frank Joquith, Utake, Tom Hirago, Toshi Kuge and "Beanie."   Photo courtesy of Tom Kuge.

remained approximately three months, from May 12, 1942, into September, 1942. In September, the War Relocation Authority (WRA) assigned the internees to three different camps, Minidoka, Tule Lake or Heart Mountain. The two Kuge families, Gisaburo and Takaye Kuge, with their children, Toshi, Kiyoko, Thomas, Chosei, Seiji and Kingo, and Yutaka Kuge, with his wife, Addie (Shinozaki) Kuge, transferred to Tule Lake. On February 6, 1943, after the War Department changed its policy with regard to Nisei serving in the armed forces, Army recruiters visited Tule Lake Camp to encourage young people to join. Toshi Kuge decided to volunteer (see "Toshiaki Kuge," this volume). In June, 1943, after Toshi Kuge had passed his medical exam, the Army sent him to Camp Shelby, Mississippi, for basic training.

After the government "loyalty oath" program, the WRA transferred those individuals who "passed" to other relocation camps. Question 28 asked: "Will you swear unqualified allegiance to the United States of America and faithfully defend the United States from any or all attack by foreign or domestic forces, and forswear any form of allegiance or obedience to the Japanese Emperor, or any other foreign government, power, or organization?" Having asserted their loyalty (by answering in the affirmative), the Kuge family was transferred to the Minidoka Relocation Center, Idaho. Tule Lake Camp became the WRA's preferred locale for those "failing" the loyalty test. Of these individuals, more than 4400 chose to be repatriated to Japan; about 300 (total) from the other nine camps chose repatriation. While at Minidoka, Thomas Kuge received his

Memorial Service For Thomas Kuge, Camp Minidoka

Attending the service, from left: Rear, Mrs. Endo, Mr. T. Sasaki, Mr. Arai, Mr. Tadaki, Mr. Sasaki, Mr. Otsuka, Mr. Endo, Mr. Sato, and Mr. Ishi. Front, Chosei, Kiyoki, Addie (holding Mark), Yutaka, Takaye and Gisaburo Kuge, Reverend Sugimoto, Mr. Shinozaki, Seiji and Kingo Kuge, and Mrs. Shinozaki. Ironically, the memorial service was held exactly three years after the family's incarceration at the Portland Assembly Center.

Photo courtesy of Tom Kuge.

draft notice. After his induction at Fort Douglas, Utah, the Army sent him to Camp Blanding, Florida, for basic training (see "Gold Star Veterans, Tamotsu "Thomas" Kuge," this volume). His older brother, Yutaka Kuge, also received his draft notice, but failed the Army's physical examination.

When the Supreme Court ruled that the WRA had no right to detain Americans at relocation centers, inhabitants started leaving Minidoka. The Kuge family decided to move to Chicago at the urging of a friend. Consequently, Gisaburo, Takaye, Kiyoko, Chosei, Seiji and Kingo settled in Illinois. Yutaka, Addie and their son, Mark, returned to Portland, Oregon. Toshi Kuge, after returning to Portland from overseas, completed his quest for a medical degree that had been interrupted three years earlier. Thomas Kuge, killed in action in Italy, was first interred in a cemetery in Italy. Later his remains were brought to the United States and now rest in the Arlington National Cemetery, Virginia (see "Thomas Tamotsu Kuge, Nisei Gold Star Veterans," this volume).

Shigeko Matsubu
Kiyomi Matsubu

Shigehachi Matsubu, Shigeko Matsubu's father, arrived in San Francisco from Hawaii after the major earthquake of 1906. Since his older brother, Toramatsu, lived in Portland, Shigehachi decided to settle in Portland. His son, Shigeko, born November 7, 1896, remained in Japan and lived with his grandparents. At age 15, the boy left Hiroshima, Japan, for the United States, disembarking in Seattle, Washington, in 1912. His father met his son there and brought him to Portland, where Matsubu and his wife, Yone, operated a combination barber shop, laundry and bath house. In Portland, Shigeko helped his father and stepmother in the business.

In 1920, the family sent for Shigeko's bride-to-be, Kiyomi Matsubu, born January 22, 1902, in Hiroshima, Japan. She arrived in Seattle on one of the last ships to carry Japanese immigrants to the United States before the act banning Asian immigrants took effect. On February 7, 1920, the couple married in Seattle before returning to Portland to live with Shigeko's father and stepmother. Shigeko and Kiyomi helped operate the family-owned business for about four years. In 1922, a daughter, Mary Umeko was born to the couple. The stepmother asked Mary to call her "Mama san" as she felt she was too young to be a grandmother. Mary remembers Mama san's skill as a barber, wielding scissors to cut hair or using a straight razor to shave male customers. According to Mary, Mama san could use the instruments equally well with her left or right hand, which permitted her, Mary said, to "accomplish much without moving about."

The laundry operated without machines except for a hand-operated wringer. Dirty clothes were soaked in bleach before being placed in soapy water in a tub in which a plunger was used as an agitator. The clothes were passed from the soapy water through the wringer into a rinsing tub of clear water. Once rinsed thoroughly, Mama san sent the clothes through the wringer and hung them to dry in a large room heated by a wood stove. According to Mary, the drying room had "a clever system with a pulley arrangement that took the damp clothing to dry in the space overhead." Once dry, the clothes were ironed on a large, padded table, then "neatly wrapped in white paper and tied with a string." Each package was priced and tagged with the customer's ticket, then placed on a shelf waiting to be claimed. Mama san kept the books, using an abacus to tally the day's receipts. Though many Japanese came to the United States believing a rumor that the streets were paved with gold, the immigrants soon learned, Mary said, that "they had to work to earn the gold."

The Matsubu Laundry, Barber Shop and Bath House

Shigeko's father, Shigehachi Matsubu, and stepmother, Yone 'Mama san' Matsubu operated this shop at 121 N.W. Second Avenue in Portland. Family members include (from L): Shigehachi, Asako, Yone 'Mama san' (holding Tetsuo), Shigeko (behind Yoshiaki), Kiyomi (holding Mary) and Tsurue. Photo courtesy of Mary (Matsubu) Hamada.

The establishment had several small bath rooms, each of which contained a bathtub. One of the rooms was reserved for family use. Customers paid a fee to use the other bath rooms to cleanse themselves. A long hall through the bath area led to the family's kitchen. According to Mary, Mama san would prepare delicacies for church gatherings. She taught Mary that "a good cook first tackles the unpleasant tasks" such as cleaning gobo (a domestic, burdock with a very coarse, dirt-laden peeling) or preparing fiddle ferns for cooking. She taught Mary to cut up a chicken, but, Mary said, "I could never do it her way." Mary was grateful for the influence that Mama san and her grandfather had on her (and her siblings) life. "Many of our Nisei friends didn't have grandparents who lived in America. We were fortunate to have ours. They truly enriched our lives."

In the spring of 1924, Shigeko Matsubu decided that it was time for him to become independent of his father. In addition to the problems created by two families living together, he found the temptations presented by card and game playing in Portland too irresistible for him. He decided to emulate relatives living in East Multnomah County and make a living for his family on a farm. But first, however, he had to learn more about farming. Shigeko's introduction to farming occurred in the hop fields near Salem. His family lived in a camp provided for pickers. There he picked hops while Kiyomi, who had an allergic reaction to hop plants, took care of the field hands' children. For about two

Newlyweds in Seattle   Mary and Mabel Matsubu

Kiyomi and Shigeko Matsubu, after their marriage in Seattle. Their first two children were Mary and Mabel (above right).   Photo courtesy of Mary (Matsubu) Hamada.

years, a Buddhist temple provided shelter for Shigeko's family on those occasions when farm work was not available. The owner of the Kato farm in Gresham provided him with his next job. In 1925, Ayako "Mabel" was born. In 1926, Shigeko obtained employment at the Urata farm in Fairview where he worked for the next two years. In 1927, the Matsubus third child, Akio "Hank" was born. In September the following year Mary started grade school at Fairview. As 1928 drew to a close, Shigeko and Kiyomi decided they had learned enough about farming to buy a place and establish a truck garden. Furthermore, because Mary had started school, it was "time to settle down and provide stability for the family."

Because Oregon laws prohibited land ownership by aliens, Shigeko Matsubu purchased 20 acres of the former Dunn place on Mershon Road in Tom Takeuchi's name. They moved to the farm in December, 1928. Mary enrolled at Corbett Grade School, from which she graduated in 1936. From December, 1928, until May, 1942, the Matsubu family farmed their twenty acres located at the intersection of Mershon and Chamberlain Roads (northwest corner). After the Matsubus moved into the house situated on the place and while living there, two more youngsters were born to Shigeko and Kiyomi: Hisashi "Tommy" born in 1931; and Mitsuru "Johnny," born in 1937. The Matsubu truck garden

On the Farm

Left photograph: (Rear) Mabel, Kiyomi and Mary Matsubu; Front: Hank and Tommy Matsubu. Right photograph: Kiyomi Matsubu and a Filipino farm hand picking cucumbers.
Photos courtesy of Mary (Matsubu) Hamada.

produced cabbage, cauliflower, cucumbers, lettuce, spinach, squash, strawberries and similar crops. Shigeko sold much of his produce at the farmers' early market; cucumbers went to the Steinfeld pickling plant. As the children grew older, the entire family worked in the fields. Kiyomi, Mary and Mabel wore the traditional Japanese white sunshade and hat. When necessary, Filipino laborers were hired for field work. These laborers were housed on the Matsubu farm in a small shack situated close to the barn. Neighborhood children, such as the Mershon youngsters, were hired to pick market strawberries at twenty-five cents per 24-hallock crate.

Mary, Mabel, Hank and Tommy attended Corbett Grade School. The school bus, driven by Harley Bates, came up Chamberlain Road, stopping for the Matsubu and Mershon youngsters on the corner. Heading east on Mershon Road, the bus then picked up the Uyetake, Berney, Rogers, Duncklee, McKay and Carpenter youngsters before reaching the highway. In addition to the public school, Nisei children attended the Japanese school located on property belonging to Harry Uyetake west of the Matsubu farm. Classes were held on a weekly basis (Saturdays), and the students were expected to learn to speak, read and write the Japanese language. Children from surrounding farms attended the school, which employed various instructors, usually from Portland, to teach the students.

After the armed forces of Japan bombed Pearl Harbor on December 7, 1941, people of Japanese ancestry living on the West Coast were suddenly

"Rose Festival" Time   Henry "Hank" Matsubu

Left: Directed by Mary Matsubu (from left), Hank Matsubu, George Sakurai, Queen Lilly Sakurai, Dick Sakurai, Mabel Matsubu and Tommy Matsubu re-enact the crowning of the 1935 Rose Festival Queen. The places in the background include the Mershon farm, the Uyetake farm, the Berney farm and the Rogers place at the crest of the hill. Right, Henry "Hank" Matsubu, whose skills playing baseball would have helped the CHS baseball team. Photos, Mary (Matsubu) Hamada.

considered dangerous to national security. Almost immediately, restrictions such as a curfew and limitations on travel were imposed. In May 7, 1942, the United States Government notified all residents of Japanese ancestry that they were to be "re-located," that is, removed from their homes and placed in "relocation centers." On May 12 (five days later), families were told to report to the Pacific Livestock Exposition Center with a minimum of personal belongings. Thus, on May 12, 1942, our neighbors of Japanese ancestry left their farms, most never to return, including the Matsubu family. At the time of the "relocation," Mary had graduated from CHS (1940), but continued to live at home; Mabel was a junior at CHS; Hank, a freshman; Tommy was in the fifth grade at Corbett Grade School; and Johnny had not yet started school.

The Matsubu family spent the summer of 1942 within the confines of the Pacific International Livestock Exposition Center. Once the Federal Government decided to incarcerate people of Japanese ancestry, construction of internment camps commenced, but the families had to wait until the facilities were completed. The Matsubu family was sent to the Minidoka Relocation

The Former Matsubu Place, 1984

This composite of two photographs taken by Mary (Matsubu) Hamada shows some more recent changes to the former Matsubu place at the corner of Mershon and Chamberlain Roads. Shigeko and Kiyomi Matsubu purchased the 20-acre farm in their cousin's (Tom Takeuchi) name as they could not own land as aliens of Japanese ancestry. They moved onto the farm in December, 1928, and lived there until May 12, 1942, when the U.S. Government forced them from their home.   Photo(s) courtesy of Mary Hamada.

Center in Idaho, where they spent the war years. While in the camp, in 1943, another child, Hiroko 'Joyce' was born to the Matsubus. After the war, when the government released the internees from camps, the Matsubu family decided to remain in Idaho. In 1952, they purchased a farm in Fruitland, Idaho, which remains in the family (2002). Kiyomi Matsubu passed away in Seattle on December 25, 1967; Shigeko Matsubu died in Seattle on June 1, 1984.

After working during the war years in Idaho, sometimes as a domestic, sometimes as a farm laborer, Mary Matsubu became the bride of Noboru Hamada, whose family owned an orchard at Parkdale, Oregon. She and Noboru had four children, Maxine, Dwight, Roger and Sandra. Mary has lived in Parkdale since her marriage to Noboru "Nob" on December 21, 1946. She and her son, Dwight, continue to live on the Parkdale farm. Mabel married Edward Inamine, and settled in New Jersey. She also had four children, Julia, Gordon, Wendy and Steven. Henry Matsubu settled in Seattle where he owned a specialty grocery store. He married Edna Hirabayashi and had two children, Jody and Kiyoko. Thomas Matsubu remained with his parents and took over the farm when his father retired. He married Helen Takemoto and they had five children, Kirk, Francine, Tracey, Benjamin and Jeff. John Matsubu married Mary Brunnette and settled in Concord, California. The couple had two children, Paul and Kiyomi, before separating. He has since remarried. Joyce Matsubu married Jack Ishida, settled in Seattle, Washington, and had two children, Jason and Jennifer.

Corbett Grade School Principal George Lusby said of Hank Matsubu: "He was the only grade school player (he could recall) that could hit a softball over the bank in left field on the fly." Those who remember Hank Matsubu for his exploits on the baseball fields at Corbett will not be surprised by the following

The Matsubu Siblings

Shigeko and Kiyomi Matsubu's children appear in a recent photograph taken at Lake Tahoe. Front, from left: Mabel Inamine, Mary Hamada and Joyce Ishida. Rear: Thomas, John and Henry Matsubu. Photo courtesy of Mary (Matsubu) Hamada.

news story that appeared in the Fort Lewis, Washington, publication, *The Flame*, on October 10, 1946:

> "Hank "Mats" Matsubu's catching and hitting paced the Fort Lewis Warriors to the Sixth Army Championship. In three games he hit .583 and drove in ten runs. Hank was chosen the most outstanding player in the tournament."

After Hank Matsubu's discharge from the Army, Babe Herman signed him to play for the Pittsburgh Pirates. He played on Pittsburgh "farm" teams in Modesto, California, Hutchinson, Kansas, and Yuma, Arizona. Hank turned down an opportunity to play professional baseball in Japan.

Mary (Matsubu) Hamada

Tatsuzo Nakashimada
Kisano (Seki) Nakashimada

Tatsuzo Nakashimada came to the United States from Japan in 1907. A railroad company employed him as a laborer in Oregon. His pay was $9.00 per month, $2.00 of which was withheld for subsistence. The hours were sunup to sundown. In 1911, Mr. Dabney of Troutdale offered Tatsuzo a job as gardener at his property located along the Sandy River, which includes the acreage now known as Dabney State Park. With stable employment, Nakashimada sent word to his betrothed, Kisano Seki, in Japan that she should come to America. He met her at the dock in San Francisco and the couple wed November 10, 1911. Mr. Dabney and some of his neighbors had built a home for the couple into which they moved after the ceremony. Mr. Nakashimada worked as a gardener for about two years. He then decided he wanted to farm. He was able to lease a place from Mr. Kendall of Troutdale located on what is now Seidl Road, and they moved to the farm in 1913. According to their son, Leke, the "house" was just a shack, but it provided shelter.

Mr. and Mrs. Nakashimada had ten children, all born in Troutdale: Shigeo, born in 1912), Rosemary (1913), Thomas (1915), Elsie (1918), Leke (1920), Takey (1921), George (1923), Mary (1925), Margaret (1929) and Betty, (1931). Shigeo, Thomas and Mary died in a terrible flu epidemic that struck in the mid-20's. George died of spinal meningitis at age four. In a period of about two years, the couple lost four of their children.

When the family moved to the Kendall property, only about one-half of the twenty acres was cleared. Nakashimada cleared the remainder "with dynamite, a pick and a shovel," according to Leke. They grew berries, including raspberries, youngberries and strawberries, and also grew cucumbers and cabbage. Later, Mr. Nakashimada gave up on raspberries and started planting cauliflower. Soon that became the principal crop on the farm. He joined the "Top of the Hill" cooperative, which was a "big mistake," avers Leke. "Pop didn't get a dime for the crops he delivered there for three years." To compound the problem, the Troutdale Bank, in which Nakashimada had placed his savings, "went belly-up" during the first years of the depression. Leke states his father "had two quarters in his pocket. That was it."

The older youngsters started school at Pleasant View Grade School on Wand Road. When the District consolidated with Corbett, they attended there. Alvin Kinney drove the school bus that transported them to school. Leke said, "Mr. Kinney was a great guy. He was fair to everyone. We used to get salmon from him every year." Rosemary finished grade school at Corbett. She did not attend

Tatsuzo and Kisano Nakashimada Family

Front, from left: Rosemary, Elsie, Takey, Margaret and Kisano. Rear, Leke and Tatsuzo Nakashimada.
Photo courtesy of Leke Nakashimada.

high school as "she had to help my father on the farm," Leke reported. Leke completed his elementary years at Corbett Grade, then enrolled at Columbian High School. One day Marion Kirkham challenged him to a ping-pong game, which Leke accepted. They played several games, which totally engrossed the two until Leke suddenly realized, the bus! Sure enough, he had missed the bus, which meant a four-mile walk home. Leke reminded Marion of his "long walk home" at a meeting of the Crown Point Country Historical Society some 60 or more years later. Leke Nakashimada graduated from Columbian High School in 1939. He lettered in both baseball and basketball. He said, "Mr. Emerson was a good coach, but he was also a great teacher." Leke had nice things to say about several of his teachers, including Mrs. Cheney, whom he had for mathematics, and Miss Rosen, whom he had for typing and English. Leke's younger sisters, Margaret and Betty, were attending Corbett Grade when the U.S. Government ordered Japanese families to report to the Pacific Livestock Exposition Center on May 12, 1942, for "evacuation" from the West Coast. Takey and the younger Nakashimada youngsters completed high school at Minidoka.

In 1929, Nakashimada was able to lease the Bramhall Place on Woodard Road. This gave him an additional 54 acres to farm since he continued to lease the Kendall property. In 1931, the family moved to the house on the Bramhall place, which gave them much more room for the family. With the additional ground, Nakashimada increased the acreage devoted to cauliflower to about

Margaret and Takey at the Bramhall Place

Margaret and Takey Nakashimada with work horses in the barnyard at the Bramhall place on Woodard Road. Photos courtesy of Leke Nakashimada.

The Rented Bramhall Home

Margaret, Elsie and Betty (right) play with a friend at their home on Woodard Road.

40 acres each year. The crop was generally sold to Pacific Fruit, which required that the heads be spotless. Since Mr. Nakashimada took great pains with the crop, he sometimes was able to sell cauliflower when other farmers left it in the field. The family had three horses to work the ground, Lady, Pete and Pack. Until the mid-thirties horses were used to do the tilling. This included plowing, disking, harrowing and cultivating. Leke remembers cultivating with Pack, who was usually the horse chosen for this work. After Mr. Nakashimada purchased a Massey-Harris tractor in the mid-30's, the family used it to do the plowing. Later Nakashimada hired "Tood"

The Family's 1924 Nash

Margaret (left) and Betty Nakashimada pose on the family's 1924 Nash, a prized possession of Mr. Nakashimada. The Bramhall barn is visible, middle left.

Photo courtesy of Leke Nakashimada.

Larson and Howard Winters to plow the entire place with their "Cat."

When families of Japanese ancestry from the surrounding area gathered at the Pacific Livestock Exposition Center in North Portland, the Nakashimadas were among them. The center's livestock area was partitioned, forming cubicles for families in the stall areas. Mattresses of straw were furnished and family members used the stalls as further partitions to separate family members. Families spent several months at this facility. Some families volunteered to go to Tule Lake, California in August, even though that camp was not yet completed. In September 1942, the Nakashimadas were sent to the Minidoka Relocation Center in Idaho. This is where they spent the war years. Leke was not among them as he had been drafted in July 1941 into the U.S. Army. Because he was on a farm, he received an extension until January 1942 (see "Leke Nakashimada, Nisei Veterans," this volume).

Rosemary married Eichi Ishida. The couple settled in N. Portland after the war and live there still (2003). She has no children. Elsie married Thomas Nakata, a veteran of World War II. After the war, the couple lived in SE Portland. She and her husband had two sons, both of whom became medical doctors. In 1946, the next sibling, Leke, married Mary Hirata, who was born and raised in Parkdale, Oregon. The couple has four children, John, Diane, Debbie and Lisa. John works as an administrator for Kaiser Permanente. Diane lives in

Tatsuzo and Kisano Nakashimada Family

From left: Rosemary, Betty, Takey, Margaret and Leke Nakashimada. The Nakashimada youngsters rode the school bus to attend school in Corbett.

Haying, Bramhall Place, 1940

Leke Nakashimada (on load) and a friend, Mickey Mori (right), prepare to take a load of hay to the barn for the family's work horses. The truck is a 1930 Chevrolet.

Photos courtesy of Leke Nakashimada.

Nakashimada Brothers at Home

Leke (left) and Takey Nakashimada pose by the family's new Buick at their home on Woodard Road. *Photo courtesy of Leke Nakashimada.*

Portland and works at Nordstroms. Debbie lives in Portland and operates a beauty shop. Lisa is a pharmacist and lives in Lake Oswego (2003). Leke Nakashimada operated his own restaurant in N.E. Portland for about ten years, then went to work for Esco Corporation, where he worked until he retired in July, 1984. He raised his family in SE Portland and has lived in the same house there since 1953.

Takey Nakashimada was also inducted into the Army out of the Minidoka. He underwent basic training in Texas and was assigned to the Third Army. Takey said, "I went wherever Patton went." He served in the European Theater and remembers well the Battle of the Bulge (see "Leke Nakashimada" and "Takey Nakashimada," this volume). He married after the war, had three children and worked for the Portland Water Bureau. He supervised the Water Bureau works located at Mt. Tabor. He also worked nights for Franz Bakery. Currently Takey lives with his wife, Mavis (Jacobson) in Portland. The next sibling, Margaret, married George Hongo, a veteran who also served in the European Theater. They lived in N.E. Portland and had three daughters. Margaret passed away in 1980. The youngest girl, Betty, did not marry. She worked in the insurance business and lives in Tigard (2003).

Tatsuzo and Kisano Nakashimada returned to the Portland area the summer of 1945, and lived with Rosemary and Elsie in a St. John's housing unit

Cauliflower, Lower Field, Bramhall Place

Nakashimada family members and relatives from Canada survey the cauliflower crop planted on the lower field of the Bramhall place. This field overlooks the Sandy River near the Stark Street Bridge. (During and after World War II, the author spent many hours working this field with a horse, Pack, previously owned by the Nakashimada family, pulling a single row cultivator.) Photo courtesy of Leke Nakashimada.

where Leke joined them upon his return from the service. As an alien, Mr. Nakashimada was not able to purchase a farm in his name before the war. After the war bitter racial feelings created a situation that made it nearly impossible for citizens of Japanese extraction, including veterans, to buy a home. Tatsuzo Nakashimada died March 5, 1952 in Portland before Leke was able to purchase a home in SE Portland. Thus Tatsuzo died before any member of his family actually purchased a place. His wife, Kisano, passed away January 5, 1969.

Leke expressed his gratitude to several neighbors, including the Larson family (Robert "Bob," Jane and their son, "Tood"), and John Seidl. "The Larson family visited my family at the Exposition Center in Portland, and came to see them off when they left for Minidoka by train," Leke recalled. "John Seidl helped the family before they left and kept in touch during the war."

Leke Nakashimada

Shintaro Okita
Tatsu (Kaji) Okita

Shintaro Okita and Tatsu Kaji married in Hiroshima, Japan, in 1897. Their first son, James, was born in Japan and was left with his grandparents when the couple emigrated to Hawaii. In Hawaii, Shintaro obtained work in the sugar cane fields. A second child, Kinu, was born in Honolulu on October 6, 1903. After the outbreak of the Japan-Russia war, the family returned to Japan. Thus, both James and Kinu spent much of their childhood in Japan. In 1912, the couple decided to return to the United States, settling in the Montavilla area on a farm. Shintaro and Tatsu Okita had six more children: George, born in 1913, Morio 'Frank,' born in 1914, Mary, born in 1916, Todd, born in 1921, Chieko, born in 1923 and Yoshito, born in 1927. At one point, according to family members, the Okitas operated a dairy, but, primarily, the family grew vegetables on a "truck garden" type farm. Mary recalled, "We moved often." Shintaro and Tatsu Okita moved to a rented farm on Corbett Hill in the late 1920s.

On the Corbett farm, the Okitas raised cabbage, cauliflower, lettuce and similar crops. They sold most of their produce through the early farmers'

Trowbridge Farm, Corbett Hill Road, 1915

Shintaro and Tatsu Okita rented this farm in the 1920s, after the Kirkham family moved to the Farquhar place in Springdale. The Okitas remained on this farm until 1933. The Sumpter family, shown in the photograph, lived on the farm in 1915. Photo, the author.

CHS, Class of 1933 (Sophomore Year)

Front, L to R: **George Okita**, *Shio Uyetake and* **Frank Okita**. *Middle: June Woodle, Mildred Larson, Lois Evans, Marie Stolin, Jeanne Larson, Beatrice Hodgson and Miss Sarah Poor. Rear, George Fehrenbacher, Lewis Faught, Charles Pulliam, Goldie Knieriem, Walter Stolin, Earnest Chamberlain, Meredyth Brown, Donald Reed, George Shepperd, Estelle Davis, Francis Benfield, Walter Jackson and O. Capon.*

CHS Cohimore photo.

market in Southeast Portland. In 1932, Shintaro Okita suffered a stroke, which required his son, George, who was a sophomore at Columbian High School, Corbett, to drop out of school to take over the farm. Because the farm seemed to be situated in a "frost pocket," and because of the distance to market, the family decided to locate elsewhere.

Consequently, the Okita family moved to a rented farm off Palmblad Road in Gresham. The youngsters, who had been attending Corbett schools, enrolled in Gresham schools, the younger children at Gresham Grade and the older youngsters at Gresham High School. Because of his father's health, George continued to take the responsibility of managing the farm. Frank Okita graduated from Gresham High in 1933, Mary, 1934, Todd, 1939, and Chieko, 1941. Shintaro and Tatsu Okita's two oldest children, James and Kinu, joined the family in the United States before the war. James settled in Burns, Oregon, and worked for the railroad. He and his wife, Shizumo, had four children, 3 boys and 1 girl. One son, Paul Okita, now lives in the Parkrose, Oregon area.

The second Okita child, Kinu, married Tsuneki Kagawa and the couple had two children, Mabel and John. Kinu and Tsuneki were visiting Japan when the World War II started and could not return to the United States until the war ended. They returned, but their daughter, Mabel, decided to remain in Japan. John was affected by radiation sickness from the atomic bomb blast at Hiroshima in August, 1945.

CHS, Class of 1934 (Freshman Year)

*Rear, L to R: Dean Burkholder, Elmer Winters, Mary Northway, Mabel Woodle, Clifford Ellis, Mr. Leslie M. Emerson, Alfred Burness, Rod Bates, George Wand, F. Cone, M. Burness, Margaret Johnson and C. Pack. Middle: L. Ellis, F. Endicott, Dorothy Frommelt, Mildred Keeton, Margaret Rogers, Lucille Frommelt, Shirley Deverell, Vivienne Shelley, Hazel Deverell, **Mary Okita** and Frank Jackson. Front: Jerome Fehrenbacher, Alfred Canzler and Charles Wilson.* CHS Cohimore photo.

Soon after his father's death in 1939, the family's eldest son, George, married Chiyo Okita (no relation). At this time, George Okita had full responsibility for managing the family's farm. George and Chiyo Okita had three children, Carolyn, Marion and Bette Ann. In 1939, George's younger sister, Mary, became the bride of Ben Kasubuchi.

On May 12, 1941, similarly to other Nikkei families in the area, the Okita family had to leave their farm. By this time George and Chiyo Okita had a daughter, Carolyn, and Ben and Mary Kasubuchi had one son, Ben. Thus, two Okita families and the Kasubuchi family joined other Nikkei families at the Pacific Livestock Exposition Center, where they spent three months awaiting the opening of the "relocation" camps. Since Frank Okita had been drafted in January, 1942, and was stationed at Fort Warren in Wyoming when the "evacuation" took place, he was not directly affected by the order.

Okita family members spent some time at the Tule Lake facility before being transferred to the Minidoka Relocation Center in Idaho, where they were interned for the next three years. After the family reached the center, Frank Okita, who had completed basic training at Fort Warren, visited his family on furlough. There, he became re-acquainted with a young lady, Mary Tashima, who had also lived in Gresham. The couple continued to correspond after Frank returned to Fort Warren for more training. As other Nisei veterans have reported, the U.S. Army seemed to have some difficulty deciding exactly

Camp Minidoka Visit

On furlough, Frank Okita visited his family at the Minidoka Relocation Center (obviously during the winter months). While there, he became re-acquainted with Mary Tashima, who had also attended Gresham High School. Photo, Mary (Tashima) Okita.

how to handle its soldiers of Japanese ancestry. First Okita served in a Supply and Service Detachment. Later, the Army placed him in Company 38, 3rd Training Regiment (see "Frank Okita, Nisei Veterans," this volume). Frank remained at Fort Warren, Wyoming until late in 1944, when he was sent to Camp Shelby, Mississippi, then overseas.

After the war, George Okita returned to Oregon and obtained housing at Vanport. He commuted to Parkrose, working on the Damonte farm. Frank Damonte had a house on the farm in which the Okita family could live and they moved from Vanport. When Mr. Damonte passed away, George and Frank Okita purchased the farm as partners. This arrangement lasted about five years until George purchased Frank's share. George and Chiyo Okita's three daughters, Carolyn, Marion and Bette Ann, attended Parkrose schools. On January 27, 1946, Frank Okita, soon after his discharge from the U.S. Army, married his betrothed, Mary Tashima. The couple found housing at Vanport, where they lived until flooded out in 1948. They then moved to the Damonte farm in Parkrose, which he and George were farming. In 1956, Frank and Mary purchased a 20-acre farm in the Pleasant Home area east of Gresham. There, they raised berries, broccoli, cabbage, cauliflower and similar crops. They sold their

Todd Okita, U.S. Army

Todd Okita (right) shown here with a fellow Nisei soldier, served his country during World War II. Apparently, he was sent to the European Theater. Photo courtesy of Mary (Tashima) Okita.

berries to Scenic Fruit or Smuckers and wholesaled the other crops through the eastside wholesale market (formerly the early farmers' market). Frank and Mary Okita had two daughters, Cheryl and Gayle, who attended Gresham schools. Cheryl now lives in Lake Oswego and Gayle, in Tule Lake, California. Frank Okita died on September 17, 1985. Mary (Tashima) Okita continues to live on the Pleasant Home farm, though it has been sold to the Frank Schmidt Nursery.

Ben and Mary (Okita) Kasubuchi returned to Oregon after the war and first lived in Northwest Portland. The couple had three boys, all of whom attended Portland schools. Their eldest son, Ben, graduated from Lincoln High in 1958; Dennis in 1961, and Alan in 1966. Alan served with the U.S. Army in Viet Nam, 1968-1969.

The sixth Okita sibling, Todd, served in the U.S. Army during World War II, though few details of his service are available. He served in the European Theater and was in the Army of Occupation, Germany. After the war, he married Dorothy Kaihara and settled in Denver, Colorado, where he worked in the wholesale produce trade. He and Dorothy raised 5 children, 3 girls and 2 boys. Todd Okita passed away on March 27, 1994. The next Okita sibling, Chieko, married Charles Itami, whose family owned the Kern Park Floral Company, N.E. 67th and Holgate, in Portland. Consequently, after the war, the couple settled in Portland. Chieko Okita passed away on June 2, 2004. She and Charles had no children. The youngest sibling, Yoshito Okita, returned to Portland, married Lois Ogawa, and the couple had two children, Ann Margaret and Richard. Yoshito and Lois Okita now live in Parkrose.

Masaru Sakurai
Chiyoko (Takeuchi) Sakurai

Masaru Sakurai was born in Hiroshima, Japan, July 20, 1897. His mother died not too long after he was born and his grandparents cared for him. His father left for the United States around the turn of the century, but Masaru remained in Japan. In 1914, after completing school in Japan, he joined his father in the United States. In the interim his father had remarried. Later, Masaru Sakurai met his future bride, Chiyoko Takeuchi, in Portland, where she had been born November 14, 1905. The couple wed in the summer of 1922 and moved to the East Multnomah County area in the late 20's with Mr. Sakurai's father and stepmother. The family first stayed with the Takeuchi family on Wand Road. Shortly, the Sakurai family purchased a place of approximately 25 acres located just north of the Takeuchi farm on Wand Road. There was a small house on the property into which the family moved. Much of the place was still covered with timber and brush, so the land had to be cleared for farming. With the use of dynamite and hand tools, the Sakurais, with the help of the Takeuchis, accomplished the task. Mr. Sakurai's parents decided to return to Japan, and he took over the farm. He planted strawberries, broccoli, cauliflower, cabbage and spinach. Horses did the tilling, which included plowing, disking, harrowing, floating and cultivating. In the early days, Mr. Sakurai often hired itinerant laborers, who lived on the farm and worked for him.

Masaru and Chiyoko Sakurai had six children, Lily, born in 1924, Richard "Dick" (1926), George (1929), Betty (1931), Edward (1936) and Judith (1938). Lily started school at Corbett Grade in 1930. Her first grade teacher was Miss Sherman and Mr. Lusby was the Principal. Her younger brothers and sisters, except for Edward and Judith, attended Corbett as well. During the 30's as the children grew older, they were able to help with the farm work. Sakurai sold much of his farm produce at the farmers' market in Portland, which meant everyone was up early to harvest the crops so that Masaru could be at the market when it opened. Lily said they usually started work at 4:30 a.m. On school days, mornings were a busy time at the Sakurai home. According to Lily, the strawberry crop was usually contracted to the Birds Eye Cannery in Gresham. Spinach was sold to a cannery in St. Johns and broccoli was sold in Hillsboro. Everything was planted by hand, strawberries, broccoli, cauliflower and cabbage. In the late 1930s, Sakurai purchased a Ford Ferguson tractor. Thereafter, the ground was worked by tractor, though some tasks, such as cultivating, continued to be done with a horse.

Masaru and Chiyoko Sakurai Family

From left, Masaru Sakurai (holding Dick), Lily, and Chiyoko (holding George). The Sakurai farm on Wand Road bordered the Takeuchi farm. They were neighbors of Ig Wand and his family.   *Photo courtesy of Lily (Sakurai) Kajiwara.*

Lily graduated from CHS in 1942. About ten days before her graduation day, the Sakurai family, together with all other families of Japanese ancestry in the area, were ordered to leave their homes by the U.S. Government. When this occurred, Dick was completing his sophomore year at CHS and George was in 8th grade. Betty was not in school because of a physical handicap (cerebral palsy). Edward and Judith had not yet started school. When the Sakurai family left home to report to the Pacific Livestock Exposition Center, they were permitted to take only what they could carry. Most of their personal possessions as well as farm implements and household belongings were left at the farm. A neighbor agreed to look after the farm and their belongings for them.

At the center, they found hundreds of Japanese families crowded together in a facility originally intended for animals. Privacy was not possible, which was particularly difficult for Lily, who was nearly eighteen at the time. Since the camps where the Nikkei families were to be interned were not yet finished, the approximate 3,000 people of Japanese ancestry housed at the center stayed there until September. According to Lily, the summer was exceptionally warm, which added to their discomfort. In the Sakurai family, seven members of the family (of eight) were U.S. citizens. The family lived in a 20-by-20 foot cubicle. In September, authorities sent the family to the Minidoka Relocation Center in Idaho.

Minidoka Camp, Twin Falls, Idaho

The entire Sakurai family, Masaru, Chiyoko, Lilly, Dick, George, Betty, Edward and Judith, lived in Barracks 9, Block 41. Presumably, the family can be found somewhere in this photograph of the residents of Block 41.

Photo, <u>Minidoka Interlude</u>, *published by its residents in 1943.*

While in Minidoka, Masaru Sakurai worked on surrounding farms where the principal crops were potatoes and sugar beets. Dick and George also worked as farm laborers during the summer months when school was out. When he was not working as a farm laborer, Masaru Sakurai worked as a janitor. All school-age children attended school in camp. Lily worked at the Stafford Grade School as a teacher. The first year she taught 4th grade, the second, 6th grade and the third, kindergarten. Dick graduated from high school in 1944. His diploma reflects the circumstances as Hunt High School, within Minidoka, awarded the document.

After the war, the Sakurai family returned to Oregon. Masaru and Dick Sakurai drove to the farm to assess the situation. They found their home in deplorable condition. The family's household goods and other belongings had disappeared, taken by parties unknown. Furthermore, Lily said, "Father and Dick felt some animosity toward the Japanese still existed." After a discussion among family members, the decision was made to sell the farm. Consequently, it was sold and the family settled in rental housing at Vanport.

Thereafter, the Sakurai family lived in Portland where Masaru Sakurai became a contract gardener. George completed high school at Roosevelt, graduating in 1946. Edward and Judith attended Failing Grade School. In 1948 the family lost much of what they had accumulated after the war in the Vanport flood. They found a place to rent, which was located at SW 1st and Sherman Street in Portland. Edward and Judith attended Lincoln High School; Edward graduated in 1954, Judith in 1956. In the mid-50's, the Sakurais purchased a home in Southeast Portland at 84th and Holgate.

George Kajiwara, U.S. Army

Pfc. George Kajiwara, 442nd Headquarters Company, stands before the unit's headquarters in Livorno, Italy.
Photo courtesy of George Kajiwara.

Masaru Sakurai took many awards for his gardening, particularly with his roses. He was also pleased and proud to pass the test to become an U.S. citizen. Chiyoko Sakurai became well-known poet in the Japanese verse, Haiku. Many of her poems were published locally and in Japan. She received many awards and much recognition for her work. Her daughter, Judith, plans to have her mother's poetry published in book form. Chiyoko Sakurai was also an accomplished singer, performing at many community events. She passed away in March, 1986. Masaru Sakurai retired at age 85. He died September 1995, age 98. Both Masaru and Chiyoko Sakurai are interred at the Forest Lawn Cemetery in Gresham.

After the family returned to Oregon, Lily worked for Holman Transfer. In 1952 she decided to travel and see the country. She traveled south through California, across the southern part of the country and up the East Coast. She ended up in New York City and found a job. While there she met George S. Kajiwara, who had settled in New York after being discharged from the U.S. Army. George Kajiwara was born in Colorado in 1925. He had served with the 442nd Regimental Combat Team in the European Theater. The couple decided to get married and make Oregon their home. They were wed December 5, 1953. They have one child, Karen, born in 1961. While Karen was in school, Lily completed requirements for a degree at Portland State University, graduating in 1975. She became a staff member at the Portland State University library, and worked there until she retired in 1994. After coming to Oregon, George Kajiwara worked for the Hyster Company, retiring in 1987 when Hyster closed its local plant. He then worked for the American Cancer Society before retiring for good in 1995.

Dick Sakurai worked at various jobs in Portland before deciding to go on to school. He enrolled at Reed College, graduating in 1953 with a degree in

Sakurai Family, Post-War

Rear, from L: Masaru, Dick, George Kajiwara, Eddie and George. Front, Chiyoko, Betty, Lily, Judy and Janice (George Sakurai's wife). Photo courtesy of Lily (Sakurai) Kajiwara.

Physics. He completed graduate work at Bryn Mawr, and taught physics at several colleges in the Midwest. He and his wife, Sandy, have two sons, Saren and Korien. The couple now lives in Troutdale, Oregon.

After graduating from Roosevelt, George enrolled at Oregon State College where he majored in biology. He worked in a laboratory for a time, after which he was accepted into the School of Medicine at Oregon Health Sciences University. After completing medical school in 1959, he did his internship at Good Samaritan Hospital. He was accepted into the residency program in psychiatry at the State Hospital in Salem. He practiced as a psychiatrist in Medford, Oregon for a time before taking a position with the United States Government in Springfield, Missouri. Later, he accepted a position as Psychiatrist for Orange County, south of Los Angeles. He now lives in Westminster, California with his wife, Janice. They have four children, Steven, Larry, Scott and Leslie.

Because of her handicap Betty did not attend school. She lived with her parents until they passed away. She did not marry. Until her death in January, 2003, she lived in N.E. Portland with a lady caregiver.

After graduating from Lincoln High School, Edward attended Reed College, from which he graduated in 1958 with a degree in mathematics. He then completed graduate work at Washington University in St. Louis. He teaches mathematics at Webster University in St. Louis, a position he has held since completing his graduate work (2003). He is married to Anna, but they have no children.

Judith, after graduating from Lincoln High, attended Reed College and graduated with a major in chemistry. She did graduate work at the University of Oregon, then attended the Stanford Foreign Language Institute. She married Hiroshi Yamauchi, a professor at the University of Hawaii. They undertook several tours to Japan in order to teach there. Judith and her husband have a daughter, Kara. After retiring from the teaching field, the couple moved to Portland, Oregon.   Lily (Sakurai) Kajiwara and Dick Sakurai.

Picking Strawberries

In the '30s, strawberries destined for the fresh market were picked into wooden hallocks. The crate was two-tiered, with 12 boxes in each tier. Depression-era pickers earned 25 cents per (double) crate. According to Lily, the Sakurai family's strawberry fields had "set" a good crop in the spring of 1942, but someone else picked the berries.

Photo courtesy of George Perry VI.

Sakajiro Takeuchi
Yaye (Sumihiro) Takeuchi

Both Sakajiro and Yaye (Sumihiro) Takeuchi were born in Hiroshima, Japan; he in 1885, she in 1895. He ventured from Japan as a teenager, and spent a couple of years in Hawaii, working on a cane sugar plantation. Next, he traveled to San Francisco to join other family members who had emigrated from Japan. In 1905, Sakajiro came to Portland, where a brother had established a barber shop. In 1911, he sent for and married his "picture bride," Yaye Sumihiro. On November 7, 1912, the couple's first son, Masao, was born in Portland. Shortly thereafter, in 1913 or 1914, Takeuchi purchased 21 acres on the 'hill,' lying adjacent to, and north of the Jasper Mershon place. Since the property was timbered, Takeuchi set about clearing it, and "cleared about an acre each year," according to his son, Hiro. Hiro, the second child, was born in 1915, at home. After purchasing the land, Takeuchi farmed for a living, raising strawberries, cabbage, cauliflower, lettuce and spinach. The latter was sold to the Birds Eye cannery in Hillsboro, but most of his produce was sold at the early market in Portland. In the earlier years, Takeuchi would start for Portland in his horse-drawn buggy around 2:00 a.m., sell what he could at the Farmer's Market and start for home. He often fell asleep on the way home, but the horse knew the route and delivered him safely to his farm.

Sakajiro and Yaye Takeuchi had three more boys, Shigeru, born in 1917, Shiro (1918), and Tadashi (1923). The older boys started school at Wilkes, but completed their elementary years at Corbett Grade School. All of the boys graduated from Corbett Grade School and completed their secondary years at Columbian High School, Corbett; Masao graduated in 1932, Hiro (1933), Shigeru (1935), Shiro (1936) and Tadashi (1941). The boys worked on the farm, helping care for the vegetable crops during the growing season and clearing land with mattocks, axes and grub hoes during the winter months. Dynamite was used to blast stumps from the ground. Quay Martin built a new home for the family in 1931; Robert Larson and the Takeuchi boys assisted in the construction. This home replaced the 10-by-20 foot "shack" in which the family had lived previously. Though a couple of rooms had been added, it became quite crowded as the boys grew older, and all appreciated their new home. Hiro told of the Japanese custom regarding passing ownership of the land to the eldest son. The younger brothers knew that Masao Takeuchi would eventually own the farm, and they had to "find jobs on their own. " Of course, Masao had to care for his parents as they grew older; which was also customary.

Mr. and Mrs. Sakajiro Takeuchi   Mr. Takeuchi Plowing

Left, Sakajiro and Yaye Takeuchi, both of whom were born in Hiroshima, Japan. Mr. Takeuchi came to Oregon in 1905. In either 1913 or 1914, the family purchased 21 acres on the "hill." Right, Sakajiro plows the land with his team.

The Takeuchi Home c1931

Quay Martin, assisted by Robert "Bob" Larson and the Takeuchi boys, built this home for Sakajiro Takeuchi in 1931.   Photos courtesy of Hiro Takeuchi.

However, during the '30s, jobs were hard to find. Consequently, the Takeuchi boys continued to work on the farm after graduating from CHS. Masao, as the eldest, began to accept more responsibility each year. On January 21, 1940, he married Masumi Ninomura. Hiro sought work in Portland, and found a job in a grocery store, where he learned the grocery business. However, the job was not permanent, and he returned to the farm to work. Later, he found a job in a different store. In 1938, he decided to go into the grocery business himself; he purchased a store at S.E. 32nd and Hawthorne. Shigeru worked at home until he was drafted into the army in July, 1941. Shiro worked on the farm for a

The Takeuchi Family

Top, from left: Hiro, Shiro, Tadashi, Shigeru and Masao Takeuchi. Front, Sakajiro and Yaye Takeuchi. The boys, all born on the "hill" except Masao, graduated from CHS.

Photo courtesy of Hiro Takeuchi.

couple of years, then worked for his brother, Hiro, until he too, was drafted into the army on October 13, 1941. Of course, the Takeuchi's youngest son, Tadashi, continued to work on the farm after he graduated.

When Japan bombed Pearl Harbor on December 7, 1941, life changed abruptly for the people of Japanese ancestry living on the west coast. According to Hiro, when the war started there were about 40 stores with owners of Japanese ancestry in Portland. Most of these owners had to sell their stores and merchandise, but because of time constraints and the "glut" of properties, most received just pennies on the dollar. Hiro, irritated by the situation, decided not to sell his store. He did sell what stock he could, gave some away and returned the balance to Hudson House, his supplier. He stored some of his furnishings at the farm and leased the building. He then waited with his family at the farm until May 12, 1942, when they reported to the assembly center. Both Shigeru and Shiro were in the army, stationed in the midwest. During this interval, Shigeru, granted leave by the army, was not allowed to visit his family at home. Nisei could not enter the Western Defense Command area, which encompassed much of Washington, Oregon and California.

The Takeuchi Farm Near Weiser, Idaho, WWII

While two of the Takeuchi brothers were in the service, Masao and Hiro (at the wheel) rented farmland near Weiser, Idaho, and helped with the war effort by farming, producing tons of potatoes, onions, sugar beets and other crops during World War II. They were permitted to farm in Idaho as it was not included in the restricted zone from which people of Japanese ancestry were excluded. *Photo courtesy of Hiro Takeuchi.*

On May 12, 1942, the Takeuchi family traveled by bus to the Portland Assembly Center in North Portland. They asked a neighbor, Ig Wand, to look after the farm. During the war, the house was rented to the McCleary family; the land to Ed Klinski. The family did not remain at the assembly center for long. Hiro volunteered to help prepare the camp at Tule Lake for the influx of Nikkei families expected to arrive soon. After Hiro volunteered, the entire family chose to go to Tule Lake. Hiro had the responsibility of readying the canteen (store) for the camp opening. During the time the family was at Tule Lake, the army granted Shiro leave. However, he too, similarly to his brother, Shigeru, could not visit his family because California was part of the Western Defense Command, and thus, "off-limits" to all persons of Japanese ancestry. Masao and Hiro, growing restless because of the confinement, volunteered to work as farm laborers in Idaho. They were placed on a sugar-beet farm near Weiser, Idaho, and worked the next year on the farm. The following year they were able to rent 80 acres of irrigated land, which they farmed together, growing sugar beets, onions, lettuce and potatoes.

When the war ended, Masao and Masumi decided to return to the home place. In 1946, Masao resumed farming, but after a few years found that

Farm Crops, Idaho, World War II

Left, Masao's son, Don Takeuchi, hauls a wagon load of lettuce from the field while his younger brother, Bob (on load), supervises. Right, sacked onions ready to be hauled from the field.   *Photos courtesy of Hiro Takeuchi.*

farming in the '50s was a losing proposition because of competition from corporate farms. In 1957, he went into the grocery business, purchasing a market on Sandy Boulevard in Parkrose. Hiro, who had opened his own grocery store earlier, helped Masao get established. Masao and Masumi had five children: Donald, born in 1941, Robert (1943), Mel (1944), Nancy (1949) and Kathy (1953). The youngsters attended Corbett Schools until they moved to Parkrose in 1962. Sakajiro Takeuchi, who died November 9, 1963, lived with Masao and his family until his death. On July 9, 1971, his wife, Yaye Takeuchi, passed away in Parkrose. (Since the Takeuchi family had left Japan before the turn of the century, no family members were killed when Hiroshima was destroyed by the first atomic bomb dropped in the war. However, Mrs. Takeuchi's family had remained in Hiroshima. Thirteen members of her family were killed by the blast). Masao Takeuchi passed away July 13, 1967, age 55. His wife, Masumi, died October 3, 1999. The Corbett farm is now owned by Masao and Masumi's five children.

After the Tule Lake camp opened, Hiro managed the canteen until he and Masao left for Idaho to work on the sugar beet farm near Weiser. When Masao and his family decided to return to the home place after the war, Hiro leased the 80-acre Idaho farm for three more years. On April 7, 1946, he married Mary Yabuki of Houghton, Washington. In 1949, he gave up farming and came to Portland, hoping to find a grocery store for sale. In May 1949, Hiro and Mary purchased Cole's Food Center at N.E. 102nd and Halsey, which they renamed the Halsey Food Center. Over the years, they made many changes and improvements to the store, including a 45,000 sq. ft. addition to floor space, living quarters upstairs and storage in the basement. They also bought the lot on the corner, removed the house and added a parking lot. Hiro was a charter member of the Gateway Boosters, and is a past president. He was also active in the Woodland Park Lions Club and a sponsor of several community and school sports activities. He and Mary had two sons, Jerry, born in 1948 and Harold L.

Shiro and Shigeru Takeuchi

Shigeru (right) served with the famed 442nd Regimental Combat Team; Shiro (left) served under General George Patton in the 3rd Army. After the war, the brothers visit Corbett Grade School, from which Shigeru graduated in 1931; Shiro, in 1932.

Photo courtesy of Shiro Takeuchi.

"Lynn," born in 1950. Both completed their elementary and secondary school years in the David Douglas District. Currently (2000), Jerry is responsible for quality control at the Oregon Iron Works. He has one son, Jared. Lynn owns an architectural firm in Redmond, Washington. He has a daughter, Erika, who earned the Washington State AAA girls singles championship in tennis in 2000. Mary (Yabuki) Takeuchi passed away May 26, 2001. Hiro Takeuchi lives in the Argay Terrace neighborhood, Parkrose.

In July 1941, Shigeru Takeuchi was drafted into the U.S. Army (see "Shigeru Takeuchi, Nisei Veterans," this volume). Shigeru came home in 1945. He helped Masao farm the home place his first year back. He then rented the Bates place, and farmed it for a few years. In 1948, he married Lucy Kubo, of Fresno, California, whom he had met while he was stationed at Camp Robinson. Lucy's family had been sent to the Jerome Relocation Camp in Arkansas, and the camp often hosted Nisei soldiers from Camp Robinson for entertainment and refreshments. In 1953, Shigeru and Lucy moved to Fresno, Lucy's home town, where Shigeru obtained employment in a grocery store. He and Lucy had three children, JoAnn, born in 1949; Keri (1953) and Brian (1955). In 1957, Shigeru and Lucy purchased a store, which they operated for the next 20 years. In 1977,

Hiro Takeuchi's Halsey Food Center

After the war, Hiro Takeuchi returned to Portland and re-entered the grocery business. After spending the war years in California and Idaho, he purchased this store located near 102nd Avenue and N.E. Halsey Street. After a span of eight years, he was back in the grocery business, a business in which he had much experience before WW II.

Photo courtesy of Hiro Takeuchi.

Shiro Takeuchi's Store, 122nd and S.E. Division

Shiro Takeuchi (center) surveys his stock of merchandise at his and Misawo's store on S.E. Division near 122nd Avenue, where they moved after closing their first store in S.E. Portland.

Photo courtesy of Shiro Takeuchi.

The Extended Takeuchi Family

Front, L to R: Keri, Brian, Sakajiro, Yaye, Susan, Kathy and Peggy. 2nd Row: Joann, Mary, Misawo, Nancy, Lynn, Jerry, Masumi and Lucy. Top: Hiro, Mel, Shiro, Tadashi, Shigeru, Masao and Bob. The only family member missing is Donald, Masao's oldest son.   Photo courtesy of Hiro Takeuchi

they leased the store and Shigeru started working at the Central Fish Market in Fresno. He worked there until his death in 2005.

Shiro Takeuchi, drafted on October 13, 1941, was sent to Camp Grant in Illinois for basic training. He applied for clerical school, for which he had to take a typing test. Although he had not touched a typewriter since taking typing from Miss Genevieve Rosen at CHS, he passed the test easily. On March 13, 1946, Shiro Takeuchi was discharged from the U.S. Army. He had spent four years and five months in the service. Shiro recalled, "If the war had not ended when it did, I would have fought with the 3rd Army in Japan" (see "Shiro Takeuchi, Nisei Veterans," this volume). After he arrived home, he helped his brothers on the farm. Later, he helped Shigeru, who had rented the Bates place. After 1948, he worked for two years in a grocery store. On January 15, 1950, he married Misawo Uyeoka, of Fresno, California. He then worked for his brother, Hiro, for about five years. In 1955, he and Misawo purchased the Busy Corner Grocery at S.E. 41st and Raymond (Hiro Takeuchi helped them get started in the business). Next, they moved to a store located at S.E. 122nd and Division, the Division Food Center, which they operated several years. Finally, they purchased a store on S.E. 86th and Woodstock, which Shiro and Misawo operated until 1981, when they retired. They have two children, Margaret "Peggy," born in 1953 and Susan, born in 1954. Both attended David Douglas

Tad Takeuchi

Tad Takeuchi enlisted in the U.S. Army after the war ended. He served in Japan in Army intelligence.
Photo courtesy of Hiro Takeuchi.

schools. Peggy attended the Health Sciences unit, University of Colorado, where she graduated with a degree in physical therapy. Susan attended Lewis and Clark where she majored in education. Later, she earned a masters degree in special education at Portland State University. She now teaches in the North Clackamas School District (2002). Both have volunteered at the Shriners' Hospital for Children.

Similarly to his brothers, "Tad" Takeuchi participated in sports. He played on the 1940-41 CHS basketball team that took 2nd place at State. After graduating from CHS in 1941, Tad remained on the farm. He accompanied his parents to the Pacific Livestock Exposition grounds and Tule Lake. Soon after Masao and Hiro left for Idaho, the rest of the family were sent to the Minidoka Relocation Center in Idaho. There, Tad worked for his two brothers on the farm they leased in Idaho. Soon after World War II ended, Tad was drafted into the U.S. Army. He served three years, including duty with the Army of Occupation in Japan, assigned to the Military Intelligence Service. During his tour in Japan, Tad was stationed at Utsunomiya. A courier, he delivered military intelligence and correspondence from his station to General Douglas McArthur's Headquarters in Tokyo. After his discharge, he attended and graduated from Reed College. He completed a doctoral program at the University of Washington and was hired to teach at Michigan State University. After three weeks, he resigned and returned to Portland. He then worked for his brothers in their stores and at the Bush Garden Restaurant. According to Hiro and Shiro, he loved to read and did not wish to take a job with any management responsibilities. Of his family, he seemed to be most affected by his wartime experiences. On June 25, 1997, Tad Takeuchi passed away, age 74.

Kaguma Toya

Yone (Ito) Toya

Photos courtesy of George Toya.

Kaguma Toya
Yone (Ito) Toya

Born in Japan on November 15, 1878, Kaguma Toya left the Islands at age 17 to avoid being drafted into the Japanese Imperial Army. He landed in Vancouver, British Columbia, and obtained employment in a logging camp. He worked in the camp for two or three years, then, near the turn of the century, decided to move to the United States. He worked as a gardener for the Mountain View Floral Company, which was located on the bluff above the Sandy River on what became an extension of Stark Street in later years. In 1914, he married Yone Ito, born in Kumamota, Japan, on April 4, 1892. Kumamota was also Kaguma Toya's hometown. When they married, he was age 36; she, age 22.

Kaguma and Yone Toya's first child, a girl, lived only two or three months, dying from the flu during the epidemic of 1918. Their second child, George, was born in 1919; their third child, Josephine, in 1920; and their fourth child, Fred, in 1923. The youngsters started school at the historic Cedar School on Troutdale Road. In 1929, because of his growing family, Kaguma decided to try farming. Since he could not own property, he rented the 18-acre Baker place located on Lucas Road about one-half mile north of Springdale. The family's nearest neighbors were the Amos Porter family, whose farm bordered the Baker farm on the west and the George "Jum" Mershon family, whose farm was located a short distance up Lucas Road. Other neighbors included the Gene Berney family, who operated a dairy farm close by, and the Henry Canzler family, who

Kaguma and Tone Toya Family

Kaguma came to the United States near the end of the 19th century. He found work as a gardener at the Mountain View Floral Company located on the bluff above the Sandy River near the Stark Street Bridge. He married Tone Ito during the time he worked for the Company. The photograph was taken in the early '20s. From left: Yone (Ito), George, Josephine, Fred and Kaguma Toya.   *Photo courtesy of George Toya.*

owned Canzler Hill to the south. The Baker farm included land on the North Slope of Canzler Hill, which land was farmed though it was quite steep.

The Toyas raised strawberries, lettuce, cauliflower, cabbage, pole beans, pole peas, tomatoes and cucumbers. The lettuce, cauliflower and peas were marketed through the Troutdale Vegetable Growers, while the beans, tomatoes and cabbage were sold at the farmers' market. Larson and Winters took the cucumbers to the Libby McNeil & Libby processing plant in Southeast Portland. The first three or four years on the farm, Ray Wilson, who lived on Jum Mershon's place, plowed the farm's acreage with Jum's team. Thereafter, M.B. McKay, who owned a caterpillar tractor with which he did custom work, plowed the 18 acres. The Toya family owned one horse, which was used to harrow, 'float' the ground and to cultivate. A barn on the property located across Lucas Road from the house provided horse stalls and a hay storage area. The three surviving Toya youngsters, George, Josephine and Fred, worked on the farm weeding seedbeds, planting (by hand) lettuce, cabbage and cauliflower, cultivating with the horse and hoeing the crops. They picked strawberries, beans, peas, tomatoes and cucumbers, cut cabbage, lettuce and cauliflower and helped with other farm chores.

Springdale Grade School

Springdale Grade School, the two-room schoolhouse that George, Josephine and Fred attended after moving to the Baker farm in 1929.   Photo, the author.

The three youngsters attended grade school in the two-room schoolhouse in Springdale. George and Josephine both completed grammar school in 1934 (she had skipped a grade), then attended Columbian High School in Corbett. Fred graduated from Springdale Grade School in 1935. In 1936, because of a dispute with his landlord, Kaguma rented a 68-acre farm in Powell Valley and the family moved. George and Josephine both graduated from Gresham High School in 1937; Fred, in 1939. George remained on the farm helping his family until he found his draft classification was to change from 4A (agriculture exemption) to 1A (draft eligible). To "get it [the obligation] over with," he volunteered to be among the first group of inductees to leave, and was inducted into the Army *for one year* on July 1, 1941 (see "George and Fred Toya, Nisei Veterans," this volume).

While in the Army stationed at Fort Snelling, George Toya married Sonoya Hirata, whom he had met when he visited Minidoka on furlough. After he returned to the Fort, he arranged for Sonoya to join him in Minnesota, where the couple married. He spent about a year in the Pacific theater (see "George Toya, Nisei Veterans," this volume). After his discharge from the Army, George Toya returned to Ontario, Oregon, Sonoya's home. He and Sonoya remained there until 1947, when they moved back to Gresham to take over the Powell Valley farm. George and Sonoya had two children, Georgene, born 1948, and Evelyn, born 1950. Both attended Gresham schools. The Toyas sold their Powell Valley farm in 1958 and moved to a newly built home on SE Kane Road in Gresham. Tragically, Evelyn died of cancer in 1965. After graduat-

On The Farm

George Toya poses beside the family's new 1939 Chevrolet truck purchased for farm use.
Photo courtesy of George Toya.

ing from Gresham High School in 1966, Georgene attended the University of Oregon, where she completed a degree program in education. She taught in Gresham schools for 25 years until ill health forced her retirement. She taught for several years at Gordon Russell Middle School. She passed away of Parkinson's disease in October, 2003. She did not marry.

After leaving the farm, George Toya obtained employment with the U.S. Postal Service transportation section, which is responsible for transporting mail by rail. The government then sent him to Stanford University to study computer science. After his training, he became a systems analyst. He worked for the U.S. Forest Service for two years, then worked for Bonneville Power for 17 years. In 1972, he retired from federal employment. Ross Perot's firm, Electronic Data Systems, then hired him as a systems analyst and he worked for that firm for ten years. During that period, George worked as a consultant at Bonneville Power with many of his former associates. George cited a couple of examples of how Ross Perot "took care" of his people. The son of an employee needed an urgent medical procedure. Perot flew the youngster in his private airplane to the Mayo Clinic and paid his entire medical bill. Perot would not permit the release of any publicity regarding the incident. On another occasion, Perot hired former special forces trained individuals to rescue an employee who was being held by terrorists.

Josephine married Charles "Chuck" Uyeda and the couple lived in Portland. In 1942, she and her family were interned with other Nikkei families at the Portland Assembly Center. After the Minidoka Relocation Center was built, the federal government sent the family to that facility. After being released, the Uyeda family returned to Portland where Chuck Uyeda worked for the North Pacific Terminal Company. After Josephine's five children, Jerry, Janice, JoAnnne, John and Sherri, were raised, she worked at the University of Portland.

George Toya Family

From Left, Evelyn Toya (in front of) Sonoya, and Georgene (in front of) George Toya at the family's Powell Valley farm.

Georgene Toya

After graduating from the University of Oregon, Georgene taught in Gresham schools until she retired because of ill health after 25 years service. Here she models a traditional Nikkei outfit for a prize-winning photograph.

Photos courtesy of George Toya.

Fred worked on the family's Powell Valley farm until the Western Defense Command removed Nikkei families from the West Coast. He, too, spent the summer months with his parents at the Pacific Livestock Exposition Center, then was sent with them to Minidoka. In 1944, he married Kimi Tainaka, whom he had met at the assembly center. Also in 1944, Fred was drafted into the U.S. Army. First he was sent to Fort Meade, then was transferred to Fort Snelling. He was at Fort Snelling when the war ended. Because the war was over and because his aging parents required help on the farm, Fred received an early discharge. When George returned to take over the farm, Fred purchased a farm near Carver, Oregon. While living there, he and Kimi had two boys, Rollin and Daniel. Presented with an opportunity to move to a farm located near Moses Lake, Washington, Fred sold the Carver farm and took his family to Moses Lake, where he farmed until his death in 1985.

Yone (Ito) Toya passed away on July 20, 1968; Kaguma Toya died just seven days later on July 27, 1968. George and Sonoya Toya now (2004) live in their Gresham home, which they had built in 1958.

Juichi Uyetake
Chise Uyetake

Both Juichi 'Harry' Uyetake and Chise Uyetake were born in Hiroshima, Japan, he November 25, 1884 and she, August 31, 1890. The Uyetakes came to East Multnomah County in 1913, first locating in a rental house on Henkle Road. In 1916, they purchased five acres on Mershon Road across the road from the Porter place. About two years later Harry purchased approximately 17 acres located on Mershon Road from the Mershon family. He moved his family into the house on the property in 1918. The main structure of the house (in which Shio Uyetake now lives) was built circa 1890. Harry and Chise Uyetake had five children: Shio, born in 1915; Kor, born in 1921; Fujie, born in 1922; June, born in 1925; and Mitzi, born in 1927.

Shio started grade school at Pleasant View on Wand Road, transferring to Corbett Grade School when Pleasant View closed in 1924. The other youngsters attended Corbett Grade School, from which each graduated. Shio, Kor and Fujie graduated from Columbian High School in 1933, 1939 and 1940, respectively (before the people of Japanese ancestry were interred during World War II). The Uyetake children also attended a "Japanese School," which was located on the five-acre parcel the Uyetakes owned on Mershon Road about one-half mile west of the home place. Nissei children living in the area attended this school once or twice a week, including a session on Saturdays. The students learned to read, write and speak the Japanese language. Other attendees included children of the Matsubu, the Takeuchi, the Sakurai, the Nakashimada, the Kondo, the Okita and the Toya families. Teachers included Mr. Nakata and Mr. Fukuda, among others. Shio Uyetake went on to attend the University of Washington, from which he graduated with a degree in Business Administration in 1937.

The Uyetakes grew vegetable crops and berries. During the 1930s, their berry crops included strawberries and boysenberries. They hired a number of area residents to pick for them including George, Clarence and Isabelle Mershon, Eva Knieriem and Norah Davis. Harry purchased seven acres immediately behind Jum Mershon's residence at the corner of Lucas Road and Mershon Road; he also purchased thirteen acres of the Baker Place on Lucas Road where the Toya family lived for a time. Thus, the family owned approximately 42 acres when the war started in 1941. After Japan attacked the United States fleet at Pearl Harbor as well as other outposts in the Pacific, the government required persons of Japanese ancestry (including U.S. citizens) to leave the area. After spending three months at the Portland Assembly Center, the internees were

Juichi 'Harry' and Chise Uyetake Family

From left, Fujie, June (in front of) Shio, Harry, Kor, (behind) Mitzi and Chise Uyetake. The Uyetakes moved to East Multnomah County in 1913, and settled on Mershon Road in 1918.
Photos courtesy of Shio Uyetake.

The Uyetake Farm

The Uyetake farm looking east from the Mershon place. Note the Louis Berney home (above the shed) and the Jesse 'Mike' Rogers' home (at the crest of the hill in the trees).

sent to "relocation camps." Authorities sent the Uyetake family to the Tule Lake Camp in California.

When the family was forced from the farm in 1942, the Uyetakes entrusted Louis Berney to take care of their property. In 1943, the family left Tule Lake for a farm in Michigan. Juichi 'Harry' Uyetake died in Michigan in May, 1944. Though they had an opportunity to remain in Michigan after the war, Chise Uyetake, Shio, Fujie, June and Mitzi returned to their home in East County.

Digging Out in 1937

From left: Harry, Fujie, Mitzi and June clear the driveway to the barn after the record snowfall of the winter of 1936-37.   *Photos courtesy of Shio Uyetake.*

Snowbound, 1937

Abandoned automobiles on the hill above the Uyetake place that same year (1936-37).

Shio took over the operation of the farm and farmed the place until 1961. During this period he raised berries and vegetables. Shio sold berries to Snider Farms and then to Scenic Fruit. The other crops, cauliflower, cabbage, lettuce and broccoli, were sold to S.T. Produce and Birds Eye Foods, which had developed a market for frozen vegetables.

On September 17, 1950, Shio Uyetake married Nobuko Mukai of Fresno, California. The couple had four children: Arlene, Donna, Vern and Lyle. All

The First Uyetake Home, ca 1920

From left, Harry Uyetake, Chise Uyetake, Shio, Yoshiko Kuwabara and Joe Kuwabara. Harry Uyetake moved his family into this home in 1918. It was built ca 1890.

Remodeled Uyetake Home, ca 1940

Harry Uyetake had his home remodeled in 1940, just before the war forced his family from the farm.   Photos courtesy of Shio Uyetake.

attended Corbett Grade and High School, with Arlene graduating from CHS in 1969, Donna in 1972, Verne in 1975 and Lyle in 1979. Arlene graduated from the Oregon College of Education (now Western Oregon University), but did not teach. She and her former husband, Vance Dunlop, built a home on the 7-acre parcel adjacent (west) of the Mershon place mentioned above, which was

Shio Uyetake Family

Rear, from left: Shio Uyetake, Arlene and Nobuko. Front, Donna, Vern and Lyle (on his mother's lap). Photo, Shio Uyetake.

later sold. She has two children, Tara and Beth, lives in Sandy (2003) and works for the US Bank. Her daughters attend Sandy High School.

Donna graduated from Portland State University, married Frank McConnell, has a son, Mark, and lives in Issaquah, Washington. Verne graduated from Oregon State University in 1979, has not married, lives at home (2000) and works as a journalist and photographer for the *Lake Oswego Review*. He also does free lance photography. Lyle attended Oregon State University from which he graduated in 1983. He married Sue Ireland, works at the Stanford University Laboratory and lives in Redwood City, California.

Kor, who did not return to Oregon after the war, completed college at the Missouri College of Mines and worked in the mining industry in Colorado after the war. He married Mary Hishinuma and had two boys, Sidney and John. Kor passed away several years ago. Fujie married Bill Furumasu and had two boys, Stacey and Russell. She now lives in Green Acres, Washington. June married Kiyo Ogawa and had one son, Steve. She now lives in Altadena, California. Mitzi married Tosh Okada and had two children, Kerrie and Dale. Kerrie Okada graduated from Oregon State University and now lives on Littlepage Road. Mitzi lives in Los Altos, California (2003).

Shio reported that farming became unprofitable in the late 50's, so he decided to take a job with a more certain income. He went to work for Kubla Khan Company, which produced canned and frozen Chinese foods. He worked for the company approximately 20 years, retiring in 1981. He also worked part-time for Kwan Ying's Kitchen as a cashier and deliveryman. Nobuko Uyetake started working at Edgefield after the children were in school, and worked there until the facility closed. She transferred to the Juvenile Justice Center where she worked until her retirement in 1984.

Chise Uyetake died February 6, 1958, after living her final years at the family's farm on the "hill."

Roy Iemon Asakawa
Kiku Asakawa

According to family lore, Roy Iemon Asakawa, after marrying his intended, Kiku, in Japan, shipped out on a freighter as a deck hand with plans for their future. Upon reaching Seattle, Roy "jumped ship," obtained work as a laborer on a railroad and started saving money to bring his bride to the United States. Later, he found work at various lumber mills. In 1912, he sent his wife the funds with which to pay her passage so that she could join him in the United States. At this time, he was living in Oregon and working at a lumber mill in Mill City. The "plan" succeeded, and the couple's first child, Toyoko "Toyo" was born in Mill City, Oregon, in 1914. In 1916, the couple's second child, a son, Nogi, was born. Shortly thereafter, Roy Asakawa found employment in Troutdale, working for A.C. Althaus at his dairy on Troutdale Road. The Asakawa family lived in a house on the property while he worked at the dairy. Roy and Kiku Asakawa had four more children, Jack, born in 1918, Katherine (1920), Ben (1925), and Walter (1929). Acting on the recommendation of Lenore Althaus, the four younger children were given "American" names.

Emmett B. Williams' Barn, Troutdale Road

When Roy Asakawa first moved with his family to Troutdale, he worked on the Althaus (former Williams) dairy farm located on the NW corner of Cochran Road and Troutdale Road. *Photo courtesy of Carol Asakawa.*

Asakawa Family ca 1933

Sitting on the porch of the family home, SW corner, Cochran Road and Troutdale Road are, from left: Ben, Roy, Nogi, Walter (on lap of), Toyo, Kiku, Katherine and Jack Asakawa.   *Photo courtesy of Carol Asakawa.*

Roy Asakawa, a thrifty individual, had soon saved enough money to purchase a 16-acre parcel across Cochran Road from the Althaus dairy farm. After the purchase, Roy Asakawa moved his family into the home on the property and started a "truck garden" farm operation. The family raised rhubarb, spinach, cauliflower, cabbage, broccoli and some berries. Similarly to other Nikkei families in the area, he sold much of his produce through the Eastside Farmers' Market. Initially handicapped by the lack of a truck, he transported his produce in the rear seat and trunk of his automobile, which permitted him to eke out a living until he could afford to buy a truck. Kaz Tamura remarked, "When he came to Troutdale, my father knew nothing about farming. Roy Asakawa took the time to teach him how to farm. Roy Asakawa was a great neighbor!"

The Asakawa youngsters attended Cedar Park School, located on Troutdale Road south of their home. After completing elementary school, the older Asakawa youngsters attended Gresham High School from which Toyo graduated in 1932; Nogi, in 1934. For some reason, Jack did not complete high school; perhaps he preferred farm work. Both Katherine and Ben graduated from Hunt High School, Minidoka. Walter started high school at the camp and remained in Idaho after the war to complete high school at Hunt.

Troutdale Grade School 7th and 8th, 1940

Front, L to R: Ed Schneider, Ronald Lee, Shirley McGinnis, Beulah Gilstrap, Shirley King, Doris Burnacci, Jean Knarr, Anna Cereghino, Al Sinner, Don Espenel and Fred Owens. 2nd Row: **Walter Asakawa***, Gary McKercher, Edward Kido, Neil Lovell, Clarence Gandy, Mr. Leslie Bass, Principal, Stan Rathman, Melvin O'Dell, Ed Burnacci, Lorall Bettendorf and Vern Rathman. 3rd Row: Jim Sunderland, Pete Wheadon, Marvin Schneider,* **Scott Cunningham***, Lawrence Schneider, Dick Owens, Billy Giancone, Willy Walker and Tom Kido.* Photo courtesy of Scott Cunningham.

Cedar Sewing Club, 1934

From left, Lillian Yayoi Tamura, Esther Lewis, Virginia Martin, Bonnie Townsend, Katherine Asakawa, Lenore Althaus (leader) and Mabel Powers

Photo courtesy of Lauretta Yamashita.

Spinach Harvest, Asakawa Farm, 1940

Harvesting spinach are, from left, Roy Asakawa, Kiku Asakawa, Nogi Asakawa, Marion German and Ben Asakawa.

Photos courtesy of Lauretta Yamashita.

Asakawa Home

The new Asakawa home located west of Troutdale Road and south of Cochran Road.

Photo courtesy of Lauretta Yamashita.

I. ASAKAWA
R. F. D. 2,
Troutdale, Oregon.

農

淺川伊右衞門園

三重縣三重郡內部村

In 1936, the North American Times documented Nikkei families living in the west. Above is Iomen Asakawa's advertisement.

Courtesy of Jeff Grover.

Toyo Asakawa married Tetusaburo Yamamoto before the war. The couple lived on the farm until the U.S. Government forced all Nikkei families from their farms on May 12, 1942. The couple had a daughter, Janet, born on the farm. The couple's second child, Roy, was born at the Minidoka Relocation Center. After the war, the Yamamoto family lived on Sauvie Island where they farmed for a living. Toyo and Tetusaburo Yamamoto had three more children, Colleen, Marlene and Susan.

Minidoka Camp, Twin Falls, Idaho

Forced from their Troutdale farm on May 12, 1942, the Asakawa family, excepting Jack, who had been drafted, found themselves in Barracks 2 of Block 31, Minidoka Internment Camp, where they spent the war years (WWII).

Photo, from <u>Minidoka Interlude</u>, *published by its residents, 1943.*

Ben Asakawa, U.S. Army

Ben Asakawa served in the U.S. Army during the Korean War, but was not deployed overseas.

Photo courtesy of Carol Asakawa.

Nogi Asakawa worked with his father on the farm until May 12, 1942. At the center, the family lived in Barracks 2, Block 31. After the war, in February, 1946, Nogi married Mary Kinoshita. The couple purchased a farm in the Sandy, Oregon, area, where they concentrated on growing strawberries and other berry crops. In the early 1980s, when farming became less economical, Nogi took a part-time job as a butcher in a meat shop in Sandy. Nogi and Mary had three children, Landon, Maxine and Julie.

Jack Asakawa, drafted early in 1941, was eventually assigned to a medical detachment of the 442nd Regimental Combat Team. Hit by shrapnel from a "tree burst," he

Walter Asakawa, After the War

In 1955, Walter Asakawa purchased a parcel of land off Troutdale Road near Sweetbriar Road. Here, his disking under a cover crop of rye and vetch, preparing the land for plowing.   Photo courtesy of Carol Asakawa.

Camp Shelby, Mississippi

Corporal George Yamashita and his bride, Katherine Asakawa, at Camp Shelby, Mississippi, where George was stationed.

Photo courtesy of Lauretta Yamashita.

suffered a disabling injury and the Army returned him to the States. Jack never married and, because of his injuries, he could not drive an automobile. After the war, he helped farm the home place with his brother, Walter. Walter purchased a tractor with special equipment for Jack, which he could operate. However, as Carol Asakawa recalled, "Jack once took out one of our sheds. He had to drive the tractor very slowly." After Walter purchased another eleven acres across Troutdale Road. Jack helped farm that acreage as well as other rented parcels in the area. Jack died on July 15, 1992, and is interred in Willamette National Cemetery (see "Jack Asakawa, Nisei Veterans," this volume).

Katherine Asakawa married George Yamashita, veteran of World War II, who served as a cook in the Cannon

Asakawa Family Members, ca 1980

1st Photo, upper left (from left): Toyo and Jack Asakawa. 2nd Photo, upper right: Mary and Nogi Asakawa. 3rd Photo, lower left: Ben and Irene Asakawa. 4th Photo, lower right: Carol and Walter Asakawa.   Photos courtesy of Carol Asakawa.

Company, 442nd Regimental Combat Team. Among other duty stations, he served at Camp Shelby, Mississippi, Camp Swift, Texas, and most likely, in Italy after the war (his name appears in Orville C. Shirey's book; see "Sources," this volume). After the war, Katherine and George bought a parcel of the former Althaus farm and built a home there. Their six children, Diane, Roger, Donna, Byron, Perry and Wayne, attended Powell Valley Grade School and Barlow High, except Byron, who died in childhood, and Diane, who attended two years at Gresham High before transferring to Barlow. George Yamashita worked at the Gresham Post Office. He passed away on May 23, 1989, and Katherine (Asakawa) Yamashita died on July 13, 1997; both are interred at the Willamette National Cemetery.

Ben Asakawa served in the U.S. Army during the Korean war, though he was not deployed overseas. He passed away on July 15, 1997, and is interred at Willamette National Cemetery.

After completing high school in Idaho, Walter Asakawa returned to the farm on Troutdale Road. In 1955, he purchased an eleven-acre parcel across Troutdale Road and south of the home place. On March 28 that year, he married Carol Murahashi, of Gresham. Walter farmed with his brother, Jack, farming the home place (16 acres), his place (11 acres) and other rented parcels. He, Jack and Carol grew rhubarb, spinach, cauliflower, cabbage, broccoli and berries, most of which were sold through the Eastside Farmers' Market, which later became a wholesale market. They also sold produce to Albertsons, Fred Meyer (some), United Grocers, Safeway and Fujii Produce. Walter and Carol Asakawa had four children, Linda, Peggy, Walter "Butch," and Scott. Walter Asakawa died on November 17, 1983.

Carol Asakawa and her son, Scott, continue to farm the family's holdings on Troutdale Road. In 2005, she will have lived on the farm for 50 years. She and her son grow Asian pears, persimmons, potted garden plants and flowers. They dry many of their flowers and use them to make wreaths. They market their farm products through the farmers' markets in Gresham and Milwaukie. In addition to her work on the farm, Carol Asakawa works in the cafeteria at Russell Middle School, Gresham (2004).

442nd Medics In the Vosges Forest, France

Medics relax for a moment during a lull in the fighting in the Vosges Forest, France. Note the dug out covered with logs to protect its occupants from "tree burst" shrapnel. Jack Asakawa served as a medic in the 442nd.   *Photo, the National Archives.*

Bukichi Fujii
Yoshino (Yamakado) Fujii

Bukichi Fujii, born January 16, 1884, in Tokuyama, Japan, came to the United States from Vancouver, British Columbia in 1899. Eventually, he settled in Troutdale on Cherry Park Road, where he purchased a 49-acre farm in his oldest son's name (Toshio Fujii). He and his first wife, Umi (Arima), had three other children that did not survive childhood . In 1918, after his first wife died, Bukichi traveled to Japan to find a bride and married Yoshino Yamakado, of Susuma, Japan. The couple returned to the United States and Bukichi Fujii introduced his bride to life on the Troutdale farm. Bukichi and Yoshino Fujii had eight children: Akiye, born in 1918, Kazuo "Kaz" (1919), Kimiko (1921), Edward Harumi (1923), Jack Kiyoshi (1925), James Mamoru (1926), Thomas Tomio (1929), and Tadato (1933). The youngsters attended Troutdale Grade School (in the building that continues to serve as a school) their elementary years, and Gresham High School their secondary years (until May 12, 1942). Fujii purchased a 79-acre, uncleared parcel of land south of Gresham, but did not farm the ground before the war. The family raised cauliflower, cabbage, broccoli, brussel sprouts and berries, including blackberries, raspberries, boysenberries, loganberries and strawberries. The "cold weather" crops were generally sold at the farmers' market in S.E. Portland and the berries were generally sold through the Gresham Berry Growers. Other Issei considered Bukichi Fujii a pioneer leader, or "taisho," whom they sought out for advice. A large, robust man, he invariably held a cigar in his mouth.

December 7, 1941, according to Edward Fujii, "was a day which most of us of Japanese ancestry will never forget as long as we are on this earth. We were busy with the usual Sunday chores such as getting all the different vegetables prepared for the early morning market...(Monday) our fellow students were very congenial to us and never really put any pressure on us for what happened on Pearl Harbor Day. I must admit that the day went along quite well and everything was handled without incident. My father, who was classified as an alien was getting different literature (as to) where he could travel and what curfew hours he had to abide by...My father was not allowed to leave the area, (which required his sons to) do a bit of adjusting to do the truck driving plus attend school...With curfew regulations in effect, we all had to adjust our schedule and make every attempt to be back home by 8:00 p.m...In the Spring of 1942, there was a bumper crop of smelt running. We were all waiting for the evacuation order so many families on the farm smoked a lot of smelt." Similar to other Nikkei families in this area, on May 7, 1942, the Fujii family

Bukichi and Yoshino Fujii

Mr. and Mrs. Fujii raised their children on their Troutdale farm, but the action taken by the Western Defense Command forced them from their home in 1942. They returned after the war, and resumed farming. *Photo courtesy of Edward Fujii.*

received orders to leave the farm and report to the Pacific Livestock Exposition Center in North Portland on May 12, 1942. Since Edward Fujii was a senior, he received his diploma from Gresham High early. He remembered Mr. Saverude as "a great person and a wonderful principal." Mr. Fujii asked a neighbor family, Andrew and Charlotte Cunningham, to live in the Fujii home, harvest the berry crops and take care of the family's personal possessions and farm equipment for the duration. He had confidence that Charlotte Cunningham, who had worked for him as field boss, would make certain that the berry crops would be cared for properly. After the Cunninghams assented, the Fujii family stored their furniture and other household possessions in one bedroom. They lubed and oiled their Caterpillar tractor, stored it in a shed and covered it. The farm equipment that the Cunninghams would need to care for the berry crops was stored in or near the barn. The horse, used to cultivate the berries, was in the pasture by the barn. When May 12, arrived, Andrew and Charlotte Cunningham took the Fujii family to the Troutdale assembly area. There the Fujiis boarded a school bus bound for the Portland International Livestock Exposition Center. Before December 7, the Fujii's oldest daughter, Akiye, had married Seiichi Nakamura, employed on an oyster farm in Willapa Bay. Before the war broke out, the couple moved to Brighton, Colorado, thus they were not affected by the order. Also, Kaz Fujii had been drafted in 1941, and was in the Army, so he

Troutdale Intermediate, 1937

*Front, L to R: Donald Snell, Stan Rathman, Shirley McGinnis, Doris Burnacci, Jimmy Owens, Jean Knarr, unidentified, **Jimmy Fujii** and unidentified. 2nd Row: Wayne Espenel, Walter Naismyth, Iris Burlingame, Mrs. Helen Fehrenbacher, Anna Cereghino, **Scott Cunningham**, Edward Burnacci and Donald Espenel. 3rd Row: Clarence Gandy, Robert Salthe, Glenn Dorches, Billy Giancone, Lloyd Snell, Guy Dorches and Vern Rathman.*   *Photo courtesy of Scott Cunningham.*

was not directly affected. Therefore, on May 12, Bukichi and Yoshino Fujii and their six youngest children entered the livestock center in North Portland. However, the family's story differs from that of most other families at the center.

Once settled at the Portland center, Fujii family members read a posted notice stating that farmers near Nyssa, Oregon needed labor to help in the sugar beet fields. Jim, Jack and Edward Fujii volunteered to help and were sent by train to a labor camp near Nyssa. There, the United States Department of Agriculture, Farm Security Administration, had established a work camp to house farm laborers urgently needed by farmers in the area. The Fujii brothers worked there for a couple of weeks, then returned to the center. Bukichi Fujii decided to take the entire family to the camp. About 100 Nikkei took advantage of this opportunity at that time. As Edward related, conditions at the labor camp were primitive. "We lived in tents and worked hard in the fields, but this was better than living at the center. We were kept busy the rest of the year harvesting fruit, sugar beets, potatoes and onions." That winter (1942-43) the government rehabilitated a former CCC camp at Adrian, Oregon, in order to house the approximate 100 field hands and their families engaged in farm work, mostly in sugar

Labor Camp, Nyssa, Oregon

Youngsters, including some of the Fujii brothers, line up for a haircut from Ben Yamihiro at the Farm Security Administration labor camp in Eastern Oregon.

Photo courtesy of Edward Fujii.

beets, but also involving other crops, including caring for cattle and sheep. In the fall of 1943, Edward Fujii decided to attend Brigham Young University (BYU) in Provo, Utah. He worked at the BYU college farm on weekends to help pay expenses. He attended two quarters before the government reversed its position on drafting Nisei, and Edward's classification was changed from 4-C (not acceptable because of ancestry) to 1-A (see "Edward Fujii, Nisei Veterans," this volume). The Fujii family remained in the labor camp until the spring of 1944, when they were able to rent 40-acres of farmland near Nyssa, on which they raised potatoes, sugar beets and onions. Edward Fujii was drafted and ordered to Boise, Idaho to take his physical.

After the Fujii family left Troutdale enroute to the Portland Center, Andrew and Charlotte Cunningham and their two children, Scott and Charlotte, prepared to move into the Fujii home. Before the move, they painted the house, inside and out. After the move, they rented their own home to a family that had come to Oregon to work in the shipyards. The first farm task facing the Cunninghams was getting the strawberries picked. Both Scott and Charlotte were experienced pickers and Mrs. Cunningham had experience as a field boss. Sufficient pickers were found and the berry harvest started. However, when Scott took the first load of strawberries to the Gresham Berry Growers, he recounted what happened. "The rednecks at the cannery went through the load crate by crate looking for bad berries. When one was found, they started dock-

Fujii Brothers at Nyssa High School

While living in the United States Department of Agriculture labor camp at Adrian, Oregon, the younger Fujii students attended school in Nyssa. Jack (left), graduated from Nyssa High in 1943; Jim (right), in 1944.   Photo courtesy of Edward Fujii.

ing us for "bad" fruit. Of course they knew the berries were from the Fujii farm." Because of this incident, the Cunninghams opened the berry fields to U-pickers. They did successfully harvest about two acres of asparagus, which was sold without incident. Charlotte Cunningham turned over the farm receipts to Mr. Boyd, an accountant in Troutdale who managed Mr. Fujii's financial affairs. This included rent money paid by tenants who lived in the farm housing previously used by farm workers and the payments from Multnomah County for the "share-crop" arrangement between the County and Bukichi Fujii from the sale of hay.

One day, a Federal Bureau of Investigation (FBI) agent stopped at the Fujii home. Apparently, someone had informed the Government that the bedroom where the Fujiis had stored their furniture held a short wave radio. The agent broke the lock and "went through the items in the room thoroughly," according to Scott. Of course, nothing of an incriminating nature was found. In a few months, this visit was followed by another. The second FBI visit concerned a report that a *tank* was stored in a shed on the property. Of course, the tank turned out to be a Caterpillar farm tractor. But these two visits illustrate the suspicion and the hysteria that gripped the country during the early months of the war.

In February, 1945, the Government allowed the Fujii family to return to their farm in Troutdale. According to Edward, the "feeling in our area (Troutdale)

Ed Fujii, U.S. Army

Edward Fujii, attending BYU, had his draft classification changed from 4C (Not acceptable because of ancestry) to 1A, and he soon found himself in the U.S. Army. *Photo, Edward Fujii.*

was quite hostile, but we were able to overcome the harassment from some of the local people." The Cunningham family moved back to their home in Troutdale, and the Fujii family prepared to resume farming. However, the Manager of the Multnomah County Farm adjacent to the Fujii farm had other ideas. Fujii had arranged with the Multnomah County to harvest hay on some of the land during their absence, and alfalfa had been planted. After fruitless negotiations concerning the situation, Fujii took matters into his own hands, disked the field and planted lettuce. That settled the matter. After his discharge from the Army, Kaz returned to the Troutdale farm, as did Ed upon his discharge. Mr. Fujii and his sons purchased more farmland in the area, including 20 acres on which the new Reynolds High School was later built. They rented other land, including a 79-acre parcel on Troutdale Road near the former Baker Pit (quarry) on Stark Street, and another 55-acre parcel near Sundial, rented from Reynolds Metals. They rented other farmland and at one point had nearly 450 acres in cultivation. The Fujiis continued to raise row crops, some of which were sold through the farmers' market while other crops went to food processors such as Birds Eye Foods on Stark Street. However, as the farm economy slowed in the late 1950s and early 1960s, some in the family decided to try other pursuits. Kaz and Jim Fujii, however, continued to farm; Kaz until encroaching development took his land. Jim Fujii's family continues to farm. The family concentrates on growing berries, primarily on rented land.

As mentioned earlier, Akiye Fujii married Seiichi Nakamura and the couple had five children, Hisae, Richard, Dennis, Vicki and Alan. On November 6, 1955, Kaz Fujii married May Nakata, born in Oregon, but who spent the war years in Japan. The couple had two children, Tim and Karen. Kimiko Fujii married Roy Yamada. The couple settled in Newburg, Oregon, where Dr. Yamada practiced dentistry. They had three boys, Russell, Randall and Rodney. Edward married Aya Iwasaki of Hillsboro, Oregon. Aya graduated from Oregon State University with a degree in Home Economics. She worked as a dietitian at Woodland Park Hospital for more than 30 years. Ed and Aya Fujii had three children, Scott, Becki and Tami. When Edward left the farm, he purchased a wholesale produce business and renamed it Fujii Produce. As Fujii Produce, Ed brokered vegetable and berry crops to large grocery chains. He sold the business in 1990, but the business remains a going concern. Jack Fujii, who served in the Army during World War II in Europe, also farmed with his brothers after his discharge in 1946. Eventually, however, he worked with his brother, Jim Fujii. Jack married, but his marriage did not last. Jack died on January 1, 1993, in Portland.

In 1944, after graduating from Nyssa High School, Jim Fujii worked on the farm his father had rented near Nyssa. When the courts ruled that the detention of people of Japanese ancestry in "relocation camps" was not legal, Bukichi Fujii returned to Troutdale. However, Jim Fujii had received his draft notice and reported to Fort Douglas, Utah, for induction. Jim Fujii spent about 18 months in the service, predominantly as a member of the Army of Occupation, Germany (see "James 'Jim' Fujii, Nisei Veterans," this volume).

Upon his return, Jim Fujii resumed farming with his father and brothers. As his brothers left the farm, he went on his own, farming the 79-acre place on Troutdale Road and other land he rented. He married Suzie "Jinx," and the couple had five children, Cheryl, Jill, Ron, Patty and Ray. Jim Fujii's son, Raymond, and his daughter, Cheryl, bought the family farming enterprises and manage several fruit stands in the area, which family members operate.

The next sibling, Thomas Fujii, graduated from Oregon State University and worked for the United States Soil Conservation Service. He married Mary Nakata, and the couple had four children, Gerald, Mark, Lisa and Shari. The youngest of Bukichi and Yoshino Fujii's children, Todato Fujii, served in the U.S. Army during the Viet Nam era. After his discharge, he served in the Merchant Marine until his death on April 21, 2003, in Sacramento, California.

Note: Fujii family members whom the author interviewed spoke highly of the Cunningham family, who managed their farm during the difficult years of World War II. They had special praise for Mrs. Cunningham, who, the Fujii siblings relate, was "a second mother" to them. They also mentioned the help extended to them by Al and Anita Espenel. Bukichi Fujii passed away on February 28, 1974, age 90.

George P. Kumazawa
Tsugi Kumazawa

George Kumazawa, born in Japan, came to the United States in 1913. He sent for his "picture bride," Tsugi Sugiyama in 1919. The couple lived on a farm in Wilsonville, Oregon. There, Kumazawa planted onions as his principal crop. The couple's first three children, Grace, Joe and Frances, were born while the family lived in Wilsonville. In the late 1920s, when Frances "was just a toddler," Kumazawa purchased, sight unseen, what he thought was a 16-acre farm near Scappoose, Oregon. He discovered that the "farm" was actually cutover forestland. It might have been suitable for farmland if the stumps and brush were removed. A disappointed Kumazawa found employment with the Clark & Wilson Lumber Company. While living in Scappoose, four more children were born to the couple, Mary, Josephine, George and Gladys. In 1935, George Kumazawa lost his life in an accident at the lumber company. Fortunately for his family, the loss occasioned an monthly insurance payment to his widow, which permitted Tsugi to provide for her children.

In 1937, after receiving entreaties from friends and relatives to return to Japan, Tsugi Kumazawa decided to join her parents there. The small insurance stipend she received monthly would, because of the favorable exchange rate, translate into a substantial income in Japan. Consequently, Tsugi Kumazawa took her seven children to Japan, where she had a home for her family built in Hiratsuka, Kanagawa-ken, Honshu Island, Japan. There, she continued to receive the monthly check from Oregon, which provided a comfortable living for the family. Grace, however, who had started high school in Scappoose, found Japan too "quaint" for her taste. Because she lacked language skills, school personnel placed her in grade four, where her classmates called her "denshin baushira," or "beanpole." In 1937, Grace decided to return to the United States. She found a housekeeping job at a Portland hotel and enrolled at Lincoln High School. At Lincoln, she caught the attention of one of her teachers, Mabel Southworth, who lived on S.W. Montgomery Street. Mrs. Southworth and her husband, Carl, invited Grace to stay with them while she attended Lincoln. Of course, Grace helped with the housework and other chores, but she appreciated the concern for her well being demonstrated by the Southworths.

Meanwhile in Japan, Mrs. Kumazawa grew fearful that her son, Joe, might be drafted into the (Japanese) army. She urged him to return to the United States. Consequently, he, too, left Japan and returned to Oregon. He obtained employment as a farm laborer with Hawley Kato, a Gresham farmer. Though his younger sister, Frances, yearned to return to the U.S., she was too young. However, in June, 1941, having received an invitation to stay with Carl and Mabel Southworth, who had moved to Troutdale, Oregon, Frances left Japan

George and Tsugi Kumazawa

 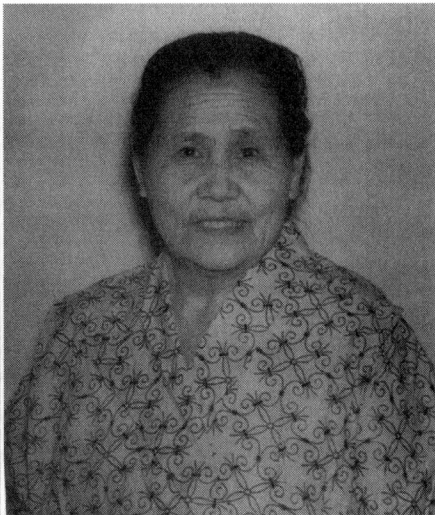

George Kumazawa immigrated to the United States in 1913. His "picture Bride," Tsugi Sugiyama, joined him on his Wilsonville farm in 1919.   Photos courtesy of Frances Ota.

for Oregon. Upon her arrival in Oregon, the Southworths opened their home to her. She enrolled as a junior at Gresham High School. Frances recalled that the Southworths treated both her and Grace as foster daughters. Frances later wrote that Carl and Mabel Southworth "were benefactors and my personal mentors."

Then Japanese planes bombed Pearl Harbor. Tsugi Kumazawa lost her monthly insurance payment from Oregon, which she had used to support her family and to build a nice home. She took a cooking job in a nearby factory. In fact, nearly every remaining member of the family worked at one of the factories in Hiratsuka producing war materiel. During the war, the Japanese population suffered from a shortage of food, affecting everyone. In 1944 and 1945, after the United States established bases within striking distance of Japan, the war brought unimaginable destruction to many of Japan's cities. On July 16, 1945, a raid by American bombers destroyed Hiratsuka, the city in which the family lived. Later George Kumazawa, a teen-ager at the time, recalled, "[The July 16 raid] lasted about 30 minutes...Our house didn't get touched, but after the bombing there wasn't anything standing between our house and a train station a mile and a half away...[The] town was flattened." Tsugi Kumazawa and her four youngest children survived the war years.

The war also affected the lives of the three older Kumazawa youngsters who had returned to the United States. Grace, with the intervention of Carl and Mabel Southworth, had enrolled at the University of Oregon. In 1940, while picking raspberries on a nearby farm, the "Dean of Women, the University of Oregon, came to the field to encourage me to enroll." Enroll she did; she had completed nearly two years at the university when the war struck. In May,

1942, the War Relocation Authority "yanked her out" of the university, forcing her to the assembly center in Portland. Her two younger siblings, Joe and Frances joined her there. A bus transported Joe from Gresham to the center and Frances, living with the Southworths, reported to an assembly point in Gresham from which a bus took her to the center. Thus, the three siblings were united at the Pacific International Livestock Exposition Center in Portland.

However, Grace soon decided that any situation would be better than "living like animals" at the center. When an opportunity came that permitted internees to volunteer for farm work in Eastern Oregon, Grace, Joe and Frances Kumazawa left the center with a group of 129 Nisei to live at a farm labor camp in Nyssa, Oregon, for employment as farm laborers. There, "In blistering hot weather, [the three] thinned lettuce, weeded and topped sugar beets, weeded and thinned onions and picked up potatoes."

Grace, determined to complete college, enrolled at the College of Idaho, completed her junior year, then transferred to the University of Missouri. At the university she met Air Cadet Ralph Giese, whom she married. After completing the program he served in the Army Air Force. Grace, a science major, graduated from the university and enlisted in the Women's Army Corps. Sent to Indianapolis for medical training, she received her discharge after VJ day since she was married. She completed graduate work at the University of Chicago. After his discharge from the Army, Ralph and Grace Giese moved to California, where they raised their three children, Robert, Vincent and Carlann. Grace's younger brother, Joe, had gone to Chicago from Nyssa. There, he learned the nursery business. When his sister moved to California, Joe left Chicago to live there as well.

In September, 1942, Frances Kumazawa enrolled as a senior at Nyssa High School, from which she graduated in 1943. That fall she enrolled in the U.S. Cadet Nurses program at Eastern Oregon State College, LaGrande, Oregon. There, she completed the pre-clinical course work after which the class transferred to The Dalles, Oregon, for the next phase of training. However, as a Nisei, Frances could not enter the coastal restricted zone. Consequently, the college arranged for her to complete this phase of her training at St. Marks Hospital, Salt Lake City, Utah. Frustrated by the fact that she could not accompany her class, Francis penned a letter to Eleanor Roosevelt, who was much more sympathetic to the plight of Japanese-American citizens than her husband, President Franklin D. Roosevelt, or others in his administration. Frances eventually received an exemption, but it came too late for her to join her classmates at The Dalles. And at St. Marks, she encountered suspicion and prejudice, which caused her to return to Eastern Oregon State College.

During this "low period, an Army recruiter appeared [and] asked [Frances] if she would be interested in joining the Army as a linguist." Frances accepted the offer and, on November 26, 1944, joined the Women's Army Corps (see

U.S. Cadet Nurse Program, Eastern Oregon State College

Above: In 1942, the Western Defense Command's exclusion of people of Japanese ancestry kept Frances Kumazawa (2nd from left, front row) from completing the nursing program in which she was enrolled at Eastern Oregon State College, LaGrande. Left: Frances Kumazawa's Certificate of Exemption, which she received about six months after writing to Eleanor Roosevelt. Photo courtesy of Frances Ota.

"Frances (Kumazawa) Ota/John Ota," this volume). On December 15, 1945, Frances married a fellow serviceman, John Ota, whom she met while both were stationed at Fort Crowder, Missouri. The ceremony took place at the home of Carl and Mabel Southworth, who arranged the entire wedding, including an appearance by the Lincoln High School choir. Frances stated, "I cannot put into words the gratitude I have for all that was done for me by the Southworths." The couple decided to make Oregon their home. Frances completed a program at a business school in Portland, Oregon, on the GI Bill. The couple moved into a unit of the wartime housing that became Vanport. When floods wiped out Vanport in 1948, John and Frances Ota purchased an acre of ground in East Multnomah County, borrowed a tent, and set about building a house. John initially built a small "starter home," which he enlarged as funds permitted. He finished the interior with beautiful woodwork and other amenities, which makes the structure a delightful, "one-of-a-kind" home. John and Frances lived in the tent while he completed the initial building. They have lived in the same home since 1948 (58 years in 2006). John and Frances Ota have one son, Jeremy Ota, who is a physician in emergency medicine with Kaiser Permamente.

Mr. and Mrs. John Ota

When John Ota and Frances Kumazawa married, they asked Carl and Mabel Southworth, who had befriended Frances years before, to participate in the wedding ceremony.

Photos courtesy of Frances Ota.

Boys' Nation, U.S. Capitol, 1963

Jeremy Ota, delegate from Oregon to the American Legion's Boys' Nation in 1963, met the representative from Arkansas, William "Bill" Clinton. Ota is 3rd from left, 2nd row (arrow); Clinton is 1st from left, top row (below arrow).

The Ota Family

Above: John and Frances Ota, with their son, Jeremy. Jeremy Ota is a physician associated with Kaiser Permanente in Portland, Oregon. Left: Jeremy Ota asks President Bill Clinton to autograph the Arkansas momento that fellow Boys' Nation delegate Clinton gave to Ota in 1963.

Photos courtesy of Frances Ota.

Jeremy, selected to attend Boys' Nation in Washington, D.C. in 1963, met a fellow delegate, William Clinton, who became President of the United States, 1993-2001. At the convention, sponsored by the American Legion, Clinton gave each of the delegates a momento of Arkansas, a miniature ceramic bathtub advertising Arkansas with the slogan, "We bathe the world." When President Clinton sponsored a reunion of the group during his presidency, Dr. Ota took his "bathtub," which President Clinton autographed for him.

Tsugi Kumazawa and her four youngest children returned to the United States after spending the war years in Japan. The family lived with Tsugi's daughter, Grace, in California. Two of Tsugi's daughters, Mary and Josephine, remained in California. Her son, George, moved to Oregon to live with his older sister, Frances, in order to attend Lincoln High School and improve his English. The youngest Kumazawa sibling, Gladys, moved to Seattle, where both she and her husband worked for and retired from Boeing.

Kumazawa Siblings, Post-War

From left: Grace Giese, Gladys Masumoto, Mary Sugiyama, Joe Kumazawa, Josephine Inouye and Frances Ota. George Kumazawa is not in the picture. Mary, Josephine, George and Gladys spent the war years in Japan.
Photo courtesy of Frances Ota.

George enlisted in the United States Army in October, 1950. After completing basic training at Fort Riley, Kansas, the Army sent him Camp Polk, assigned to the 45th "Thunderbird" Division. There, since the 45th was headed for duty in Japan, the division commander quickly appointed Kumazawa to be his interpreter. During his tour in Japan, George Kumazawa met a young Japanese lady, who became his bride. After completing his military obligation, George Kumazawa returned to Japan where he now (2006) lives.

As an interesting aside, one of Grace Kumazawa's daughters married a young man who started his employment career with Microsoft Corporation. The couple became one of many "Microsoft millionaires," for whom the company's stock options and employee stock awards created much wealth.

Frances Ota retired as Office Manager and Head Secretary from a regional office of the Disabled American Veterans, Portland, Oregon, after serving with the organization for more than 40 years. She is everlastingly grateful for the support received from individuals such as Carl and Mabel Southworth and Azalia E. Peet, a former missionary in Japan, who questioned the need for the relocation of Nikkei families from California, Oregon and Washington. After John Ota's honorable discharge from the U.S. Army, he worked as an engineer in the Portland Office, Army Corps of Engineers. His work involved planning for the development of the Columbia River basin's hydro-electric potential.

Katumi Mishima
Sakae (Nagata) Mishima

Katumi and Sakae Mishima, both of Fukuoka, Japan, came to the United States in the early 1920s. He first worked as a farm laborer in California, picking grapes, then moved to Oregon to work at a salmon cannery in Warrenton, Oregon. Next, he decided to try farming, and rented 20+ acres near Sundial Beach, which had a "shack" in which his family could live. Typical of farms in the Troutdale area at that time, his principal crops became cabbage and cauliflower. From Sundial, Mishima rented a place on N.E. Halsey, across from the County "Poor Farm." Here, also, the principal crops were cabbage and cauliflower, which were sold at the farmers' market in S.E. Portland. Katumi and Sakae Mishima had four children, Yoshio, born in 1921 (in Japan); Richard, born in 1925, in Fairview; Harry, born in 1929, in Fairview; and Henry, born in 1934, in Troutdale. Excepting Yoshio, the children started elementary school at Troutdale Grade School, but switched to Fairview after the family moved to N.E. Halsey Street. The Mishimas sent Yoshio to Japan to stay with his grandparents, and he completed his schooling in Japan, returning to the United States in 1938, age 17. Richard attended Gresham High School and was a sophomore when the war started on December 7, 1941. The Western Defense Command forced the family from the farm on May 12, 1942 about three weeks before the end of the 1941-42 school year.

Katumi and Sakae Mishima

Katumi and Sakae. Mishima came to the United States in the early 1920s, and found a farm near Sundial to rent. Thereafter, he and his sons farmed near Troutdale until May 12, 1942.
Photo courtesy of Richard Mishima.

The Mishima family was ordered to report to the Portland Assembly Center. Once

The Mishima Family

Top, from left: Harry, Richard and Yoshio Mishima. Bottom, Katumi, Henry and Sakae Mishima. Richard was drafted in 1944, and served with the 442nd Regimental Combat Team in Europe. Harry served in the Army during the Korean War. Henry became a dentist and established a practice in Gresham. Photo courtesy of Richard Mishima.

there, however, Mr. and Mrs. Mishima decided to answer a call for farm workers from Eastern Oregon, and traveled by train to the camp in Nyssa, where they found work in the sugar beet, potato and onion fields. Initially, they lived in the same camp as their Troutdale neighbors, the Fujii family, but they soon found a farmer who had living quarters for his help, and the Mishimas moved to his place. Thereafter, the Mishimas and their sons worked as farm laborers on a farm near Ontario, Oregon. Richard completed high school at Ontario

High, graduating in 1944. Harry started high school in Ontario, but the war ended before he graduated. Henry, who had started school at Fairview, attended Ontario Grade School when the family moved to the Ontario farm.

After the war ended, Katumi and Sakae Mishima returned to the area. However, since they had been renting the place in Troutdale, they had to find a place to live. Mr. Mishima found work and housing on a farm in Canby, Oregon, and moved his family there. He worked at the Canby farm until the spring of 1947. After Richard returned from the U.S. Army, the family purchased a 20-acre farm in Boring. There, the Mishima family raised cabbage, broccoli, rhubarb, strawberries and raspberries. Katumi Mishima passed away in 1963, age 61; Sakae Mishima, who lived 24 years after her husband's death, died in 1987.

Of the four children, Yoshio, classified as an alien, did not serve in the armed forces during the war. After the war, he rented a farm in Boring, started a nursery and eventually worked at Mt. Hood Community College as a gardener. He married Aster Takao, a practical nurse. The couple had five children, four of whom survived childhood. Richard, after graduating from Ontario High School, was drafted and inducted into the U.S. Army (see "Richard Mishima, Nisei Veterans," this volume). Upon his return from the service in 1947, he worked with his family on the Boring farm. In 1953, he traveled to Japan to find a bride and, on October 26, 1953, married Kumiko Ike of Fukuoka, Japan. The couple remained in Japan for approximately 6 months before he brought his bride to Oregon. The couple had two sons, Eric and James. After returning from Japan, Richard continued to farm in Boring for a couple of years, but found making farming pay a difficult proposition, so he obtained a job at a nursery, where he worked for approximately 10 years. When he quit the nursery, he found employment with the Multnomah County Parks Department, where he worked until he retired. Richard and Kumiko now live in their home in Troutdale.

After graduating from Gresham High in 1947, Harry Mishima decided he would not farm. He served in the U.S. Army during the Korean War. After his discharge, he attended Oregon State University and went to work for the Bonneville Power Administration. His younger brother, Henry Mishima, graduated from Sandy High School. He completed an undergraduate program at the University of Oregon. He then applied for admission to the Oregon Dental School, completed that program and established a dental practice in Gresham. He married Julia Quan, and the couple had three children, Henry Jr., Kathy and Thomas.

Hikosaku Murahashi
Suga (Hayashi) Murahashi

Hikosaku Murahashi (born in 1874) and Suga Hayashi (born in 1877) were married in Kumamoto, Japan, in the 1890s. The couple had two children, Ichiki (born in 1897) and Toyoki (born in 1900). In 1902, Hikosaku immigrated to the United States through Canada, and the family joined him about ten years later, settling on a farm in Gresham (NE corner of Kane Road and Division Street). The couple had three more children, Sueki, Shizue and Misue, all born in Gresham. The oldest son, Ichiki Murahashi, married his "picture bride," Ayako Hayashi, in 1924. Ichiki and Ayako had four children: Hikoki, Martha, Carol (all born in Gresham) and Miyoko, (born in Japan). The family raised cauliflower, blackberries, loganberries and boysenberries. They marketed their berries through local canneries and the cauliflower through the Eastside Farmers' Market.

In the early 1930s (1933?), Hikosaku and Suga Murahashi decided to return to Japan, taking their two youngest children with them. In 1935 (approximately), Ichiki Murahashi took his son, Hikoki, with him to downtown Gresham

The Murahashi Family, Gresham ca 1921

The Murahashi family displays their important belongings, including their truck, their team and their automobile. Family members, from left: Ichiki, Suga (behind) Misue, Hikosaku (holding), Sieki, Toyoki and Shizue. A cousin stands to the right holding an unidentified infant.   Photo courtesy of Carol (Murahashi) Asakawa.

Camp Minikoka, Block 32

The Toyoki Murahashi family was interned in Mindoka, living in Barracks 9, Block 32. Oscar was age eleven, Larry, age ten, and Roy, age 7, when the family reached the camp. They lived in the camp for about three years.

Photo, from <u>Minidoka Interlude</u>, published by its residents, 1943.

to make a purchase. On their return home, some incident caused Hikoki to fall off the truck bed on which he was riding. He sustained a severe head injury and started having seizures. Ichiki and Ayako Murahashi decided to return to Japan with their family so that Hikoki could receive the blessings (and possibly a cure) by "visiting one-thousand shrines," a Japanese (Shinto) tradition.

Meanwhile, Hikosaku and Suga Murahashi's second son, Toyoki, had married Kazue Yokote, of Portland. The couple had three children: Oscar, born in 1931, in Fairview; Larry, born in 1932, in Troutdale; and Roy, born in 1935, in Fairview. When his older brother, Ichiki, and his family left for Japan, Toyoki and his family moved to Gresham to manage the family farm. On May 12, 1942, the Western Defense Command ordered the family to report to the Pacific International Livestock Exposition Center in Portland. Subsequently, they were sent to the Minidoka Relocation Center near Twin Falls, Idaho. The Murahashi family were incarcerated in Barrack 9, Block 32. In 1945, Toyoki and his family returned to the Gresham farm and resumed its operation. Toyoki died in 1961; his wife, Kazue, in 1979.

The members of the Murahashi family who returned to Japan suffered several misfortunes. In 1940, Hikoki, despite the best efforts of his family and others to effect a cure, succumbed to the injury suffered in Gresham. In 1941, Ayako Murahashi died in childbirth, though her newborn, daughter, Miyoko, survived. On December 7, 1941, the armed forces of the Empire of Japan attacked the United States at Pearl Harbor, and the family remained in Japan during World War II. Carol Murahashi remembered her years in Japan. She had "culture shock" in adapting, she remarked, "as my mother had insisted, when

Shizue Murahashi

Photo courtesy of Leke Nakashimada.

we lived in Gresham, that we speak English." Thus, when Carol started school in Japan, she had to learn to speak, read and write Japanese. Another "shock" was the food. Carol thought, "I'll never eat that, but I did!" Her father raised rice and "every tiny plot was used." The land was terraced so that the small fields could be flooded. "My father had to get out early to make certain we got our (irrigation) water." She also recalled seeing U.S. bombers fly over their farm on their way to bomb Japan's cities. Her father admonished the children to "hide," but Carol usually stood and watched. She remembered the bombing of Nagasaki on August 9, 1945. "First the sky turned red, then black. We did not know what had happened." (Nagasaki, on the western coast of Kyushu, is approximately 50 miles from Kumamoto.) When the war ended with Japan's defeat, Carol Murahashi remarked, "I took the first available boat back to the United States (late 1940s)." She stayed with her Aunt and Uncle Toyoki Murahashi in familiar surroundings, the family's Gresham farm. She enrolled at Gresham High School, from which she graduated in 1952, four years late. In 1955, Carol Murahashi and Walter Asakawa married (see "Roy Asakawa/Kikuno Asakawa," this volume).

In 1949, both Hikosaku and Suga Murahashi passed away. In 1953, Carol's sister, Martha, returned from Japan with her husband, Don Ikeda, and daughter, Lucy. The couple had three more children, all born in Gresham, Amy, Robert and Karen.

Note: Nagasaki, Japan, capital of Nagasaki Prefecture, is located at the head of Nagasaki Bay, Kyushu Isalnd, and is one of Japan's best natural harbors. Three days after the bombing of Hiroshima, Japan, a second nuclear device (plutonium bomb) was dropped from a B-29 on Nagasaki, destroying about one-third of the city. Some 66,000 people were casualties, killed or injured.

Sakaju and Seki Naemura

Sakaju Naemura
Seki (Katayama) Naemura

Sakaju Naemura, born and raised in the small village of Yanae, Japan, came to the United States in the early years of the 20th century. He first worked in the forests of Oregon and Washington as a logger, then became a cannery worker for the Columbia River Packers' Association (CRPA), which operated several canneries along the river from Astoria, Oregon to Ellsworth, Washington (east of Vancouver). When salmon were in the river, Naemura worked at one of the firm's canneries. During the off-season, Naemura worked as a farm laborer, primarily in East Multnomah County. In 1916, he returned to his home village in Japan to find a bride. There, Naemura met and married Seki Katayama, also a native of Yanae. Shortly after the ceremony, he and his bride returned to the United States.

The couple rented a house in Montavilla, Oregon, though Naemura's job took him to different locations along the Columbia River. In 1918, their first child, Shigeru "Joe" was born, followed by Emiko "Amy," in 1920. The couple sent Amy to live with relatives in Yanae, Japan. The Naemuras had two more children, Setsuko, born in 1923, and Roy, born in 1925. In 1930, when a farmer

Seki Naemura and Children

Seki Naemura with Setsuko and Roy while living (temporarily) at a CRPA cannery on the Columbia River.
Photo courtesy of Setsuko Okino.

living in Pleasant Valley needed help, Naemura moved his family to the farm, where they lived in a small shelter built for farm laborers. Joe, who had been attending Russellville Grade, transferred to Pleasant Valley School. In Pleasant Valley, both Sakaju and Seki Naemura worked on the farm, as did the youngsters when they became old enough. However, Sakaju Naemura always departed to work in the CRPA's canneries during fish runs. In 1934, the Naemuras had finally accumulated sufficient money to pay for Amy's passage to the United States. She returned from Japan that year. She enrolled at Pleasant Valley School in order to become more proficient in English.

In 1936, Naemura moved his family to a house on Bridge Street in Fairview, Oregon. The eldest Naemura son, Joe, who had graduated from Gresham High School, enrolled at Oregon State College that fall, where he completed two years as an engineering student. From an early age, Joe had an interest in radio, crafting a crystal set from parts during his grade school years. Soon this interest gravitated to short-wave radio, with which he became quite knowledgeable and proficient. This skill led Joe to enlist in the Merchant Marine as a radioman. He became an operator on the *Herman Frasch*, a freighter. In 1940, a Coast Guard officer told the ship's captain that he must discharge Naemura, his radio operator. The captain demurred, but the officer insisted. Consequently, Joe lost his job. This event presaged some of the future problems to be visited upon American citizens of Japanese ancestry. Naemura then volunteered for the Army. However, during basic training, Army medics thought he might have contracted tuberculosis. Sent to a hospital in Walla Walla, Washington, doctors confirmed the diagnosis. Joe Naemura stayed at the hospital until he recovered after which he received a medical discharge. He then completed college and the University of Oregon accepted him as a student at the medical school in Portland. He became an anesthesiologist, which specialty he practiced at Providence Hospital until his retirement. Joe married twice. The first marriage, to Miyeko Tamura, resulted in five children (see "Minekichi Tamura," this volume); a second

Sakaju Naemura

Sakaju Naemura does his laundry during a stay at a cannery belonging to the CRPA, which firm employed him for many years.
Photo courtesy of Setsuko Okino.

marriage gave him two more children, Ted and David. Joe Naemura now (2006) lives in Gresham.

Amy Naemura was attending Fairview Grade School when the war broke out. She, her parents and her younger brother, Roy, were interned at the Minidoka Relocation Center after spending the summer of 1942 at the Pacific International Livestock Exposition grounds in North Portland. While at Minidoka, Amy married Toshio Oda. The couple had one son, Keith, before they separated. Upon Amy's release from the center, she completed a program to become a dental technician. She married Ray Matsushita and they had twin girls, Lennie and Carrie. The family resided in Portland.

After graduating from Gresham High School in 1941, Setsuko Naemura married Toshio "Tosh" Okino, who owned a farm north of Boring, Oregon. Together with others of Japanese ancestry, Setsuko and her husband gathered at the Gresham fairgrounds, each with the "one suitcase of belongings" permitted, for transport to the assembly center in Portland. In the five days allowed for "evacuees" to store or sell the belongings that would not fit in a suitcase, Tosh and Setsuko disposed of a new tractor and a new automobile. According to Setsuko, they received "just pennies on the dollar." After a very uncomfortable summer in Portland, beset by flies, overcrowding and lack of privacy, the couple traveled by train to Minidoka, near Twin Falls, Idaho. The barracks room to which they were assigned had no interior walls, an "army-issue coal stove," and just one electrical outlet, which held a single light bulb. The WRA located the Minidoka Relocation Center in a desert area buffeted by strong winds, which carried dust except when snow laid on the ground. Either dust or snow filtered through cracks, making miniature drifts around windows, doors and other openings. Winter temperatures frequently dropped below zero, which, with the usual winds, made the barracks uncomfortable at best. The daily coal ration, one bucket, had to be used sparingly. One positive thing occurred on Christmas Day, 1942, when a Quaker church group distributed presents to every internee in the camp, young and old. Setsuko Okino felt much comfort from this gesture, feeling great joy because "people [not in the camp] thought about us and remembered us at Christmas time." Summer temperatures frequently exceeded one hundred

Roy Naemura

Roy Naemura drafted after graduating from Nyssa High School, Nyssa, Oregon, died in Italy while serving in the U.S. Army.
Photo courtesy of Setsuko Okino.

degrees, with no escape, though some internees took a dip in the irrigation canal on the camp's southern boundary. U.S. Army sentries patrolled the outer fence with their "guns pointed inward."

In camp, Tosh worked as a coal swamper, loading and unloading coal for a wage of $16.00 per month; Setsuko earned $8.00 per month waiting tables in the block mess, which served three meals each day. Because $24.00 per month barely covered their expenses, they could not save any money for future needs. During their internment at the camp, Tosh and Setsu Okino had two children, Gary and Richard. In 1944, the couple asked to be paroled from the camp so that they could work as farm laborers. The WRA granted their request and they moved to Ontario, Oregon, where they obtained employment on a farm. Tosh and Setsuko Okino picked up potatoes, picked up and topped onions and performed other farm jobs. Their pay, typical for farm labor, was much higher than their wages at the camp. While in Ontario, Setsuko learned that her brother, Roy Naemura, had been killed in action in northern Italy. The family held a memorial service for him in Ontario. Before the ceremony, Setsuko stopped at a beauty shop to have her hair done. The operator told her, "We don't wait on Japs." Setsuko kept her bitter feelings to herself.

Early in 1945, Tosh Okino and three other Niesei returned to Gresham to determine the "reception" the Nisei might face. The first day the four experienced no problems, but the second day, signs appeared in many shops proclaiming: "No Japs Wanted." Consequently, Tosh Okino decided not to return with his family to the Gresham farm they owned because of the "welcome" that might await them. Therefore, the couple, who had left their farm in the care of its former owner, waited a year before returning to Gresham. According to Setsuko, "We were essentially penniless. We needed the money we earned as farm laborers to get by." Fortunately, the former owner allowed them to delay payments on the farm until they had recovered from their government-forced exile. Finally, in 1946, the Tosh and Setsuko Okino resumed the farm life that had been interrupted some four years earlier. They had stored furniture and

Tosh and Setsuko Okino Farm, Gresham

Tosh and Setsuko farmed this 40-acre place on Boring Road (now 282nd Avenue), with the help of their children, Richard, Eugene, Gary and Karen.

Photos courtesy of Setsuko Okino.

Tosh and Setsuko Okino With Their Family

The Okino family gathers to celebrate Tosh and Setsuko's 50th wedding anniversary. From left, Gary, Karen, Richard, Setsuko, Eugene and Tosh Okino. Each of the children chose to pursue a professional career, rather than taking over the farm.

other household goods in a locked area of the barn. They discovered that a tenant had reported the locked room to the FBI, whose agents required the former owner to open the area so that the G-Men could examine its contents.

Of course, the agents found no contraband. After their return to the farm, Tosh and Setsuko Okino primarily raised berry crops, though they also planted broccoli, cauliflower and cucumbers.

After returning to Gresham, the couple had two more children, Eugene and Karen. All four youngsters attended Orient Grade School and graduated from Gresham High. The eldest, Gary, completed his medical degree on the "hill." As a physician, he specializes in anesthesiology. Richard attended Oregon State University, took graduate work at Stanford, worked in the communications industry for American Telephone and Telegraph and works for them still (2006). Eugene completed his undergraduate work at Oregon State University in electrical engineering and completed a graduate program in business administration at the University of Washington. He first worked at the Bremerton Naval Yard on a project to convert diesel-powered submarines to nuclear power. He then obtained employment at Boeing, where he has worked since. Karen attended Oregon State University and earned a degree at Portland State University. She married Eric "Rick" Saito, who became a partner in the architectural firm, McKenzie/Saito. The firm is now called the Group McKenzie; Saito serves as a consultant.

Roy Naemura enjoyed his high school years at Gresham High School. Always an extrovert, he made close friends, participated in extra-curricular activities and joined Explorer Boy Scout Troop 635. He made model airplanes that flew and took second place in a model airplane contest held for Oregon students as an eighth grader. Forced to leave Gresham High during his junior year, he nevertheless maintained a positive outlook. He left Minidoka to stay in a labor camp near Nyssa, Oregon. In 1943, he graduated from Nyssa High School. When he reached draft age, the board ordered him to report to Fort Douglas, Utah, for induction. Since other Nisei drafted at the time were sent to Camp Blanding, Florida, that is probably where the Army sent Roy Naemura for basic and advanced infantry training. Sent overseas, he was assigned to Company B, 100th Battalion, 442nd Regimental Combat Team, as a replacement. He was killed in action on April 15, 1945, in the battle to break the German Gothic Line in Northern Italy (see "Roy Naemura, Gold Star Veterans," this volume).

In the 1950s, after Issei were permitted to file for U.S. citizenship, Seki Naemura studied diligently to earn her citizenship papers. She was very proud to become a citizen of the country for which her son gave his life. At the ceremony, she selected the name "Helen" to be her given name.

In the 1970s, Tosh Okino, together with other members of the Gresham-Troutdale Japanese American Citizens League, worked to create a Japanese garden within Gresham's main city park. The garden was meant to be a gesture of goodwill to the Gresham community in which so many families of Japanese ancestry lived.

Josuke and Tsutano Nakata

Josuke Nakata
Tsutano (Kato) Nakata

Joe Josuke Nakata immigrated to the United States in 1906, settling in Oregon. In 1920, he sent for an acquaintance, Tsutano Kato, to come to the United States to become his bride. Nakata had rented a home and about 40 acres on Columbia Boulevard in Portland, which he was farming at the time. The couple had four sons, Alfred Yutaka, born in 1921, Albert Takeshi (1923), Harry Akira (1925) and Frank Wataru (1926). With a partner, Joe Nakata established one of the first, if not the first, farm stands on Columbia Boulevard (1770 NE Columbia Blvd.). A typical truck garden operation, Nakata grew beans, cabbage, cauliflower, cucumbers, lettuce, spinach, tomatoes and similar vegetable crops. Most of his farm produce sold in the fruit and vegetable stand he operated with a partner with the same surname, though they were not related. Some produce sold through the early farmers' market in southeast Portland; a cannery usually took the spinach. When the family harvested spinach, Frank recalled, "We always got up about 4:00 a.m. to cut the spinach while it was wet. Pop insisted it would weigh more."

The boys all attended Woodlawn Grade School during their elementary years. When he was about ten, Albert started taking piano lessons. Naturally, he wanted a piano, which his father purchased for him. Unfortunately, the heavy

The Nakata Boys

From left: Frank, Harry, Albert and Alfred Nakata. The boys grew up on a farm on Columbia Boulevard, where their father sold produce through a fruit and vegetable stand.   *Photos courtesy of Frank Nakata.*

instrument went through the floor of the rented dwelling. Mr. Nakata had to replace the floor. Thus, the instrument became quite an expensive purchase. Though Frank admired his brother's talent, he remembered, "We had to listen to Albert practicing scales on that piano by the hour. It wasn't always pleasant." He also recalled how the family used newspapers to cover the walls; his father could not afford real wallpaper. Both Alfred and Albert attended and graduated from Jefferson High; Frank completed two years at Benson Tech. After completing elementary school, Harry traveled to Japan, arriving home before the war in time to be "evacuated" with his family in May, 1942. After the attack at Pearl Harbor, an unknown person reported Joe Nakata to the FBI, accusing him of making a claim that he possessed enough "explosives to blow up several bridges." The FBI promptly arrested him. He and other suspects were sent to a prison in Missoula, Montana. Nakata did not rejoin his family until his background had been thoroughly investigated. Meanwhile, authorities sent other family members to the Portland Assembly Center, Oregon (except Alfred, who had moved to Ontario, Oregon).

After spending about three months at the Portland center, the WRA sent the Nakata family to the Minidoka Relocation Center, Idaho, with other evacu-

U.S. Army Days

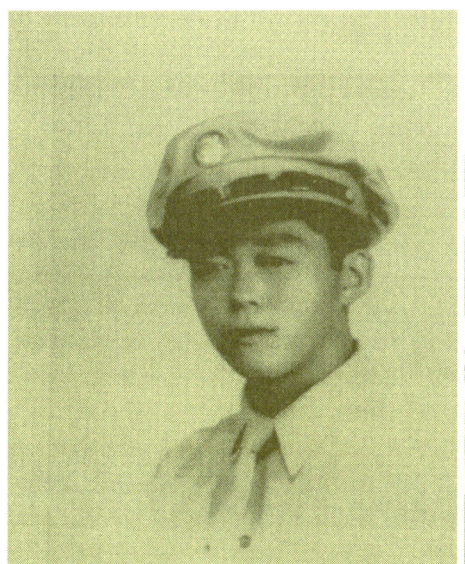

Left: Alfred Nakata, while serving with the Army of Occupation, Germany, died "in the line of duty" in a vehicular accident. Right, Frank Nakata (right) with a friend, Paul Salizar, whom he met in basic training. The two kept in touch for more than 40 years.

ees. There, Joe Nakata joined them after the FBI completed its investigation. When the camp developed its agricultural potential, Nakata became a foreman for a farm crew. Both Harry and Frank Nakata completed their secondary years at Hunt High School, Minidoka. Albert Nakata, somewhat of a prodigy on the piano, left the camp to attend the University of Denver, where he majored in music. During the summer months, three of the Nakata boys usually worked outside the camp. One summer, Frank, together with seven other internees (from Hood River) worked for the Filer Orchard in Idaho Falls, pruning apple trees. Another summer he, Alfred and Harry worked on the Conforth Ranch, Ontario, as farm hands. The following year Harry and Frank returned to the Ranch, where they packed celery and carrots, carload after carload, for shipment by rail. Asked about his thoughts with regard to being imprisoned, Frank replied, "At my age, it really didn't bother me that much. I didn't have to get up at 4:00 a.m."

On April 5, 1945, Alfred enlisted in the U.S. Army. Inducted at Fort Douglas, Utah, he completed basic training in Texas. The Army assigned him to a heavy (infantry) weapons unit, Company H, 2nd Battalion, 3rd Infantry Division. Sent to Germany as part of the Army of Occupation, Alfred Nakata died "in the line of duty" on June 7, 1946, in an vehicular accident in Berlin, Germany. The next sibling, Albert Nakata, was drafted. Inducted at Fort Lewis, he completed basic training after which he volunteered for the Military Intelligence Service. He served two years, including time in Japan, where he acted as an interpreter, Army of Occupation. Frank Nakata, also drafted, reported for induction at Fort Lewis on April 27, 1946. He completed basic training at Lackland Air Base in San Antonio, Texas. He received his honorable discharge for "the convenience of the government" on April 25, 1947.

After his discharge from the Army, Albert "Al" Nakata devoted his working life to music. He taught piano for many years. Later in his life, he took up the sport of running, and competed in many racing events. He became well known for his achievements in the sport and continued his involvement even after he suffered from heart problems, which necessitated a pacemaker. He married May Fujita and the couple had two children, Nancy and Gail.

Both Harry and Frank went into the automobile business. Harry started working in a body and fender shop. Eventually he opened his own shop. He married Kyoko Kamada and the couple had two children, Dennis and Steven. After completing training in the automotive trade on the GI Bill, Frank started working at Lomac Motors, Portland, rebuilding engines. During the period his brother, Harry, worked for Gill Motors, Frank became convinced that body and fender work had greater appeal, so he joined his brother at Gill Motors to learn the business. Thereafter, he worked for a number of body shops, including Cascade Auto Body in Vancouver, Washington, which employed him for several years. Ron Tonkin Honda became his final employer. The organization "needed a body and fender man," and promised Frank that he would "have the easy jobs" because of his age. He worked there for about 4 years. He recalled, "They really treated me well. Even after I left, they invited me to their employee parties." He had fond memories of Brad Tonkin, Ron Tonkin's youngest son, who "always treated the employees well." Frank Nakata married Ruth Watanabe, who grew up on a farm in Milwaukie, Oregon. The couple had three children, Janyce, Julie and David.

After the war, Joe and Tsutano Nakata returned to Portland and found an apartment at St. Johns Wood, a housing project for shipyard workers during the war. According to Frank, "The family came back empty handed. Both my father and mother worked as farm laborers, picking berries, cultivating, weeding, hoeing and harvesting other crops. We were in bad shape." Later, the parents lived with Frank and Ruth Nakata. Joe Josuke Nakata died in 1982; Tsutano passed away in 1989. Albert Nakata is also deceased.

Etsuo Namba
Shizuno (Nakayama) Namba

Etsuo Namba immigrated to the United States before World War I, landing in Seattle. Since the railroads were hiring aliens of Japanese extraction, he sought work with the railroad, and found employment with the Union Pacific out of Portland. He worked as a section hand for the Union Pacific between Portland and Pendleton for approximately three years. He sent for his betrothed, Shizuno Nakayama, also of Okayama, Japan, with whom he had an "understanding" before he left Japan. Similarly to other Japanese immigrants, Etsuo decided to try farming for a living, and rented a small farm in Gresham, Oregon. In the early 1920s, he found a 62-acre farm at the intersection of Birdsdale Road (201st) and N.E. Sandy Boulevard, which he leased from Florence Donald.

Etsuo and Shizuno Namba had five children, all born in Oregon: Emiko, born in 1918, in Gresham; Tomomi "Tom," (1920); Maria, (1922, in Fairview); Kenji "Kennie," (1925) and Akio "Art," (1927). The youngsters attended Fairview Grade School their elementary school years, then enrolled at Gresham High School (GHS). Emiko graduated from GHS in 1936; Tom in 1938; and Maria in 1940. Kennie Namba completed three years at GHS, but his high school education at GHS was interrupted when Nikkei families were interned on May 12, 1942. Art had completed nearly a year at GHS before his education was interrupted for the same reason. Tom started college at Oregon State College, and had completed more than 1½ years before the family's internment. Both Kennie and Art Namba completed high school at Hunt High School in Minidoka.

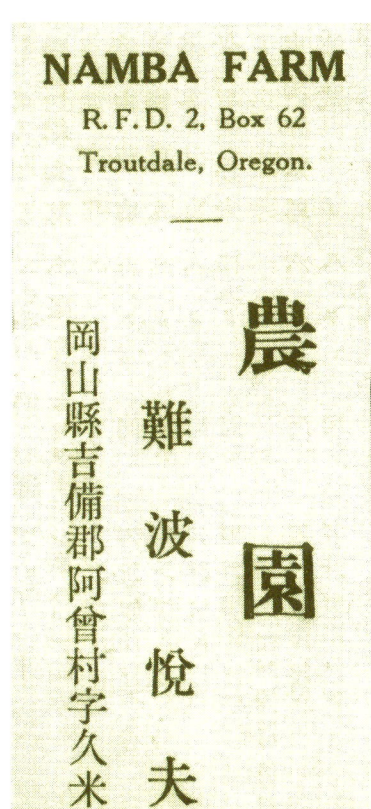

Ad, 1936 North American Times

During the years the Namba family farmed the 62-acre place located on Sandy Boulevard, Etsuo Namba planted about one-half the acreage to berries; black raspberries (black caps). loganberries, raspberries and strawberries. The balance was planted to vegetable crops, including cabbage, cauliflower, brussel sprouts, celery, cucumbers and tomatoes. The family usually planted only one or two acres of the celery as that crop took much

Etsuo and Shizuno Namba

Etsuo and Shizuno Namba settled on a farm in Fairview in the early 1920s. They farmed it until their daughter, Emiko Kikkawa, took over after World War II. Of course, the family was interned during the war.   Photo courtesy of Kennie Namba.

care and required lots of water. Etsuo obtained irrigation water for his celery from the Columbia Slough that coursed along the northern border of the farm. In that era, celery could not be sold unless the stalks were white. This required the placement of boards alongside the plants to keep them shaded so that chlorophyll would not form in the stalks, turning them green (now, of course, celery is sold green). The berry crops were sold to various canneries in Gresham while the vegetable crops were sold almost exclusively at the Eastside Farmers' Market on Belmont Street.

On May 12, 1942, the Namba family, including Emiko, who had married Kazuo Kikkawa, a kibei who had returned from Japan, was interned with other Nikkei families. They were confined at the Pacific International Livestock Exposition Center from May 12 until September 10, 1942 (see "Internment," this volume). Together with other Nikkei families, the U.S. Government sent them to the Minidoka Relocation Center, near Twin Falls, Idaho. Because Emiko was married, she and her husband had separate quarters. The other Namba family members, Etsuo, Shizuno, Tom, Maria, Kennie and Art, were assigned to Block 34, Barracks 6A. While the family was confined at Minidoka, Etsuo did not have a permanent "camp" job, but did work for neighboring farmers during the growing season. Tom and Kennie worked for an Idaho farmer, who Kennie said, "was good to his Nisei crew." In January, 1943, the government of

Namba Farm ca 1940

Left, Emiko (Namba) Kikkawa holds her daughter, Joyce, in the automobile. Kennie Namba pets the family's dog. Right, Shizuno Namba picks strawberries for the cannery.   Photos courtesy of Kennie Namba.

the United States reversed its policy, taken shortly after the attack at Pearl Harbor, that made it possible for Nisei, both men and women, to volunteer (or to be drafted) for service in the armed forces. Tom Namba immediately volunterred and was sent to Camp Shelby, Mississippi. Shortly after Kennie became eighteen years of age, he too, volunteered. The Army sent Kennie Namba to Camp Blanding, Florida, where he underwent basic training (see "Nisei Veterans, Kennie/Tom Namba," this volume).

After the war, Etsuo and Shizuno Namba and Emiko (Namba) Kikkawa and her husband returned to the Sandy Boulevard farm from which they were forced in 1942. Actually, Emiko and her husband had purchased a 10-acre parcel before the war, to which they returned. Etsuo planned to renew the lease he had with Florence E. Donald for the property he had farmed before the war. However, in the interim, the Oregon Legislature had passed the Oregon Alien Land Law, which prohibited "ineligible" aliens from owning or leasing land. Rather than circumventing the law by leasing it in one of the children's names (the usual practice), Kennie Namba and his father decided to fight the exclusion in court.

After Multnomah County issued an edict prohibiting Florence Donald from leasing the land to Etsuo Namba, Mrs. Donald and the Namba family filed a

Work Crew, Minidoka Interlude

Front, from left: Kennie Namba, Masami Takenaga and Mr. Empey (farm owner). Rear: John Nazaki (in front of) Bob Nishino, Mino Okazaki, George Tambara, Kaz Yamaguchi and Dan Hinatsu (in cab).   Photo courtesy of Kennie Namba.

lawsuit in a Multnomah County Circuit Court. They contended that the Oregon's Alien Land Law violated constitutional provisions that provide for due process and equal protection under the law. The plaintiffs also maintained that the Federal Government is responsible for laws relating to aliens and immigration. The Circuit Court issued a decree upholding the legality of the law. The plaintiffs appealed the case (Namba et al v. McCourt and Neuner [John D. McCourt, District Attorney, Multnomah County and George Neuner, Attorney General, State of Oregon]) to the Oregon Supreme Court. In its opinion, the Supreme Court justices wrote:

> "It was the purpose of those who understand the situation to prohibit the enjoyment or possession of, or dominion over, the agricultural lands of the State by aliens ineligible for citizenship, — in a practical way to prevent onerous competition by the Oriental farmer against the American farmer.
>
> It is obvious that the argument must be rejected. We have been employing the term 'ineligible aliens,' although the Japanese aliens are virtually the only persons embraced within the term. All of our Japanese aliens are at least twenty-five years of age, and since most immigrated to America about 1910, most of them are middle age or beyond it. No one claims that any danger to our general welfare lurks in this small group of people who long ago lost the bloom of youth. The Ex-

The Namba Siblings (post war)

From left, Art Namba, Tom Namba, Maria Asai, Emik Kikkawa and Kennie Namba.
Photo courtesy of Kennie Namba.

clusion Act makes it certain that their dwindling number will not be increased.

The several hundred alien Japanese to whom the Alien Land Law is applicable came to our State lawfully under laws enacted by Congress. They are here lawfully and are entitled to remain. Many of them are parents of United States citizens, and some of them are mothers and fathers of American soldiers who gave a good account of themselves in the recent war.

Our country cannot afford to create, by legislation or judicial construction, a ghetto for our 'ineligible aliens.' And yet if we deny to the alien who is lawfully here the normal means whereby he earns his livelihood, we thereby assign him to a lowered standard of living. We know of no basis upon which these two acts can be sustained.

…It is clear from Oyama v. California, supra, that Oregon Laws 1945, Chapter 436, infringe upon the equal protection clause of the Fourteenth Amendment. We hold that it is invalid. …The cause is remanded to the Circuit Court to enter a decree favorable to the appellants, in conformity with the views herein expressed.

Reversed." (emphasis added)

Kennie Namba, his father, Etsuo Namba, and Forence Donald prevailed. After serving in the United States Army and returning as a wounded and

Tent City, 442nd Regimental Combat Team, Italy

Since Ruth Inukai left Minidoka to work in a war plant in Minneapolis, Minnesota, which produced 'pup' tents for the Army, Kennie Namba may have slept in one of the tents she helped produce in France and Italy. Photo courtesy of Kennie Namba.

decorated veteran, Kennie Namba decided that he had to speak out against the injustices committed against his and other families of Japanese ancestry. He and his wife, Ruth, have became advocates, not only for the interests of Nikkei families, but also for Nisei veterans, who served with distinction in World War II (and later wars). The two have made numerous public appearances for their cause. They have appeared on television, been interviewed for newspaper accounts and, generally, avail themselves of any opportunity to tell the positive story of the contributions made by people of Japanese ancestry to the betterment of their homeland, the United States of America. Kennie, who always considered himself an American, said: "One of the more difficult situations for me to deal with was the realization, after we were interned, that many of our friends and neighbors did not regard me as a loyal American."

When Etsuo and Shizuno Namba returned to their farm, they found that all of their farm equipment, tractors, implements, a truck, hand tools, etc., had been stolen. Mrs. Donald had provided a corner in the huge barn for storage. Etsuo Namba had partitioned it off and secured the large implements and vehicles (he thought) with chains and locks. Though he had the title to the tractor, the truck and proof of ownership for the equipment, Multnomah County informed him that nothing could be done. Consequently, he had to resume farming without his tractor, truck and other farm implements. After they returned

Kennie Namba's and Ruth Inukai's Wedding

From left, front: Mr. and Mrs. Tomori, Kazuo Inukai, Ishino Inukai, Richard Inukai, Maria Namba, Mrs. Hasegawa, Mr. Hasegawa and Etsuo Namba. Rear: Takako Inukai, Ruth Inukai, Reverend Sherman Burgoyne, Kennie Namba and Tom Namba. Reverend Burgoyne intervened to allow the marriage to take place in the church.

Photo courtesy of Kennie Namba.

from Minidoka, Etsuo and Shizuno Namba lived with their daughter, Emiko, and her husband, Kazuo Kikkawa. Etsuo Namba passed away in 1979; Shizuno Namba in 1984. Emiko and Kazuo Kikkawa continued to farm the place on Sandy Boulevard until their retirement. The couple had four children, Joyce, Gail, Marcia and Elaine. Emiko Kikkawa now lives in N.E. Portland at Summerplace (148th and N.E. Halsey).

After his discharge from the U.S. Army, Tom Namba married May Date and settled in Seattle. He became a dentist and established a practice in Seattle. The couple had four children, Ralph, Jimmy, Larry, Gary and Dean. Tom Namba passed away in 1990. The next Namba sibling, Maria Namba, graduated from Gresham High School in 1940, after which she was interned with other family members at Minidoka. After the war, she married a Hood River farmer, Taro Asai, whose family owned an orchard above the town of Hood River. The couple had four children, Marta, Tara, Janelle and Kevin. Maria lives in Hood River. Her son, Kevin Asai, now manages the family's Hood River orchard.

Because Kennie Namba service record reflected the fact that he had attended a Japanese school, the Army sent him by airplane to Fort Snelling,

Art Namba

Art Namba, who served in the Army during the Korean War.
Photo courtesy of Kennie Namba.

Minnesota, to train for the Military Intelligence Service. However, when the war in the Pacific ended, he had accumlated enough points to be discharged, and decided not to re-enlist to serve an additional two years with the Army of Occupation in Japan. While at Fort Snelling, he made contact with an acquaintance, Shige "Ruth" Inukai, whom he had earlier met at Minidoka. She had volunteered to go to Minneapolis, Minnesota, in order to work in a factory that produced "pup" tents for military use. When the Army sent Kennie Namba to Fort Lewis to be discharged, Ruth accompanied him on the train. They planned a stop in Hood River, where Ruth's parents lived, after which Kennie would continue on to Fort Lewis to be discharged. Arriving in Hood River, they decided to buy some groceries for Ruth's folks and stopped at a local market. They made their selections and took them to the cash register. The clerk said, "We don't serve Japs." Kennie, still in uniform, told the clerk of his service in the Army. The clerk repeated the slur; "We don't serve Japs." Kennie and Ruth left the store sans groceries and stopped at a nearby Safeway store, which sold them what they wanted. Relating this incident to Ruth's parents, they were told that the Hood River Post, American Legion, had removed the names of all Nisei soldiers from its posted "Honor Roll" of service men and women.

In 1946, after receiving his discharge at Fort Lewis, Kennie Namba and Ruth Inukai married. Initially, a local church refused them the use of the church for the wedding. However, a local minister, Reverend Sherman Burgoyne, took matters into his own hands and agreed to marry them. They remember Reverend Burgoyne for his kindness to them. The couple lived in Hood River with Ruth's parents for a time before settling in Portland.

In Portland, Kennie Namba worked as a log scaler for about a year before deciding to take advantage of the GI Bill. He enrolled at the University of Portland, where he majored in business and economics. After gaining his degree, Pacific Power and Light (PPL) employed Namba as a right-of-way and property agent. Kennie Namba worked for PPL from 1953 until his retirement in 1983. Because of requirements connected with his employment, he com-

Kennie and Ruth Namba's Family

Front: Ruth and Kennie Namba. Rear: Rocky Welsick, Ross Welsick, Diane (Namba) Welsick, Wesley Welscik, Teresa Namba, Kaeti Namba and Bryana Welsick.

Photo courtesy of Kennie Namba.

pleted two years of a four-year program in law at the Northwestern School of Law. Kennie and Ruth Namba have two children, Teresa and Diane. They now live near Glendover Golf Course in N.E. Portland.

The youngest of Etsuo and Shizuno's children, Art Namba, who had completed much of his freshman year at GHS, finished high school at Hunt, Minidoka. He served in the U.S. Army during the Korean War. Interested in photography, he completed photography school and was employed by the firm, Graphic Arts. He worked at this business, eventually serving in a management position, until his retirement. Art Namba married Jan (surname not known). The couple had one child, a son, Randy Namba.

The Onchi Family

From Left: Mizu Onchi, holding Jim Sadaki, Yukeseburo Onchi (behind) Mitsue, George Shigeru and Hidekichi Onchi.   *Photo courtesy of Joe Onchi.*

Ikisaburo Onchi
Mizu (Takeshita) Onchi

Ikisaburo Onchi served in the army of the Empire of Japan during the Russo-Japanese War, 1904-05. He emigrated from Japan after that experience and found employment, first in Hawaii in the cane fields, then in Mexico. He entered the United States in 1909, joining his father, Hidekichi Onchi, in Portland. In 1911 or 1912, he arranged for his "picture bride," Mizu Takeshita, to come from Japan, and the couple married. The settled on a rented farm in Montavilla, where the couple's children were born, Mitsue, George Shigeru, Jim Sadaki and Joe Masayuki. Onchi and his father planted vegetable crops,

Onchi Farm, Gresham

From left: Mizu Onchi, Mrs. Kinoshita (mother of the Kinoshita boys), Frank Kinoshita, Joe Onchi, Tom Kinoshita and Jim Onchi.   Photo courtesy of Joe Onchi.

which were primarily sold at the farmers' market in East Portland. In 1924, Hidekichi Onchi returned to Japan with Mitsue and George. The family wanted the two youngsters to attend school in Japan.

The family remained at the Montavilla farm until about 1930, when Onchi rented a farm in Gresham. The 30-acre farm, known as the Pullen place, was located on the northeast corner where Birdsdale (now 202nd) Avenue intersected Division Street. In addition to the Pullen place, Onchi rented adjacent ground. He planted berry crops, strawberries, raspberries, loganberries, youngberries and boysenberries, as well as vegetable crops. The family marketed the berry crops through the Gresham Berry Growers; the vegetable crops at the Eastside Farmers' Market. In 1931, Ikisaburo Onchi suffered an accident while working with a horse pulling a sled loaded with potatoes. A chain link on one of the traces broke, causing the sled to swing and catch Onchi underneath a runner. He didn't seek medical care, the wound became infected and he died within a year. Because of the accident, his eldest son, George, returned from Japan. Ikisaburo Onchi died in 1932.

All preparation of farm ground for planting was accomplished with horses, plowing, disking, harrowing and "floating" the ground (the latter smoothed the surface). After crops were planted, cultivating was done with a single-row cultivator pulled by a horse. Generally, one of the boys, either George, Jim or Joe, did the work requiring the use of horses. After her husband died, Mizu Onchi

Jim and Joe Onchi, With Friends

From left: Jim Onchi, Tosh Yoneyama, Joe Onchi and Frank Kinoshita, at the Gresham farm on Birdsdale Avenue.   *Photo courtesy of Joe Onchi.*

had to depend upon her sons and hired men to help her manage the farm. A Gresham business man, Les Walrad, helped the family by extending them fertilizer and other items on credit. The debt was repaid when the crops were sold. George, who had enrolled at Gresham Grade School to improve his English, had to leave school in order to manage the farm and support the family.

Through the depression years, the Onchi family managed to eke out a living. Ikisaburo Onchi had purchased a Model A Ford flatbed truck before his death, which George used to take crops to market. When prices improved after the outbreak of war in Europe in 1938, the family purchased its first tractor, a Farmall. Having survived the trauma of Mr. Onchi's death and the hard times of the 1930s, by 1940, because of improving prices for farm produce, Mizu Onchi and her sons looked forward to more prosperous times. Perhaps because of the improved outlook, George Onchi married Sachi Mishiro, daughter of a farm family that lived on Vashon Island, in Washington.

However, the family did not share in the better times brought about by improving prices for agricultural products. When Japanese carrier aircraft bombed Pearl Harbor, suddenly people of Japanese ancestry became suspect. The government reacted by notifying those of Japanese extraction, citizens and non-citizens alike, to report to a "relocation center." The Onchi family assembled, together with other Nikkei families, at the county fairgrounds in Gresham. They were transported to the Pacific International Livestock Exposition grounds in

Joe Onchi at the Farm   Joe Onchi and Sachi Onchi

Left, Joe Onchi at the farm on Birdsdale Road north of Division. Right, Joe Onchi visited his family at the farm before the government interned family members on May 12, 1942. The lady is Sachi Onchi, his brother George's wife.   Photos, Joe Onchi.

North Portland. However, neither Joe Onchi nor Jim Onchi were among them. After graduating from Gresham High School in 1939, Joe Onchi had taken a job in the produce business in California, hoping to save money to attend college. In 1941, he received his draft notice and, in November of 1941, was inducted into the U.S. Army (see "Joe Onchi, Nisei Veterans," this volume). Similarly, the draft board sent Jim Onchi his notice and, on February 27, 1942, he too, was inducted into the Army.

Therefore, members of the Onchi family reporting to the assembly center included Mizu Onchi, George Onchi and his wife, Sachi Onchi. After spending about three months at the Portland center, the War Relocation Authority (WRA) sent the Onchi family to the Tule Lake Camp, California. During the family's stay at the Portland center, Sachi Onchi gave birth to the couple's first child, Mary Ann. The family remained at Tule Lake for more than a year before being transferred by the WRA to Camp Jerome, Arkansas. While incarcerated at Tule Lake, George and Sachi Onchi's second child, Raymond, was born. Finally, from Arkansas, the WRA transferred the Onchi family to Heart Mountain, Wyoming, a desolate, cold and isolated camp where their imprisonment ended in 1945.

The family returned to the Gresham area, but, of course, they had no home in which to live since they had been forced from their rented farm at the out-

The Onchi Family at the Tulelake Camp

Joe Onchi, on leave from Camp Robinson, Arkansas, visits his family at the Tulelake Camp in Northern California. From left, Sachi, George (holding) Mary Ann, Mizu and Joe Onchi.
Photo courtesy of Joe Onchi.

break of war. The Mishima family, who owned a farm on Troutdale Road, invited Mizu Onchi, George and Sachi Onchi and the children to move into a shed on their farm which had previously been used to house farm workers. When Joe Onchi returned "home" after his discharge from the medical center at Fort Lewis, he moved into the "shed" with the other members of his family. The Onchi family remained as guests of the Mishima family for approximately two years.

George Onchi then found a farm to rent on Troutdale Road, located across from the Tamura Farm about one-mile south of the intersection of Troutdale Road with Stark Street. He and Sachi Onchi had four more children, Ronald, Georgene, Norene and Vicki. After a move to a second rented farm, George Onchi purchased a lot in Gresham where he had a home built for his family. He was able to rent farm land across the road from this home. His youngsters attended Gresham schools; the younger children graduated from Barlow High School. Mizu Onchi lived with her son, George, and his family until her death in 1974. George Onchi passed away in 1991.

Jim Onchi completed his military service as a member of the Army of Occupation, Germany. After his discharge in 1946, he returned to Oregon, but "had no place to go." He married Fumi Yumibe and the couple moved into rental housing in Vanport. According to Jim, the Vanport flood of May, 1948, "left us penniless. We lost our furniture, household goods, photograph albums, souvenirs, everything." He and his wife rented an apartment in Wood Village at Fairview Homes, another war housing project. He first worked for a home builder, learned the business and started his own home building business. He built several homes and other structures in Gresham. He and Fumi Onchi had five children, Curtis, Gary, Dwight, Harvey and Kelvin. As his business prospered, Jim Onchi built a home for his family in North Portland. His five boys chose to attend Benson High School rather than a high school in the neighborhood. The couple's eldest son, Lt. Curtis Onchi, was killed in action in the Viet Nam War. Jim Onchi built a new home for his family near Mt. Scott, where he and Fumi Onchi now live.

After Joe Onchi's discharge, he lived with his brother George's family on Troutdale Road. Onchi decided to take advantage of a government program that paid those veterans wounded in action a special educational benefit that paid for a college education. First he completed a two-year pre-optometry program at Multnomah College. He then applied for admission to Pacific Univerity's optometry school. Accepted, he completed the four-year program, took his state qualifying examination and became a licensed optometrist. Encouraged by businessman Les Walrad and his former high school principal, Mr. Saverude, Joe Onchi opened an clinic in Gresham.

In 1949, Joe Onchi married Toby Ninomiya, born in Troutdale, Oregon. When she reached school age, her parents sent her to live with relatives in Japan to attend school. She returned to Troutdale in 1932, but shortly thereafter her parents moved to Brooks, Oregon, where her father had found a job. She completed high school in Salem, Oregon. When ordered to an internment center, the Ninomiya family reported to Salem, Oregon, as ordered. From Salem, they were taken to the camp at Tule Lake, California. Later the WRA transferred the family to the Minidoka Relocation Center in Idaho. Released in 1945, Toby Ninomiya returned to Portland and located an apartment. While living there, she met and married Joe Onchi. After Onchi completed the optometry program at Pacific University, the couple moved into a home located on N.E. Glisan near Birdsdale, Avenue. In 1955, they had a home built in Gresham so that their children, Douglas, Valerie and Gregory, could attend Gresham schools. For a time, Valerie Onchi practiced optometry in her father's clinic. She has since moved to a group practice in Vancouver, Washington. Onchi's nephew, Raymond Onchi, established a dental practice in the same building. Joe and Toby Onchi continue to live in their home located on Fifth Street off Norman, in Gresham.

Rikizo Shiiki
Asa (Shiraishi) Shiiki

In 1912, after his marriage to Asa Shiraishi, Roy Rikizo Shiiki came to the United States. In 1915, he returned to Fukuoka, Japan, to see his wife. However, he returned to the United States alone; his wife did not come until 1917. The couple had hopes that they could save sufficient money working in the United States to give them a good start when they returned to Japan. In 1918, they located in Gresham, where their first child, Addie Arie was born (1918). Asa Shiiki picked berries and other crops to earn $75.00 to purchase a Singer sewing machine, a prized possession. The family soon found a farm to rent on Powell Boulevard, where Asa Shiiki believed raising chickens would be profitable. Consequently, they raised a flock of chickens and started selling eggs. A custom among families of Japanese ancestry leads to numerous exchanges of gifts. In the Shiiki's case, the obvious choice was eggs. Asa Shiiki gave away so many eggs the Shiiki's found that raising chickens was not profitable. Roy Shiiki grew vegetables, which he sold at the farmer's market in Portland. Asa Shiiki wheeled her daughter in a buggy to the fields to help with the harvest. In time, Roy moved his family to a rented farm on Hogan Road, the August Houseman place. There, he planted strawberries, cane berries and vegetable crops, including broccoli, brussel sprouts, cabbage, carrots, cauliflower, cucumbers and turnips. A Gresham cannery, McLoughlins, purchased the berry crops and the cucumbers were contracted to Libby, McNeil and Libby in Portland. Of course, Shiiki continued to sell much of his other farm produce at the farmers' market.

The couple had four more children: Kisae, born in 1920, Sumie, born in 1922, Tom Tan (1924) and Ray (1927). Asa Shiiki used her sewing machine to make clothes for her girls. Roy purchased the material needed at the Yamhill market and Mrs. Shiiki used catalogs and advertisements to get ideas for clothing. She cut the material without a pattern, hoping to duplicate a finished dress or another article of clothing she saw on paper. The results of her creativity were very satisfactory. The youngsters completed their elementary school years at Hillsview Elementary School in Clackamas County. After completing grade school, they attended Gresham High School (GHS). Addie graduated from GHS in 1936, Kisae, in 1938 and Sumie, in 1940.

The Alien Land Law prevented Roy and Asa Shiiki from purchasing a farm. However, when Addie became twenty-one in 1939, being a citizen, she could own land. The couple decided to purchase a farm in her name. Roy Shiiki

The Shiiki Family

Rear, from left: Kisae, Addie, and Sumie Shiiki. Front, Ray, Asa, Roy and Tom Shiiki.
All photos courtesy of Ray Shiiki.

consulted a manager at McLoughlin's cannery in Gresham, who said he would help them find a place. The manager located a farm for sale in Damascus and made arrangements for the purchase in Addie's name. However, the farm lacked a place to live and they continued to rent the farm on Hogan Road. They made their payments, paid property taxes and prepared the land for crops. Unfortunately, Johnson grass had taken over the fields, which required the family to work the land with a springtooth harrow pulled by a horse to bring the roots to the surface. The roots were then piled in stacks, dried and burned. Since a small segment of a root would generate a new plant, the effort to eliminate Johnson grass continued as long as they worked the ground.

Roy Shiiki first planted strawberries, then planted his usual truck garden crops. On December 7, 1941, Japanese aircraft bombed Pearl Harbor. The following spring, preparation of the ground for planting continued as usual, and an early crop had already been harvested. Abruptly, on May 7, 1942, the Shiiki family, together with all families of Japanese ancestry in the area, received notice to report to the county fairgrounds in Gresham on May 12, 1942, to be "evacuated." Shiiki hurriedly sold the new GMC truck he had purchased at a great loss; he also sold a new, 1941 Pontiac automobile he had acquired. During the five-day period of time allowed, Roy and Asa Shiiki found that the "help" given to them by a manager at McLoughlin's cannery had been fraudulent; the farm that they thought they had been buying in Addie's name was

Scenes, Shiiki Farm, 1920s and 1930s

Upper left: Kisae Shiiki picking strawberries. Upper right: Roy Shiiki holds Tom in front of a load of berry crates from McLoughlin's cannery. Middle left, Ray Shiiki, standing in front of the family's new automobile (early 1930s). Middle: Asa Shiiki holds Ray. She worked in the fields with other family members. Middle right: Tom and Ray Shiiki at the farm on Hogan Road. Below left: Roy Shiiki picking strawberries. Lower right: Roy Shiiki with a load of carrots delivered to the shipping shed at Troutdale.

Hillsview School ca 1932

Front, from left: ??, ??, Eddie Imhoff, Jack Taylor, Doug Bednar, ??, and ??. Second row: Miyeko Fujimoto, Sumie Shiiki, ??, Bill Bjornsted, Kazuo Kato, Tom Shiiki and Bob Hoffmeister. Third row: Mary Jean Peterson, teacher, Jim Bjornsted, Hap Forsyth, Bill Riggs, _?_ Adam, Bob Derrick, ?? and ??. Fourth row: ??, ??, Bob Bjornsted, Thurma Riggs, Ken Bjornsted, Mariam Olson and Al Hoffmeister.

actually in the manager's name. However, they were neither in a position to contest the matter, nor did they have time to do so; the farm they thought was theirs was not.

Mr. McLoughlin, cannery owner, fired the manager on the spot when he learned what had happened, but that ended the matter. Thus, the Shiiki family not only lost the farm they were "purchasing;" they lost the labor they had expended in preparing the land for planting. In addition, they lost their crops to be harvested in 1942. The manager harvested the strawberry crop, which ripened about three weeks after the "relocation." In addition, seedbeds of cabbage, cauliflower and other crops were in, and the plants would be ready to transplant in a few weeks.

On May 12, the Shiiki family proceeded to the fair grounds with the belongings they were permitted to take. Tom, who was scheduled to graduate from Gresham High in a couple of weeks was not allowed to remain in order to participate in the ceremony, but the school did forward his diploma to him. Of course, Ray, who had nearly completed his freshman year, was not allowed to finish the year. When the busses pulled away from the fairgrounds, a few of the boys' friends followed the bus transporting the Shiiki family to the Portland

Ray and Tom Shiiki, Kendo

Ray (left) and Tom Shiiki participated in Kendo, the traditional Japanese sport of fencing.
Photo courtesy of Ray Shiiki.

Assembly Center. Ray and Tom were able to visit with Bob Hoffmeister and some others, who met them at the fence surrounding the livestock buildings. Eventually their friends had to leave. An angry Ray broke down when he realized that he, a citizen of the United States, was being imprisoned because he was of Japanese ancestry. The Pacific Livestock Exposition buildings and grounds were to house several thousand families of Japanese ancestry until suitable camps could be constructed.

Family members were assigned different jobs at the assembly center. Ray became a bus boy in the cafeteria. After a month on the job, payday came and checks were distributed to the help. Ray did not get an $8.00 check. When asked about the oversight, he was told he had to be sixteen before he could be paid. He quit. Next, he volunteered to work at a labor camp in Nyssa, Oregon. At Nyssa, he weeded row after row of sugar beets. After less than a month, he returned to the assembly center with a full wallet; he was paid well for farm work even though he was not sixteen.

In September, 1942, the Shiiki family together with other families from the assembly center in Portland, Oregon, were sent by rail car to Twin Falls, Idaho, thence to the Minidoka Relocation Center. They were assigned to Barracks 6C, Block 31. Since Addie had married before the war, she and her husband were assigned a separate room. Consequently, six family members were housed in room 6C. Authorities assigned Roy Shiiki the job of taking care of the boiler, which provided hot water for Block 31. Asa Shiiki worked as a dishwasher in the mess hall. Kisae and Sumie Shiiki soon departed for Colorado, where they had obtained employment as housekeepers. Tom Shiiki, drafted, reported to the induction center for a physical, which he failed. Subsequently, he went to Spokane, Washington, where he found work with the Spokane, Portland and

The Shiiki Farm, Hogan Road

Top left: Mary and Ray Shiiki take a load cauliflower harvested from their farm. Top right: Ray and Mary Shiiki, who raised their family on the farm. Below: Workers pulling broccoli plants for transplanting, Shiiki farm, include, from left: Mary Shiiki, June Shiiki, David Lestiko (standing), Jack Gifford, Trey Rose, Verda Gifford, Steve Rose and Doris Gifford. Photos courtesy of Ray Shiiki.

Seattle Railroad Company. Ray graduated from Hunt High School at the camp, then started college at Miami University in Oxford, Ohio. Drafted in the summer of 1945, he traveled to Fort Douglas, Utah, to be inducted (see "Ray Shiiki, Nisei Veterans," this volume).

Since the Shiiki family had lost the farm they thought was theirs, upon their return to Oregon they moved into rented quarters at Vanport. Tom had obtained employment with the Schnitzer brothers at their Alaska junkyard. The Hoffmeister family had kept in touch with the Shiiki family during their internment at Minidoka. Al "Shorty" Hoffmeister contacted Ray and Tom with news that he had located a farm for rent on Hogan Road with a small house. Roy, Asa, Tom and Ray Shiiki soon moved to the farm. When Vanport flooded in

Ray and Mary Shiiki's Children

From left: Gail, Rik and Lon Shiiki, at home on the family's Gresham farm. The youngsters attended Gresham schools. Photo courtesy of Ray Shiiki.

1948, Addie and her husband, Don Onishi, also moved to the farm. Thus, after a six-year hiatus, the family resumed farming.

A neighbor, Bob Wilson, who became a close friend, offered to rent his 113-acre farm to the family on a "share" basis. Ray asked if Wilson wanted "papers," to which he responded, "do you." When Ray replied, "no," Wilson thrust out his hand and said, "a hand shake will do for me." The brothers accepted and farmed the acreage for the next two years, which worked out well for both them and Wilson. Wilson then proposed that the brothers buy the farm outright, giving them very generous terms. Ray and Tom Shiiki accepted his offer, thus becoming farm owners rather than tenants. Ray remarked, "After some of the things that had happened to us over the war years, Bob Wilson's honesty and fair dealing made us feel much better." The farm had excellent soil, which their hard work could make productive. The brothers purchased an additional 40 acres of the original place that had been sold to Poly Schedeen. A few years later, the partners purchased a 100-acre woodland that adjoined their property on the west. Thus, Ray and Tom Shiiki owned 153 acres of farm land as well as 100-acres in trees when they sold the place in 1990. Their former farm and acreage is now part of the Persimmon Golf Course complex.

Ray Shiiki married Mary Muramatsu, whose family lived in Parkrose before the war. The couple had three children, Rik, Lon and Gail, who attended Gresham schools.

Minekichi Tamura
Sute Tamura

Minekichi and Sute Tamura purchased 32 acres on Troutdale Road from a Mr. Jones in 1919. According to their grandson, Kazuma "Kaz" Tamura, they knew absolutely nothing about farming, but learned quickly. "My grandfather was a smart man," Kaz asserted. Minekichi left Japan with his wife for Hawaii, most probably in 1907. The couple's first three children were born in Japan: George Genchiro in 1898, Seiko, in 1900, and Kuniji, in 1906. Around 1912, George Tamura ventured to the mainland with hope of finding employment and perhaps, better circumstances for the family. He found work and wrote to his father in Hawaii, suggesting that he should also come to the mainland. Once here, Minekichi found work in a sawmill near Seattle. For the next few years, Minekichi and George worked at different sawmills in the Seattle – Tacoma area, and saved money. When sufficient money had been saved to bring the rest of the family to Seattle, Minekichi sent for them.

In 1915, the family moved to Linnton, Oregon, where Tamura found employment at a Linnton sawmill. In 1917 or early 1918, Minekichi and Sute Tamura decided to open a restaurant, with the hope that his days as a mill worker had ended. In 1919, fire destroyed the restaurant, which ended that dream. However, rather than return to the mill, Minekichi, with his two sons to help, decided to try farming. Fortunately for Minekichi, a neighbor, Roy Asakawa, volunteered to help him learn to farm. And, as Kaz mentioned, his grandfather "caught on quickly. He had too." By that time, the Tamuras had a fourth child, Mary Yoneko born in 1917. From 1919 to the present (excepting the war years), a member of the Tamura family has operated the farm on Troutdale Road.

In 1919, George Tamura traveled to Japan and returned with his bride, Toyoko Aoki, of Tokyo. The couple had four children, Kazuma "Kaz." born in 1921; Takashi, (1922); Lillian Yayoi (1924); and Miyeko, (1927). The youngsters attended Cedar Grade School, located on Troutdale Road just a short distance north of their farm. Kaz completed his freshman year at Gresham High, but then transferred to Benson Tech, from which he graduated in 1939. Both Lillian and Takashi graduated from Gresham High School in 1941; Takashi a year late because he spent a year in Japan. The war interrupted Miyeko's high school years and she completed high school in Caldwell, Idaho. Of George's siblings, Seiko Tamura married, but did not get along well with her husband; she returned to Japan to live. Kuniji Tamura farmed with his father on the Troutdale place until about 1932, then rented a farm in Barton, Oregon. He

Tamura Family ca 1930

From left, Kuniji, Mitsuru, Takashi, Lillian, Kaz and George Tamura. At this time, the Tamura family farmed the acreage on Troutdale Road. Photo courtesy of Kaz Tamura.

married Mitsuru Fujimura, and the couple had four children, Richard, Carol, Darlene and Terri. Yoneko, the youngest sibling, remained on the farm, and also attended Cedar School and Gresham High School.

The Tamura family operated the Troutdale farm as a "truck garden," growing berries, spinach, tomatoes, celery and cauliflower, but the latter two were the principal crops. The Tamuras could grow celery because they had irrigation water from Beaver Creek, which flows through the farm. The Tamura family sold much of their produce at the Eastside Farmers' Market. Some crops, such as cucumbers, were sold on contract to food processors. Kaz cited his grandfather's sagacity in building three green houses on the farm, which permitted them to start plants so that an early crop could be raised; a crop that often came on the market without competition. This generally meant (1), that the crop could be sold, and (2), that the price would be higher. One year, Kaz recalled, his grandfather planted cauliflower on February 7. Snow fell on February 8, covering the field, but the plants survived and produced a good, early crop of cauliflower.

As with other Nikkei families, the "exclusion order" of May 7, 1942, forced the Tamura family from their farm. The family stored its furniture, photographs and personal possessions that could not be taken with them in a room in their fairly new home (built in 1930) on Troutdale Road. The farm, with an early

Tamura Family ca 1947

Rear, from left: George, Toyoko and Kaz Tamura. Front, Minekichi, Sute and Helen Tamura. Helen is holding her son, Paul Tamura, and Minekichi Tamura is holding a portrait of his father.   Photo courtesy of Kaz Tamura.

crop of cauliflower nearly ready for harvest, was rented to Fred Fernandez, a Filipino farm worker whom Tamura had previously employed. Kaz commented, "(Fernandez) made the profit. He made good money. All of our work counted for nothing." With very few exceptions, this typifies the experience of our neighbors of Japanese ancestry after May 12, 1942. The proceeds from spring crops, such as strawberries, potatoes and, in the case of the Tamuras, cauliflower, benefited those who harvested the crops, rather than the families that planted and cared for them.

On May 12 the Tamura families reported to the Portland Assembly Center, where they remained the summer of 1942. That fall, when the Minidoka Relocation Center opened, the U.S. Government sent many Nikkei families there. Kaz remembered that he and other able bodied Issei and Nisei left Minidoka to work for Idaho farmers, harvesting potatoes, sugar beets and onions. In March, 1943, the entire family, excepting the elder Minekichi and Sute Tamura, were paroled from Minidoka to a Farm Security Administration camp near Caldwell, Idaho. There, they lived in a comfortable two-bedroom house and worked in the area's sugar beet, potato and onion fields. Kaz Tamura, drafted in 1941,

Tamura Family at Home

From left: Minekuchi, unidentified, Helen (behind), Pamela, Yonoko, George and Kaz Tamura, at home in the early 1950s. *Photo courtesy of Kaz Tamura.*

took his physical, but was classified 4-F because of health problems. Later his classification was changed to 4-C (not acceptable because of ancestry), which insulted and bothered him as it did other Nisei. On February 12, 1944, he married Helen Taniguchi of The Dalles, born in 1922. His younger brother, Takashi Tamura, drafted early during World War II, was discharged after about 6 months because of a medical condition. He settled in Cleveland, Ohio, where he lived the rest of his life. He passed away on March 29, 1986.

When the war ended, the Tamura family returned to Oregon, but could not return to their Troutdale farm as their home had burned the previous winter. With it went all of the family's stored possessions, including, unfortunately, all of the family's photographs taken before the war. Because of the fire, the Tamuras rented a farm near Carver, Oregon, which Kaz Tamura purchased the following year. His uncle, Kuniji Tamura, also bought a farm near Carver where he and his wife, Mitsuru Fujimura, raised their four children. Meanwhile, Minekichi and Sute Tamura and their oldest son, George Tamura and his wife, returned to the home place. In 1962, after Sute Tamura died in 1959, Minekichi Tamura decided to return to Japan to live with his daughter, after which George managed the farm. George's younger sister, Seiko Tamura, had never left Japan. She married, but her husband was killed in action in the Philippine Islands during World War II. Minekichi Tamura spent the final 10 years of his life in Japan with his daughter. Minekichi Tamura died in 1972, age 97 years. Yoneko Tamura, the youngest of Minekichi and Sute Tamura's four children, married

Kaz Tamura on the Farm

Kaz Tamura seeds his field with rye, used as a cover crop. Rye kept the hillsides from eroding and provided organic material when plowed under.

Photo courtesy of Kaz Tamura.

Mas Migaki, whose family owned a farm in Dallesport, Washington. The couple later planted the acreage to cherry trees, which orchard their children now manage.

Kaz and Helen Tamura had two children, Paul, born in 1946, and Pamela, (1949). Both youngsters attended Carver Grade School, then Clackamas High School, from which Paul graduated in 1964; Pamela in 1967. Paul completed a program in pharmacy at Oregon State University, but first had a service obligation to meet. After serving in the U.S. Army during the Viet Nam war, he became a pharmacist in Eugene, Oregon, where he now lives with his wife, Laura (Hada), and daughter, Kimberly. Pamela attended Portland State University, majored in physical education and taught at Catlin Gabel. She married Mike Oja, whose father owned a sawmill in Sandy, Oregon, which Mike now manages. Pamela and Mike Oja have two daughters, Teresa and Valerie. When George Tamura passed away in 1970, Kaz took the responsibility of farming the home place as well as his place in Carver. He raised berries, cauliflower, spinach and similar crops, selling to Safeway, United Salad, United Grocers and Ed Fujii Produce. Kaz Tamura's mother, Toyoko (Aoki) Tamura, passed away in 1984; on July 29, 2000, he lost his wife, Helen (Taniguchi) Tamura. He now lives on the family farm on Troutdale Road, but no longer actively farms. His Carver farm is rented.

After the war, Kaz Tamura's younger sister, Lillian Tamura, married Henry Daty and the couple settled in New York. She and Henry had one child, Michael. The youngest sister, Miyeko Tamura, married Joe Naemura, a physician, and

Kaz, Helen and Pamela's Family

Kaz and Helen Tamura are surrounded by, from left, Valerie, Teresa, Mike and Pamela (Tamura) Oja. Pamela and her family live in Sandy where her husband, Mike, owns a sawmill.   Photo courtesy of Kaz Tamura.

the couple settled in Portland after the war. She and Joe had five children, Joseph, Lori, Tracey, Jeanine and William. Recently, Miyeko Naemura suffered a stroke, and she now lives with her daughter, Tracey, in Ridgefield, Washington.

Internment

Immediately after the attack at Pearl Harbor on December 7, 1941, President Franklin D. Roosevelt issued a proclamation that categorized all nationals and subjects of the nations with which we were at war as "enemy aliens." On February 19, 1942, the President issued Executive Order No. 9066, which authorized and directed the Secretary of War "to prescribe military areas in such places and of such an extent as he or the appropriate Military Commander may determine, from which any and all persons may be excluded, and with respect to which the right of any persons to enter, remain in, or leave, shall be subject to whatever restrictions the Secretary of War or the appropriate Military Commander may impose at his discretion." President Roosevelt cited the successful prosecution of the war as requiring "every possible protection against espionage and against sabotage to national-defense materiel, national-defense premises, and national-defense utilities," as the rationale for the order.

In response, on May 7, 1942, Lieutenant General J.L. DeWitt, Military Commander, Western Defense Command, issued exclusion orders that affected approximately 110,000 individuals, in the Command's words, "of Japanese ancestry" living in California, Oregon or Washington. The orders, issued in the spring of 1942, excluded "all persons of Japanese ancestry, both alien and non-alien" from certain defined areas in the three states. Essentially, people of Japanese ancestry were forbidden to enter a zone from the Pacific coastline eastward approximately 200-250 miles wide. The orders specified the items that each person "must carry:"

(a) Bedding and linens (no mattress) for each (family member)

(b) Toilet articles for each member of the family

(c) Extra clothing for each member of the family

(d) Sufficient knives, forks, spoons, plates, bowls and cups for each member of the family

(e) Essential personal effects for each member of the family

No pets of any kind. No personal items and no personal goods will be shipped to the Assembly Area. The Government will provide storage for household items (refrigerators, stoves, etc.) if crated, packed and plainly marked with the name and address of the owner.
        Signed: J.L. DeWitt, Lt. General, U.S. Army, Commanding

General DeWitt, Commander, Western Defense Command, certainly had a significant role in the government's decision to exclude "all persons of

U.S. Army Personnel Post Exclusion Order

The Western Defense Command posted notices in the government established "exclusion zones" informing "all persons of Japanese ancestry, both alien and non-alien [U.S. citizens]," to report to a designated "assembly center."   Photo, U.S. Signal Corps.

Japanese ancestry, both alien and non-alien," from the entire west coast. He is quoted as remarking, "A Jap is a Jap," which certainly reveals his attitude toward these immigrants and their families, most of whom were U.S. citizens. Farming, logging and fishing engaged approximately 46% of the interned workers (with farming dominant); 23% worked in the wholesale or retail trade. Such occupations would not be advantageous to an individual engaged in espionage. In contrast, only 3.7% of those employed worked in a manufacturing job. Obviously, the government had not planned for a mass "evacuation" prior to the outbreak of hostilities. Immediately after Pearl Harbor, authorities imposed curfews and constraints on travel, prohibited the ownership of guns, cameras and other items, and placed other restrictions on persons of Japanese ancestry. Any individual violating these restrictions was subject to arrest and imprisonment. Within days after the attack, approximately 2000 individuals of Japanese ancestry had been arrested and imprisoned. Joe Josuke Nakata, rumored to have a store of dynamite, was arrested and sent to a prison in Missoula, Montana.

However, no facilities for holding the approximate 110,000 Americans of Japanese ancestry who lived in the restricted area had been built. Consequently, the government instituted a crash program to provide facilities to hold the internees. In Oregon, the choice was the Pacific International Livestock Exposition grounds and buildings. In Southern California, one choice was the Santa

The Evacuation

Above: "Evacuees" being interviewed by personnel of the Farm Security Administration. The government's plan was to help farmers dispose of their farm equipment and other possessions at a fair price. The effort failed, as the stories of families (section 1) confirm. Below: "Evacuees" crowd the Los Angeles train station awaiting transport to the Santa Anita assembly center. Photos, U.S. Signal Corps.

Anita race track, with its extensive grounds and buildings. In total, the government selected 15 locales for "assembly centers." Large fairgrounds

Guard Tower, Tanforan   Construction, Manzanar

Left: A tower for use by Army Military Police to guard the internees at the Tanforan Assembly Center near San Francisco, California. Right: Construction crews build the barracks, etc., to be used at the Manzanar assembly center, Owens Valley, California. This assembly center became Camp Manzanar under the jurisdiction of the War Relocation Authority.   Photos, Acme Newspictures, Inc. and the U.S. Signal Corps, respectively.

or racetracks were preferred. A former Civilian Conservation Corps camp in Arizona became a site (Mayer). A closed California lumber mill with company housing was selected as a site (Pinedale). The State of Washington had just one center, at Puyallup. The government located 12 centers in California: Marysville, Sacramento, Tanforan, Stockton, Turlock, Salinas, Merced, Fresno, Tulare and Pomona, in addition to the Pinedale and Santa Anita centers, already mentioned. Two sites, Manzanar (California) and the Colorado River Relocation Center, Poston, Arizona, housed evacuees immediately. Both later became permanent "relocation" camps. Hastily built, structures to house the influx of internees were inadequate, which created problems of overcrowding, poor sanitation, a lack of privacy and other issues described in the accounts found herein. Before the evacuation took place, about 4,800 individuals of Japanese ancestry relocated voluntarily, moving to areas outside the restricted zone. A few residents, less than 500, were exempted from the order for various reasons. One U.S. Navy veteran, who had served honorably for many years, was exempted. Frances Kumazawa, enrolled as a student in a nurses training program, wrote Eleanor Roosevelt to ask for an exemption so that she could complete the program with her class. Mrs. Roosevelt's interceded and Frances received an exemption, but it came too late to help.

While the internees waited in these "assembly centers," an Army program to provide more permanent internment camps for the prisoners proceeded. The United States government established ten Internment Centers west of the Mississippi River (populations given are the peak reached):

(1) Minidoka, Idaho, to which most of the internees from Oregon were sent. This 68,000 acre site of desert sageland housed 9,397 well-guarded prisoners.

The Santa Anita Assembly Center

Above: Internees disembarking from busses undergo baggage inspection upon their arrival at the Santa Anita Racetrack Assembly facility. Below: The government hastily built these barracks to house the approximate 18,000 internees who reported to this assembly center. Photos, Santa Anita Assembly Center and the U.S. Signal Corps, respectively.

Temperatures ranged from the extreme heat of summer to twenty-five below zero in the winter.

(2) Tule Lake, Northern California, to which some of the "evacuees from Oregon were sent, was located on a 26,000 acre site in Modoc County. It was a

Tule Lake "Relocation Center"

The Tule Lake Center, in Northern California, held more than 18,000 internees. Eventually it became the camp of choice for those whom the government classified as "troublemakers."   Photo courtesy of Kazuko Hara.

hot, dry, desert area covered by grasses and tule. The "lake" was a reclaimed lake bottom 4000 feet above sea level. Many of Tule Lake's 18,789 inhabitants were supposedly "trouble makers." Often, that meant the detainees had objected to their treatment by government officials and their loss of civil rights.

(3) Manzanar, Southern California, occupied a 6000 acre site in the Owens Valley. Mount Whitney and Mt. Williamson were visible in the distance. Here, the barracks had red roofs and the camp was not enclosed by barbed wire; the desert provided security. It held about 10,000 prisoners

(4) Poston, Western Arizona, was located on the 90,000 acre Colorado Indian reservation. Actually Poston contained three camps, intended to house between 5,000 to 10,000 prisoners each. The inhabitants of Poston suffered from the almost unbearable heat during the summer months. During the winter months, it was more comfortable. Poston's three camps held 17,814 Nikkei.

(5) Gila, South-Central Arizona, had the Superstition Mountains as a back drop. This desert camp had whitewashed buildings with red roofs. The soil was favorable for raising gardens, which its "guests" utilized to advantage. Gila held 13,348 prisoners.

(6) Topaz, Central Utah, held many families from the San Franciso area. The camp, with its square-mile barbed wire enclosure and black, tarpaper barracks

was quite similar to others. The terrain was an absolutely flat plain covered with sagebrush. Topaz housed 8,130 prisoners.

(7) Heart Mountain, North-Central Wyoming. This most northern of the camps was flat, treeless, desolate, and subject to high winds. The tarpaper-covered barracks had black roofs, but a few buildings had beige walls and red roofs. Winters were extremely cold, but the summer months were more comfortable. Heart Mountain housed 10,767 prisoners.

(8) Amache, South-Eastern Colorado, was located on a small hill in an arid and dusty flatland. Nearby farmers grew melons and fruit and about one-half of its 10,000 acres was under cultivation when the center opened. Winters were long, lasting from October until the beginning of May. Amache held 7,318 prisoners.

(9) Rohwer, Southeast Arkansas. Both Rohwer and Jerome were located in a swampy lowland in Arkansas, covered with lush vegetation. The swamps held water moccasins and the forest, rattlesnakes. Rohwer held 8,475 prisoners.

(10) Jerome, Southeast Arkansas, surrounded by swamps, did not have the usual barbed wire fence. Gardens thrived and rains were frequent. On one occasion, a local resident of Dermott, Arkansas, shot at a visiting Nisei soldier. Jerome housed 8,475 Nikkei.

The 1940 census registered approximately 110,000 persons of Japanese ancestry living in the three Pacific Coast states of California, Oregon and Washington, most of whom were incarcerated in the above centers. Some were

Relocation Center, Amache, Colorado

This view shows a typical "block" of 12 barracks, a recreation hall, laundry and bathhouse, and a mess hall (center). Each barracks had "two small, two medium and two large apartments."   *Photo, the War Relocation Authority.*

paroled, that is, allowed to leave the centers to farm in Idaho or other areas. And, of course, those Nisei serving in the armed forces were not interned (in most instances). Shortly after Pearl Harbor, the selective service re-classified Nisei 4-C (not acceptable because of ancestry). At this time, the armed services ordered its Nisei soldiers to turn in all equipment and return home. George Azumano, among others, took the proffered discharge and complied. Many commanders objected, however, and the government soon reversed this action. Nevertheless, the classification, 4-C, continued to be used until a directive issued on January 22, 1943, reversed the policy.

On June 11, 2002, Lily (Sakurai) Kajiwara, Leke Nakashimada and Shio Uyetake spoke to the members of the Crown Point Country Historical Society about their experiences some sixty years earlier, when they and their families were forced from their farms by the United States Government. Shio described his families departure from their home on Mershon Road, bound for an assembly point in Troutdale. "Your President (the author) and his sister stood alongside the road as we passed; both were crying. That memory has stayed with me all of these years." Lily, Leke and Shio recounted some of the unpleasant experiences that they and other families of Japanese ancestry suffered during the World War II years. Our Nikkei neighbors became victims of a reflected rage directed toward the Empire of Japan, a fury encompassing anyone and anything "Japanese," including, unfortunately, our neighbors of Japanese ancestry. Fortunately, by their account, the inflamed passions of the time did not affect either their schoolmates, their teachers or most of their neighbors.

Certainly apprehension grew after December 7, 1941, with U.S. outposts in the Pacific being attacked and conquered one by one, with bad news following bad news day after day. Nikkei families received notices regarding curfew times and travel restrictions, but the children, educated in our schools, knew that they were secure, as the founding documents of our government guaranteed to each of its citizens certain inalienable rights, which included liberty, security in the home and justice for all. When the Western Defense Command posted its notices in East Multnomah County on May 7, 1942, commanding "all persons of Japanese ancestry, both alien and *non-alien,*" to report to an assembly center, our Nikkei neighbors were dismayed and bewildered. But the unimaginable and unexpected had happened; they complied with the edict. In the five days provided, possessions were sold, including farm animals, farm equipment and automobiles. The Sakurai family arranged a sale of their automobile to a buyer who agreed to take possession at an assembly point in Troutdale. Thus, the Sakurai family's last trip in this automobile was to Troutdale where the car was delivered to the buyer and the family boarded a school bus bound for the Portland International Livestock Exposition Center. A neighbor, Robert "Tood" Larson, drove the Uyetake family to the Troutdale assembly point in his car. Other Nikkei families made similar arrangements as they were permitted to bring only those personal effects, extra clothing, toilet articles, bedding, linens and eating utensils that could be carried.

After the posting of the notice, Bukichi Fujii approached Andrew and Charlotte Cunningham and asked them if they would consider taking care of the farm. Fujii had hired Mrs. Cunningham as his field boss because of her skill in dealing with the youngsters hired to pick strawberries, raspberries and loganberries. After carefully considering the plea, the Cunninghams agreed to live in the Fujii home, to harvest and care for the berries and, essentially, to manage the farm. Scott Cunningham recalled that when Mr. Fujii left their home after his parents had agreed to look after his farm, "tears were streaming from his eyes." The Fujii family packed their furniture and other possessions in one bedroom; the Caterpillar tractor, covered and well lubed, was locked in a shed; the other farm implements and the horse for the Cunningham's use were either in or near the barn. Mr. and Mrs. Cunningham took the Fujii family to the Troutdale assembly area, where they exchanged tearful good-byes. Soon, each school bus departed with its apprehensive passengers, bound for the Portland International Livestock Exposition Center in North Portland.

Upon their arrival at the center, the "evacuees" were processed, assigned quarters and questioned regarding skills. The responses soon led to each individual being assigned to a task; U.S. Army methodology through and through. Dick Sakurai remembered his first job: his father directed him to take the provided sacks and fill them with straw from a pile on the premises. Dick remarked, "If I had known how that straw would pack down I would have filled them much fuller." About 10 days after being confined, George Sakurai responded to a friend's (George Perry) letter: "We have good beds, but the mattresses? Alas! They are of straw."

Doctors, nurses, cooks, waitresses, latrine orderlies, janitors and other workers came from amongst the prisoners. The center was fenced on all sides, with a large common area to the east, which provided space for a ball field. Center buildings, designed for livestock, had been "remodeled" for human habitation. Stalls were removed and eight-foot plywood walls installed to form "rooms" approximately 20-by-20 foot in size. A floor of green lumber had been laid to cover the gutters that formerly held animal waste; a flap of canvas covered the entry "door." Army cots lined one wall for the occupants' use.

For the Sakurai family of eight, confinement in a 20-by-20 foot cubicle afforded no privacy for family members whatsoever, the situation not only common to every family at the Center, but to individuals as well, as single individuals were grouped together. Compounding the problems experienced by the Sakurai family was the fact that one child, Betty, afflicted by cerebral palsy, could not walk to the community toilets, which created much anguish for her and her family. Another problem mentioned by numerous individuals came

Scenes, Portland Assembly Center

No. 1: Kitchen scene. Cooks prepared meals "under caucasian supervision." No. 2: Waitresses served "family-style meals" in the mess hall. No. 3: Laundry room. No. 4: Men's community washroom.   Photos, U.S. Signal Corps.

about because of the lack of ceilings. Any noise, such as a crying infant, disturbed all the "neighbors."

The internees ate at a community mess, were seated at a designated table and were served by the same waitress each day. The inmates showered at a community facility found in each building; toilets and wash basins were located in the same area. A night visit to the toilets, in addition to the long walk, might awaken others as the unfortunate pattered along the passageway to the facility. The queue to use the showers caused much frustration and the thought; how might this wait be avoided? [But no solution!] The internees could venture outside to get a breath of fresh air and to look upon the "world," since the windows in the buildings were so high that the only thing visible from within was the sky. One teen-ager, visiting with a former classmate beyond the fence, suddenly realized, for the first time, that he was a prisoner.

The Sakurai family's room was located in the swine area, that is, where pigs were kept during livestock shows. As the green lumber comprising the floor dried, gaps opened in the floor. Rather than helping provide for some movement of air, however, the cracks became an opening for flies; thousands of flies that bothered everyone. And as the days grew more hot as summer progressed, the number of flies increased. Flies were into and on everything. A

More Scenes, Portland Assembly Center

No. 1: The carpenter shop. Since internees coule not bring household furnishings, furniture was great demand. The shop tried to meet these needs. No. 2: Family quarters. A "brother and sister" make up one of the cots that lined the wall behind the young man. No. 3: The paint shop, which finished items that came from the carpenter shop. No. 4: Workers repair radio sets. Internees were allowed radios without long or short wave bands. No. 5: This dormitory at the Portland Assembly Center housed single men.   Photos, U.S. Signal Corps.

Dormitory, Single Men, Portland

This dormitory at the Portland Assembly Center housed single men.

Photo, U.S. Signal Corps.

Internees Leave Portland for Camp Minidoka

From all accounts, these happy faces reflect the joy of the internees as they left the Portland center for Camp Minidoka. They had suffered through a miserably hot summer dealing with overcrowding, noise, waiting in line at toilet facilities, innumerable flies, etc.

Photo, The Portland Oregonian.

The Minidoka Relocation Center

The Twin Falls North Side Canal (right) gave the Camp its southern border. Each "block" was bound by twelve barracks with the dining hall, laundry and sanitary building and recreation hall within. The road to the entry gate came in on the west side (below); the agricultural fields lay to the east (top). Photo, Mindoka Interlude.

common comment of those who spent the summer of 1942 at the center concerned the infestation of flies and the discomfort that this caused. Some families managed to leave the Center by volunteering for farm work in Idaho or Eastern Oregon. However, most families endured the hardships through the summer, hoping that the "relocation camps" under construction might be an improvement.

Typical Housing Block, Relocation Center

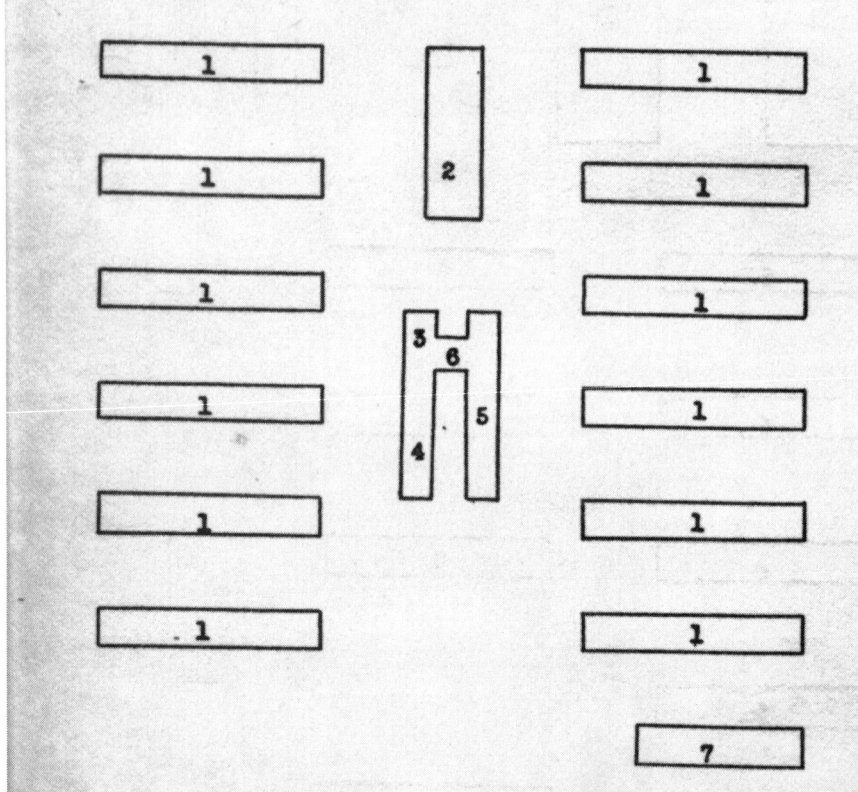

Key: 1. Barracks; 2. Mess Hall; 3. Women's Latrine; 4. Men's Latrine; 5. Laundry Room; 6. Boiler Room; 7. Recreation Hall Western Defense Command

    The government sent most of the prisoners held at the Portland center to the Minidoka Relocation Center (Minidoka) near Twin Falls, Idaho. In early September, trains carrying many of our neighbors left Portland bound for Twin Falls and the camp. The U.S. Government had constructed a complex of blocks, each of which included 12 barracks, a dining hall, a laundry and sanitary building and a recreation hall. The camp had its own hospital, administration buildings, schools, postoffice, churches (3), library and storage buildings. It also had manned guard towers, a headquarters building for its military police and a guarded entry gate. The camp encompassed thousands of acres of desert land that could be farmed if it could be irrigated. Each barracks had six rooms, two of a smaller size, two of an intermediate size and two of a larger size. The "small" rooms could accomodate 2-3 people; the "intermediate," 4-5 people; and the "large," 6-8 people. Thus, each of the buildings could accomodate between 24 and 32 people, which implies a capacity of between 288 and 384 for each block. Since the camp population peaked near 9400, or approximately 260 persons per block, the camp population never reached its theoretical ca-

Block Mess

At Minidoka, each block had its own mess hall, where inhabitants of the twelve block barracks ate three meals a day. The internees performed all tasks related to feeding the inmates, food preparation, serving and clean up. Photo, U.S. Army Engineers.

pacity. The barracks had board siding covered by tarpaper. The interior walls were not finished, thus the studs with fire stops were exposed. The fire stops became shelf space. A coal-burning, pot belly stove provided heat for each room. Seasoned lumber must have been in short supply because the builders used green lumber for the floors. As it dried, the boards shrank, which left cracks and holes where knots had dropped out. Tin can lids provided the means to cover knot holes. A single light fixture with one bulb provided light. There were no outlets for appliances or for a radio. Some families used an adapter with the light fixture so that an electrical appliance could be used.

Since private enterprise was not permitted, a number of co-ops became established in the camp, including a canteen, a dry goods store, a flower shop, a shoe repair shop, a radio repair shop, a mail order service desk, a dry cleaning and laundry shop, a watch repair shop, a barber shop, a fish market, a telegraph office, an optical shop, a beauty shop, bus service and places where movies were shown. Since many of its residents had been farmers, the agriculture section became an important and useful project for the internees. In 1943, more than 200 acres had been cleared and irrigation water obtained. That year, camp farms produced over 100 tons of produce with the expectation that by year end, the poultry farm would produce 1000 eggs per day and 4800 meat birds for winter use, while the hog farm would deliver 25 pigs per week to the block

Camp Minidoka Coal Division

Above: Since every family's "room" had a coal heat stove, the camp required lots of fuel. This is the crew that supplied coal for heating. Since George Yamashita worked in the Coal Division, he is likely in this photograph. Left: A standard U.S. Army issue coal stove of the type used by Mindoka's residents. Photo above courtesy of Lauretta Yamashita. Left photo, the author.

mess halls. The agriculture section also included a cannery, a pickling plant and a tofu plant. Insofar as possible, the camp's occupants provided the labor needed to operate and sustain the facility, which was, in essence, a small city.

The Sakurai family was included among the Portland Center contingent that arrived on September 10, 1942. Since the family included eight members, the administration provided them a large room with eight army cots in barracks 9, block 41. Later, when it became obvious that the camp had the room, the administration assigned a small adjacent room to the Sakurai family, which provided them more space and a modicum of privacy for family members. The Sakurai family ate at the common mess in their block and used its laundry and sanitary facilities. Because the block occupants shared the shower and toilet facilities, problems such as waiting in line to take a shower and the inconvenience of walking to and sharing toilet facilities continued to be a nuisance. Because of Betty's handicap, Dick Sakurai built her a "potty chair" so that she could take care of those needs in the family's quarters.

The administration assigned Masaru Sakurai to a janitor job in the block mess. Later, he drove a delivery truck. During the growing season, Sakurai requested and received a parole to take a job at a farm outside the camp, which jobs paid considerably more than "camp" jobs, which paid him $16.00 per month. When these "outside" jobs ended, he returned to Minidoka. Since

Stafford Grade School Staff

Stafford Grade staff members include, front row, L to R: Lily Sakurai, M. Murakami, E.M. Fitzsimons, S. Iwami, B Murakami, N. Ochiai. 2nd row: E. Yamashita, I. Nispel, R. Smith, A. Morton, C. Stull, E. Kleinkopf, T. Heyerdahl, unidentified. Back row: R. Lambert, M. Schmidt, M. Johnson. Bottom: Hunt High School staff members.

Photo, the Minidoka Interlude, *published by its residents.*

Chiyoko Sakurai had children to care for, she did not have an additional job. Because Lily had graduated from Columbian High School, Corbett, Oregon, the administration assigned her to teach at the camp's Stafford Grade School. She earned the professional level salary of $19.00 per month, the same as doctors, nurses and other professionals. Dick and George Sakurai both attended Hunt High School, established in the camp. During the harvest, they obtained a parole to work on farms outside the camp. Edward started first grade at Stafford School where his sister, Lily, taught. Later, Judith also started school at Minidoka. The experiences of other families incarcerated at Minidoka were most likely very similar to those experienced by the Sakurai family.

In December, 1944, the United States Supreme Court ruled that the War Relocation Authority (WRA) had no right to detain loyal Americans in relocation centers. Thus the Western Defense Command's exclusion order, with regard to loyal American citizens, was revoked, effective January 2, 1945. This affected Dick Sakurai directly, as he had been paroled to attend Miami of Ohio University. While attending, he received his draft notice and reported for his

Staff, Hunt High School

Dick Sakurai, who became a physics major, thought that his mathematics teacher, Ecco Hunt, had a positive effect on him and other students at Hunt. She had served as a missionary in Burma, and fled when the Japanese invaded that country. Miss Hunt is 4th from the left of those standing.

physical. The examination revealed that he had contracted tuberculosis (TB). The University, unaware of the result, allowed him to complete the term. Upon his return to Minidoka, however, the camp administration told him that he could stay at Minidoka only if he paid room and board. Consequently, he chose to join his father, who was working on a farm outside the camp. The WRA announced that, because of the Supreme Court decision, all relocation centers, including Minidoka, would close before the end of 1945. Consequently, its residents were faced with the task of rebuilding their lives that had been so abruptly disrupted some three years previously. The Sakurai family returned to Portland, but did not return to their farm. Dick Sakurai enrolled at Reed College, where a physical examination confirmed the existence of TB. However, Reed's health service sent him to the hospital at the Oregon Health Center, where the disease was treated, enabling him to continue his studies at Reed, where he completed a major in physics (see "Masaru Sakurai," this volume).

Unfortunately, closing the camps neither remedied nor ended the discriminatory practices experienced by our neighbors of Japanese ancestry. Because of the provisions of the alien land law, many had been tenants rather than owners. Because of their internment, these Nikkei families had missed four lucrative years for farmers; farm owners sold everything they could produce at favorable prices. Because of the depression years preceding the war, their internment and the forced liquidation of assets, these families had little capital. When

Internal Security Section

Suematso "Pops" Ando served on the camp's Internal Security Section, which handled law enforcement matters. The police had few miscreants to deal with.
Photo courtesy of Roberta Ando.

released, many of the families were penniless. The number of Nikkei families moving into apartments at Vanport, Fairview Homes and other "temporary" wartime housing units is testimony to their plight. Josuke and Tsutano Nakata, who farmed and operated a fruit and vegetable stand on Columbia Boulevard before the war, had to take jobs as farm laborers in order to survive.

Many Nisei commented about "No Japs Wanted" signs posted in stores and other businesses when they returned to East Multnomah County. Kazuo Fujii, returning from the European Theater, where he had fought in four major campaigns, found the signs posted in several Troutdale business establishments. Tosh Okino, accompanied by three former residents, returned to determine the "welcome" that awaited them in Gresham. Initially, there was no problem. However, overnight the signs went up, obviously the result of an organized effort. Because of this experience, Okino remained in Ontario an additional year before returning to his farm..

Lily Sakurai's father and a brother stopped to talk to a former neighbor who lived on Woodard Road. He told them, "We don't want any Japs here." As a consequence, the Sakurai family decided to sell their farm. Shio Uyetake stopped to get a haircut at the barbershop located in the Springdale Hotel building. The proprietor, who had cut Shio's hair before the war, told him, "I don't give haircuts to Japs."

Fortunately, many friendships formed before the war endured. And when others began to learn of the exploits of the 442nd Regimental Combat Team, attitudes started to change. Because of their intelligence, educational achievements, discipline and work ethic, most Nisei prospered after the war. The fact that they essentially recovered in one generation is also a testament to their resilience, their equanimity, their work habits, their thriftiness and their family values.

Girls' Softball Champions, Area B, June 1944

Front, from left: Sumi Niiya, Hiro Shiogi, Katie Matsuda, Toshi Heyamoto, Alice ???, Yutako Kimura and Hisa Kimura. Standing: Chickie Ishihara, Ruth Kamata, Mary Higurashi, Lily Kobayashi and Sjusie Heyamoto. Photos courtesy of Ray Shiiki.

Camp Minidoka "American Legion" Baseball Team

Front, L to R: Aki Namba, Tosh Saito, Bob Fukutomi (bat boy), Sun Tsuji and Ray Shiiki. Middle: Ted Okita, Lindy Sata, Sho Sakakibara, Jim Kuga, George Aoyama, Tom Hayashi and Terumasa Oka. Top: Hank Matsubu, Sab Nakahara, Joe Tsnunemitsu, Bob Aoki, Charles Kinoshita, Ray Mitsudo and Coach Tak Akiyama. The team's record was 9 wins, 1 loss. Since the camp had no American Legion sponsor, several of its members played for the Twin Falls post. Five players, including Hank Matsubu, Ted Okita, Sho Sakakibara and Ray Shiiki, made the American Legion all-star team.

Nisei Veterans

American citizens of Japanese ancestry (Nisei) served honorably in both the European and Pacific Theaters of war during World War II and after hostilities ended, in the Armies of Occupation. While the exploits of the Nisei 442nd Regimental Combat Team are well known, less known is the service of Nisei soldiers in other units. Also, little is known of the exploits of Nisei soldiers in the Pacific Theater as the U.S. Army kept secrecy tight regarding its use of Americans of Japanese ancestry in the Military Intelligence Service (MIS). U.S. military leaders did not want the Japanese to discover the role played by Nisei in the Pacific Theater..

The formal use of Nisei soldiers started on May 26, 1942, when General George C. Marshall issued orders establishing the Hawaiian Provisional Battalion, consisting of 1300 men and 29 officers. The Army sent the newly formed 100th Battalion to the mainland for training, assigned to the Second Army at Camp McCoy. All of the unit's officers were white; many Nisei believed the officers were selected to keep close watch over them to be certain of their loyalty. The 100th made such a favorable impression during its training that the

Camp Shelby, Mississippi

Camp Shelby, Mississippi became the "home" of the 100th Battalion after the Army brought the Hawaiin Provisional Battalion to the mainland. Because the 100th made such a favorable impression, the War Department established the 442nd Regimental Combat Team, which also trained at Shelby.   *Photo courtesy of Lauretta Yamashita.*

Leke Nakashimada Visits Camp Minidoka

According to Leke, after the attack at Pearl Harbor, "the Army didn't seem to know what to do with us (Nisei). First, we were ordered to turn in all of our equipment and return home. Shortly, however, this order was rescinded. The Army sent many of us to Fort Riley, Kansas, where we cut grass, picked up litter and did odd jobs." After his family reached Minidoka, Sgt. Leke Nakashimada was able to visit his family. This incongruous photograph was taken at the entry gate. The soldiers manning the guard tower behind Sgt. Nakashimada had their guns trained inward, guarding about 9000 internees, including the Nakashimada family. *Photo courtesy of Leke Nakashimada.*

Insignia, 442nd Regimental Combat Team

Soldiers of the 442nd proudly wore the insignia (upper left on sign) of the unit on their shoulder.   Photo courtesy of George Kajiwara.

government changed its policy with respect to its Nisei soldiers. Heretofore classified as 4-C (not acceptable because of ancestry), the War Department issued a directive dated January 22, 1943, that provided for the use of Nisei soldiers in combat, effective February 1, 1943. In February the Army sent the 100th Battalion to Camp Shelby, Mississippi, which became the training facility to be used to train Nisei volunteers for combat. President Franklin D. Roosevelt announced the formation of the 442nd Regimental Combat Team (RCT) open to Nisei, both from Hawaii and the mainland. The RCT consisted of a headquarters company, an anti-tank company, an artillery company, a medical detachment and a service company. In June, 1943, the 442nd RCT arrived at Camp Shelby for training. In August, 1943, the 100th Battalion left Camp Shelby for North Africa where they were attached to the 34th Division.

On September 26, 1943, the 34th Division landed at Salerno, Italy, and the 100th Battalion suffered its first combat casualty on September 28. In two days of combat, the unit lost 2 men killed in action and 7 wounded. The Battalion gained its first decoration when Private Masao Awakuni knocked out a tank with his bazooka and earned the Distinguished Service Cross. While the Battalion was engaged in combat in Italy, the 442nd RCT trained in Mississippi. The latter embarked for Italy on May 1, 1944, and landed in Naples about one month later. The 100th Battalion then became part of the RCT. On June 16, 1944, the 442nd went into combat and soon gained a reputation as an effective fighting unit. Because of its outstanding combat record, the Regiment became

Headquarters, 442nd RCT, Italy

1st/Sgt. Omoki stands before the Headquarters of the 442nd Regimental Combat Team in Livorno, Italy, in 1945. Photo courtesy of George Kajiwara.

one of the most highly decorated units in the Army. One of the more telling bits of information about the 442nd is the fact that the unit suffered an estimated 3600 casualties (Purple Hearts). After rescuing the "Lost Battalion" in the Vosges Forest of N.E. France, I Company had just four riflemen and a weapons squad fit for duty; K Company had just 17 riflemen. General John Dahlquist ordered a review of the 442nd RCT. When the regiment stood in review, he remarked, "I ordered the entire regiment to stand for review." The RCT's commanding officer replied, "This is what's left of the 442nd."

The 442nd RCT participated in eight major campaigns in Europe, earned seven Presidential Unit Citations and its soldiers received more than 1,250 individual decorations for valor. The 100th became known as the "Purple Heart Battalion" because of it numerous casualties. Other U.S. divisions fighting alongside the 442nd RCT named them "the little iron men." Of our Nisei veterans, Jack Asakawa, Kaz Fujii, Yosh Kinoshita, Toshiaki "Toshi" Kuge and Shigeru Takeuchi fought with the 442nd throughout the its Italian and French campaigns. Bob Ando, Menow Hara, Art Iwasaki, Ike Iwasaki, Thomas Kuge, Roy Morihiro, Roy Naemura, Leke Nakashimada, Kenji Namba, Tom Namba, and Joe Onchi served as replacements. Richard Mishima and George Nishimura, also replacements, took part in breaking the Gothic line. George Kajiwara, Leke Nakashimada, Frank Okita and George Yamashita (husband of Katherine [Asakawa] Yamashita) served as a replacements in the RCT toward the end of the conflict in Europe. Soldiers in the 442nd RCT earned the following decorations:

    1 Medal of Honor*   (21)**

    47 Distinguished Service Crosses*   (33)**

    342 Silver Stars with 12 Oak Leaf Clusters* (559)** with 38 O.L.C.

442nd Regimental Combat Team

Soldiers of the 442nd receive a Presidential Unit Citation at the public square in Livorno, Italy, 1946. Photo courtesy of George Kajiwara.

810 Bronze Stars with 38 Oak Leaf Clusters*

2490 Purple Heart Medals***

Note: *As recorded by Orville C. Shirey, Officer of the 442nd. in 1946. **An article in an American Legion magazine reported that members of the 442nd RCT had been awarded 21 Medals of Honor. The author of the article raised the number of other awards as indicated. Apparently, as a result of an examination completed in 1996, the Defense Department upgraded several of the units' Distinguished Service Cross Awards to the Medal of Honor, thus the discrepancy between the unit record and later data reported in the Legion account.

*** [Shirey did not include Purple Heart Medals awarded to members of this unit wounded in action who were hospitalized and subsequently transferred to the Zone of the Interior...It is thought that the total number of Purple Heart Medals should be approximately 3600, including 500 Oak Leaf Clusters to the Purple Heart Medal.

As recorded by the *100th - 442nd Directory* (1967), the RCT suffered 671 killed in action (KIA) of which about one-half (334) were from the 100th Battalion; one-half (337) from the other units. C Company of the 100th had 99 infantrymen KIA; of the later arrivals to Italy, L Company, 3rd Battalion, had 45 infantrymen KIA. Fourteen (14) medics were KIA. The infantry battalions

B-29 Bomber

After completing 30 missions in the European Theater, Sgt. Ben Kuroki volunteered for service in the Pacific Theater, where he completed 28 missions as a gunner in the B-29, "Most Honorable Sad Saki."   Photo, the author.

took the heaviest losses, with some 641 of the KIA suffered by the combat infantry companies.

Some Nisei soldiers served in other units in Europe, despite the Army's apparent reluctance to permit this to happen. Takey Nakashimada served as a gunner in a Sherman tank (later a Pershing tank) under General George Patton in the 3rd Army. General Patton must have been impressed by the example set by the Nisei soldiers imbedded in the 3rd Army as replacements destined for the 3rd Army included other Nisei soldiers. For example, Shiro Takeuchi served as a replacement in the 3rd Army. John Ota served as a medic throughout the war, but did not serve overseas. Todd Okita, also served in the European Theater as a member of the Army of Occupation, Germany, but other details of his service are not known. Jim Onchi also served in the Army of Occupation.

While unusual, there are certainly other instances of Nisei serving in units other the 442nd. Sgt. Ben Kuroki, of Hershey, Nebraska enlisted in the Army Air Force shortly after the attack on Pearl Harbor. During basic training, he spent more than his quota of time on KP. Assigned to the 93rd Bombing Group, his name was dropped from the roster when the unit moved to Fort Myers, Florida before its deployment overseas. The 409th Squadron Adjutant, Charles "Chip" Brannan interceded and Ben remained with the Group. When the Group's bombers moved to Grenier Field, New Hampshire, enroute to England, Kuroki's name again disappeared from the roster. This time, the unit's chaplain questioned superiors and the Group Commander, Colonel Edward "Ted" Timberlake responded, "Bring him along." Ben Kuroki became so adept at armaments,

Behind Enemy Lines in Burma

Brigadier General Frank D. Merrill, flanked by T/Sgt. Herbert Miyasaki of Hawaii (left) and T/Sgt. Akiji Yoshimura of Colusa, California (right), interpreters trained by the MIS, relax for a moment during the campaign in Burma, which was fought behind enemy lines. U.S. Army photo.

taking apart and re-assembling 50-caliber machine guns, that when a vacancy occurred, he became a tail-turret gunner on a B-24. He completed the requisite 25 missions, then volunteered for 5 more. In combat, he became a member of a team where "nobody questioned my lineage. Rapport was unbelievable." Upon completion of his 30th mission [on which his turret cover was holed by flak], Ben Kuroki returned to the States where his unusual story made headlines. He made numerous appearances, including a stop at the Minidoka Relocation Center, where he urged young Nisei to enlist.

Sgt. Ben Kuroki, because of his experience, was assigned to a B-29 Superfortress outfit forming in his home state of Nebraska. He volunteered as a gunner, but again encountered discrimination. War Department regulations prohibited a Nisei from being assigned to a bomber destined for use in the Pacific theater. In this instance, it took a telegram to Secretary of War Henry L. Stimson, who excepted Sgt. Ben Kuroki from the regulation, allowing him to remain with the 484th Squadron. Thus, when the unit proceeded overseas, Sgt. Ben

Soldier Comforts Japanese Youngster Found on Saipan

Sgt. Hoichi Kubo, MIS, reassures a Japanese youngster found on the battlefield on Saipan by American infantrymen. Sgt. Kudo received the Distinguished Service Cross for his efforts in approaching armed Japanese in caves to convince them to release non-combatants and sometimes to surrender, rather than fighting to the death.

U.S. Army photo.

Kuroki traveled with it. His B-29, the "Most Honorable Sad Saki," part of the 484th Squadron, 505th Bombardment Group, operated out of Tinian, Marianas Islands. There, he completed 28 additional missions as a B-29 gunner, including several missions over Tokyo. Thus Sgt. Ben Kuroki fought both in Europe and in the Pacific as a turret gunner, first in a B-24, then in a B-29. Because of the aforementioned War Department regulation, he is likely the only Nisei to serve as a crew member on a B-29 in the Pacific theater, but as the following stories illustrate, Nisei sometimes overcame the 'official line' to serve in unusual [and unsung] roles in World War II.

In November, 1942, the Military Intelligence Service, U.S. Army, started training its first cadre of sixty Nisei and Caucasian soldiers in the Japanese language, anticipating the need for trained linguists who could read and speak Japanese. After completing about six months of intensive training, this first group was deployed to the Pacific Theater, including stations in Alaska, Australia, Fijii, New Caledonia and Tonga, under heightened security arrangements. These men interrogated prisoners, translated captured documents, monitored enemy radio traffic and conducted other intelligence missions. They proved to

MIS Language School, Fort Snelling, Minnesota

Students attending the MIS language school at Fort Snelling, Minnesota, lived in these beautiful, old barracks. During Sgt. Ray Shiiki's stay, he lived in the first building on the left.   *Photo courtesy of Ray Shiiki.*

be so valuable, military commanders requested more trained Nisei intelligence operatives. Nisei MIS personnel served from the Aleutians to New Zealand and from Hawaii to Burma. They were attached to some 128 units to translate captured enemy documents, interrogate prisoners-of-war, penetrate enemy lines to eavesdrop on conversations, disrupt enemy operations and intercept enemy communications. Nisei soldiers of the MIS joined Merrill's Marauders in Burma, serving as interpreters and translators. Japanese prisoners and documents provided much information because Japanese leaders believed that no foreigner had sufficient knowledge to read and understand the Japanese language. Nisei soldiers, MIS, were also attached to British, Indian, New Zealand, Australian and Chinese forces.

According to MIS historians, several notable exploits of the war in the Pacific involved Nisei soldiers in the Counter Intelligence Corps (CIC) or the MIS. These include: Roy Matsumoto, attached to General Frank D. Merrill's Marauders in Burma, who, for his exploits, was later inducted into the Ranger Hall of Fame at Fort Benning, Georgia. Fourteen Nisei soldiers fought behind Japanese lines with General Merrill's force in Burma. Richard Sakakida, recruited by the CIC before the war, served under General Douglas MacArthur in the Philippines. Captured, he withstood months of torture before gaining the confidence of his captors. He was able to relay information about Japanese plans to General McArthur's headquarters through his contact with guerilla forces. When the U.S. Army retook the Philippine Islands, Sakakida was rescued and served many more years in the Army. Another feat by the Army's MIS was the translation by two Nisei soldiers of the Japanese 'Z Plan.' a top secret Japanese naval and air war plan retrieved from a downed Japanese aircraft by a Filipino fisherman. With advance knowledge of the enemy's intent, the U.S. Navy met and annihilated Japanese naval forces that guarded Japanese positions in the Philippine Sea and the Marianas. Another exploit credited to Nisei MIS operatives was the interception and translation of radio messages regarding the flight plan of an aircraft carrying Admiral Isoroku Yamamoto, Commander of the Japanese Pacific Fleet, to Bougainville, Solomon Islands. With knowledge of Yamamoto's flight plan, U.S. P-38 fighter planes from Guadacanal intercepted Yamamoto's aircraft and its six escorts and all were shot down. Admiral Yamamoto planned the December 7, 1941, attack at Pearl Harbor.

Even less known than the service of Nisei soldiers in the Pacific theater, is the fact that some 300 Nisei women served in the armed forces of the United States. An acquaintace of Betty Hiagu (later Betty Nishimura), Alice Shimoyama, served in the Women's Army Auxiliary Corps (WAAC [later WAC]). When the war broke out in 1941, her family lived in Kent, Washington. With the exception of Alice's older brother, Siego, who was in the Army, the government interned her family, along with other persons of Japanese ancestry, in a "relocation center." Eventually the family was transferred to the Minidoka Relocation Center, Idaho. After seven months in the camp, Alice and three of her sisters found employment as domestics in Chicago, Illinois. In February, 1943, the sisters spotted an ad encouraging women to join the WAAC. Alice applied, but was not accepted until about a year later. In March, 1944, she started basic training at Camp Oglethorpe, Georgia. In May, 1944, she transferred to the Maxwell Army Air Force Base in Alabama. She applied for the MIS language school at Fort Snelling, Minnesota and was accepted in June, 1945. In her class of 51 students, only three were not Nisei. She completed the intensive training after the war ended. Her assigned station was Camp Ritchie, Maryland, where she reviewed Japanese military documents. After her discharge, she obtained employment as a civilian translator at the occupation headquarters, Tokyo, Japan. In addition to Siego and Alice Shimoyama, their sisters, Neba, Mitori and Nellie, also served in the armed forces. Grace Kumazawa served in the Women's Army Corp as did her sister, Frances Kumazawa, who volunteered for the MIS (see "Frances Kumazawa Ota/John Ota, Nisei Veterans," this volume).

Several other Nisei veterans from this area served in the U.S. Army's MIS, including: Ed Fujii, John Kondo, Ray Shiiki, Fred Toya, George Toya and Tadashi Takeuchi.

Bob Minoru Ando

Bob Minoru Ando, son of Suematsu and Masaki (Yokote) Ando of Troutdale, received his draft notice early in 1942. Prior to 1906, Suematsu and Masaki Ando immigrated to Oregon from Hawaii, where both had worked in the sugar cane fields. Originally, both emigrated from Kumamoto, Japan. Upon their arrival on the mainland, the couple settled on a farm in Montavilla. Later, they moved to a farm in Rockwood, then to Troutdale. In each case, except for the Troutdale farm, Ando rented the ground. The family raised berries, including raspberries, but also grew vegetables. At Troutdale, because Frank Ando was of age, the Andos purchased a farm. By the time Mr. and Mrs. Ando settled in Troutdale, they had five surviving children, Frank, Denny, Mae, Bob and Tom.

Initially, because the draft classification for Nisei changed to 4-C, Bob Ando thought he might not be permitted to serve. However, on March 12, 1942, he was inducted into the Army at the Presidio in Monterey, California. The Army sent him to Camp Robinson, Arkansas for basic training. After completing basic he was transferred to Fort Harrison, Indiana for advanced training in an engineering unit. Early in 1944, Bob Ando volunteered for service in the 442nd Regimental Combat Team. He transferred to Camp Shelby, Mississippi, where he trained in heavy infantry weapons..

Pvt. Bob Ando, Camp Robinson

Pvt. Ando completed basic training at Camp Robinson, Arkansas.
Photo courtesy of Roberta Ando.

In August, 1944, Bob Ando and other replacements traveled by train to Newport News, Virginia for deployment overseas. On August 23, the replacements boarded a troopship. On August 24, the ship left Chesapeake Bay bound for the European Theatre. On September 7, 1944, the vessel docked in Naples, Italy. From Naples, a British transport took the replacements to Marseille, France. Shortly thereafter, the command assigned Pfc. Bob Ando to M Company, 3rd Battalion, 442nd Regimental Combat Team. During the time that Pfc. Ando served, the 3rd Battalion was involved in a battle to clear German

Pfc. Bob Ando at Fort Harrison, Indiana

Above, Pfc Ando (right) and Jimmy Taketa prepare for an inspection at Fort Harrison, Indiana. Both served in an engineering detachment. Left, Bob Ando visited his family at Camp Minidoka, Idaho, before being deployed overseas. The building is a structure in the camp, perhaps the barracks in which his family resided.

Photos courtesy of Roberta Ando.

defenders from the town of Bruyeres, France. The 3rd Battalion also participated in the rescue of the "Lost [Texas] Battalion," which had been surrounded by German troops in the Vosges Forest, France. During this campaign, Ando suffered two wounds. The first, relatively minor, was treated at an aid station; Ando returned to duty. The second, likely shrapnel from an overhead "tree burst," caused a severe wound to his left arm. In addition, shrapnel penetrated his upper body and chest. The severity of the wound sent him to a hospital.

On December 26, 1944, the medical detachment, 442nd, evacuated Bob Ando from France by hospital ship. On January 12, 1945, he arrived in the states and was transported to Madigan Convalescent Hospital, Fort Lewis, Washington. From January until September 25, 1945, Pfc. Bob Ando convalesced, either at Madigan or at the Baxter General Hospital, Spokane, Washington. Doctors could not remove all of the shrapnel from his chest; some fragments were too close to his heart. Pfc. Bob Ando received the Purple Heart

Pfc. Ando Returns From France

Left: George Ishida, with crutches, and Bob Ando, kneeling, convalesce from wounds suffered in the Battle of Bruyeres, France. Right: During his convalescence, Pfc. Ando visited his parents and siblings interned at Camp Minidoka, Idaho. Photos, Roberta Ando.

with one Oak Leaf Cluster, the Combat Infantry Badge, the European-African, Middle Eastern Theatre ribbon with one battle star and the good conduct medal.

On May 12, 1942, the Ando family reported to the Portland Assembly Center as ordered by the Western Defense Command. The family disposed of the Troutdale farm at what must have been a "fire sale" price. In September, they transferred via train to the Minidoka Relocation Center, Idaho. During the war, Mae Ando died from complications of an earlier surgery. Bob Ando visited his family at least twice while they were interned at the camp. The first visit occurred after he had completed basic training; the second occurred during the time that he convalesced from his wounds while stationed at Fort Lewis, Washington.

After his honorable discharge, Bob Ando attended business college, then found employment with the U.S. Postal Service. In 1947, he married Sakae Fujii. The couple settled in Portland where they raised their three daughters, all of whom attended and graduated from Marshall High School. Roberta Ando continued her education, graduated from the University of Oregon and then completed a graduate program at the University of Southern California. Diane Ando Harder graduated from Portland State University and completed a program in nursing. Sandi Ando Lessert graduated from Oregon State University with a degree in engineering.

Suematsu and Masaki Ando Family ca 1928

Above, from left: Tom Ando, Unknown, Suematsu, Masaki, Mae and Bob Ando. It is believed that this photograph was taken at the farm Suematsu Ando rented in the Rockwood area. Far left: Pfc. Ando shortly after his discharge in 1945. Near left: Bob Ando and Sakae Fujii married in 1947. They have three daughters, Roberta, Diane and Sandi. Photos courtesy of Roberta Ando.

After the war, the Ando family's eldest son, Frank, resumed farming. His younger brother, Denny, worked in the wholesale produce business. The youngest sibling, Tom Ando, worked for the postal service, handling mail transported by train. After the war, Suematsu and Masaki Ando lived with their son, Frank, on his farm. Masaki Ando passed away in 1950. Suematsu "Pops" Ando died in 1957.

Bob Ando passed away in 1998. His wife, Sakae, his three daughters (2006) and four grandchildren (Robert Harder, James Lessert, Kaylin Harder and Mariko Harder) survive him.

Jack Asakawa

Jack Asakawa, born on September 21, 1918, served in the medical detachment, 442nd Regimental Combat Team. Drafted early in 1941, before the attack on December 7, 1941, Jack Asakawa's service was affected by that event. Trained as a medic, he first served with the Army in Alaska. However, Jack Asakawa, hearing of the formation of the 442nd, volunteered for service with the regiment, and the Army transferred him from Alaska to Camp Shelby, Mississippi, where he joined the RCT. Consequently, he trained there and was then sent overseas when the 442nd was deployed to Italy in May, 1944. Once in combat, the medical detachment suffered horrendous casualties. Kaz Fujii was not surprised. "If a soldier was hit, our medics had one mission in mind - get to them and take care of their wounds, regardless of the danger. Tree bursts, machine gun fire, whatever, the medics were there." The call, "medic! medic!" bought them on the run, regardless of the circumstances. Medics of the 442nd received 125 purple hearts, 50 Bronze Stars, 29 Silver Stars and 1 Croix de Guerre. Medic T/5 Richard Fukana received the Silver Star and a Purple Heart with 4 Oak Leaf Clusters. Fourteen medics of the 442nd were killed in action. While details of Pvt. Jack Asakawa's service are not known, he received the Purple Heart Medal for wounds suffered during combat with the 442nd. He took shrapnel wounds in the head and shoulders, which Kaz Fujii immediately ascribed to "tree bursts," wounds typically suffered by those whose tour included combat in the Battle of Bruyeres, Vosges Forest, Northeast France. Because Jack Asakawa's injuries disabled him, the Army returned him to the United States once he was in condition to make the voyage home.

Jack Asakawa, U.S. Army

Jack Asakawa, drafted early in 1941, trained as a medic before volunteering for service with the 442nd Regimental Combat Team. He was stationed at Camp Shelby, Mississippi, before being deployed overseas.
Photo courtesy of Lauretta Yamashita.

Jack Asakawa, Hospitalized Stateside

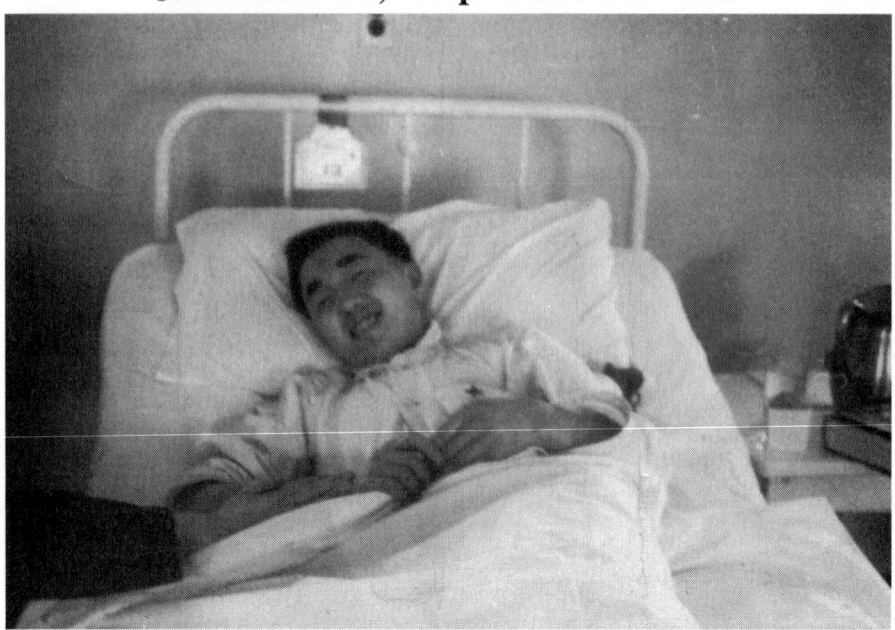

After Jack Asakawa suffered serious wounds in combat, the Army returned him to the United States for treatment and to recuperate. Photo courtesy of Lauretta Yamashita.

Because of the severity of his injuries, Jack Asakawa could not drive an automobile. He received a pension from the United States government because of his disability. He never married and lived on the family farm located on Troutdale Road at its intersection with Cochran Road. Though limited in the work he could do, he farmed with his family, particularly with the help of his brother, Walter Asakawa. Walter purchased a tractor and modified it so that Jack could do some tasks. Walter's wife, Carol, recalled, "He had to do tractor work at a slow speed. Once he took out the back wall of our shed, which collapsed." However, with the help of his family, he was able to continue farming until his death on July 15, 1992. Certainly Pvt. Jack Asakawa deserves the recognition of his country for the sacrifices he made and for the injuries he suffered as a medic in the 442nd RCT.

Edward Fujii

Edward Fujii, living with his family on a rented farm in Vale, Oregon, because of the forced "relocation" of persons of Japanese ancestry, received his draft notice in late 1944. However, he did not report for induction into the service until June, 1945. He took his physical in Boise, Idaho, after which the Army sent him to Fort Douglas, Utah, for processing. Next, the Army transferred Fujii to Camp Fannin, Texas, for basic training. As the planned invasion of Japan became more certain, the Army needed more soldiers trained for the Military Intelligence Service (MIS). Consequently, the Army selected great numbers of Nisei soldiers to serve in the MIS, including Edward Fujii, who was sent to Fort Snelling, Minnesota, for the intensive training required. According to Edward, there were about 5000 Nisei stationed at Fort Snelling at the time he was there. Nisei soldiers of the MIS had performed brilliantly in the Pacific, and by 1945, the Army had decided that these specialists could perform a much-needed role in the invasion and occupation of Japan.

While at Fort Snelling, Fujii worked in the orderly room and remained at Fort Snelling as others were deployed overseas. The war ended without the necessity of an invasion of the home Islands of Japan. Consequently, the need for thousands of trained MIS operatives disappeared. At this time, the Army transferred Edward Fujii to Fort Campbell, Kentucky, to train as a radio operator. In November, 1946, Edward Fujii received his discharge from the U.S. Army. He returned to the farm his family owned in Troutdale, and resumed farming. While he served willingly, the fact that the U.S. Government classified him and his fellow Nisei 4-C (not acceptable because of ancestry) always rankled Edward Fujii. "It was an unwarranted insult," he remarked.

Ed Fujii, U.S. Army

Ed Fujii was serving in the MIS as the war ended, but was not deployed overseas. *Photo courtesy of Ed Fujii.*

Both of Ed's younger brothers, Jack and Jim Fujii, were drafted, Jack, in 1944 and Jim, in April, 1945. The Army sent Jack to the European Theater, where he served in Belgium. He also served in the Army of Occupation, but details of his service are not available. Jim entered the service close to the end of the war.

James "Jim" Fujii

While working in the labor camp at Nyssa, Oregon, Jim Fujii attended and graduated from Nyssa High School (1944). When the federal courts ruled that detention of people of Japanese ancestry in internment camps was not legal, Jim's father, Bukichi Fujii returned to Troutdale. However, Jim Fujii had received his draft notice, which ordered him to report to Fort Douglas, Utah, for induction. Consequently, on February 16, 1945, Fjuii was inducted into the United States Army.

The Army sent him to Camp Walters, Texas, for basic and advanced infantry training. Upon completing the training regimen, Jim, granted a two-week furlough, visited his family in Troutdale. He then proceeded to Fort Meade, Maryland, for deployment overseas. From the port of embarkation, the troopship took Jim Fujii and some 6,000 other troops to France for occupation duty. The Army dispatched Fujii to a new U.S. base at Zirendorf, a city about 20 miles from Nuremburg. There, he learned to speak German and met many German people who "were good to the troops." The Americans were generous with food items and were frequently asked by the townsfolk to visit homes. Fujii spent about a year in Germany. Jim Fujii remarked, "When things settled down, we were sent home." Back in the states, he received his honorable discharge at Fort Lewis.

Pfc. Jim Fujii, U.S. Army

Jim Fujii, drafted in 1945, served with the Army of Occupation in Germany for approximatel one year.
Photo courtesy of Raymond Fujii.

Upon his return, Jim Fujii resumed farming with his father and brothers. Eventually, he farmed his own and rented land in and near Troutdale.

Kazuo Fujii

Kazuo 'Kaz' Fujii was among the first group of draftees from East Multnomah County inducted in June, 1941. He had graduated from Gresham High School in 1937, and worked with his father and siblings on the family's farm located on Cherry Park Road in Troutdale. The Army sent Kaz Fujii to Fort Warren, Wyoming, for basic training, which lasted approximately 13 weeks. The Army then sent him to Randolph Field near San Antonio, Texas, for advanced training. When the armed forces of the Empire of Japan bombed Pearl Harbor on December 7, 1941, Fujii's First Sergeant gave him a forty-five and ordered him to stand guard at a base gate. In March, 1942, the Army transferred Fujii to Perrin Field, Sherman, Texas, where he served in the motor pool and with a quartermaster company. Kaz remained at Perrin Field for approximately a year, then the Army sent him to the 86th Heavy Pontoon Battalion, Camp Howard, Augusta, Georgia, for training. Kaz said the "colored" and "white" segregation signs bothered him, as he wasn't certain "which to use." About a month later, when the War Department activated the 442nd Regimental Combat Team, the Army sent him to Camp Shelby, Mississippi, where he was assigned to the 232nd Engineering Company. The 442nd's precursor unit, the 100th Battalion, had established an excellent training record at Camp Shelby, which led the War Department to change its policy with respect to Americans of Japanese ancestry. This led to the formation of the 442nd RCT.

The 442nd RCT consisted of the 1st Battalion, Companies A,B,C and D; 2nd Battalion, Companies E, F, G and H; 3rd Battalion, Companies I, K, L and M., the 552nd Field Artillery Battalion, Companies A, B and C, the 206th Army Band; and the 232nd

Kaz Fujii, U.S. Army

Kaz Fujii, combat veteran with the renowned 442nd RCT, came home to "No Japs Wanted" signs.   Photo courtesy of Mary Okita.

Combat Engineer Company, to which Kaz Fujii was assigned. The 232nd was the only outfit within the RCT composed entirely of Nisei officers and men from its inception. While the 100th Battalion engaged in combat operations in Italy, the 442nd underwent advanced combat training at Camp Shelby. Kaz Fujii had to re-take basic training, then combat and unit training. As a member of the 232nd, his training included setting and clearing minefields. In the middle of April, 1944, the 442nd headed for Norfolk, Virginia, for overseas deployment. After a 28-day voyage, on May 29, 1944, the 442nd (minus the 1st Battalion) disembarked at Naples, Italy, and was attached to the 34th Division. The $34^{th's}$ 100th Battalion took the place of the $442^{nd's}$ 1st Battalion, but kept its original designation. The 442nd commenced combat operations on June 26, 1944, relieving the 517th Parachute Infantry Regiment and the 142nd Infantry Regiment near Suvereto.

Kaz Fujii's introduction to combat started immediately. On June 27, as he drove a truck load of munitions toward the front, his right, rear, front dual hit a land mine. The ensuing blast flattened the truck and Kaz and a passenger were thrown into the air. He believes the truck's cab saved his and his passenger's lives. He refused to go to an aid station, though the concussion caused damage to his hearing and left him with a life-long problem with tinnitus. The refusal to seek medical attention certainly kept him from receiving the Purple Heart medal that he deserves. The RCT took the towns of Sassetta and Castagneto, then advanced toward Livorno, an important seaport for the Germans. Kaz witnessed the aftermath of a gigantic tank battle near Castellina, Italy, that left the area littered with renmants of Sherman tanks, a few Panzers and hundreds of bloated bodies of men and animals. The stench was hardly bearable, but the scene remains etched in his mind as one of the most depressing sights he witnessed during his combat experiences. Combat Engineers describes the role assigned to the 232nd quite well. On occasion, the company had to provide personnel for patrols. One night, Kaz's patrol forded the Arno River to determine which German units were in the area. He said the water was "more than waist deep, and we didn't encounter a single German."

Whenever the RCT encountered an obstacle that hindered the infantry's advance, kept it from receiving supplies or disrupted communications, the Combat Engineers responded. The Germans used mines extensively as they withdrew; mines in the roads, in grape arbors and in open fields. The $232^{nd's}$ mine experts were called upon to clear the mines so that the advance could proceed. During combat operations, Kaz Fujii drove a truck to and from the front lines loaded with supplies. On occasion, German artillery tried to zero in on the convoy, and "we could see the explosions getting closer and closer." Usually, Kaz said, they tried to speed up to outrun the incoming shells or to change speeds to confuse the enemy gunners. The Engineers also provided the means for crossing rivers and streams. Though some were fordable, supplies had to be brought forward, which required the 232nd to provide bridges or a stream by-

Pfc Kaz Fujii

After the Battle of Bruyeres, men of the 232nd had an opportunity to relax in Nice, France, before resuming combat in the Po Valley, Northern Italy.

Photo courtesy of Kaz Fujii.

pass. In September, 1944, the Army withdrew the 442nd RCT from the front to Naples, where they awaited orders. On September 27, the RCT embarked from Naples for Marseille, France.

In France, the 442nd joined the Seventh Army attached to the 36th Division. On October 14, 1944, infantry battalions of the RCT prepared to launch an attack on German positions the following day. A favorite tactic of the German defenders was the use of roadblocks, which the Combat Engineers were called upon to remove. Often, German snipers were posted nearby, and when the engineers started to work, they came under fire. Another German tactic was to cover the roadblock with an enfilading crossfire from emplaced machine guns, which certainly caused the 232nd's complement to earn its "combat" designation. In the mountains of France, the Germans felled trees across roads covered by sufficient firepower to make clearing the obstacle a hazardous undertaking. In the village of Bruyeres, the 232nd cleared two massive roadblocks, the first as Americans entered the town on October 18, 1944; the second the following morning. During this campaign, the Combat Engineers, supported by the 111th Engineer Company, tried to clear the Belmont-Biffontaine Road east out of Bruyeres. Tied down by enemy fire, a company observer worked his way forward to a point where he was able to provide information to artillery that enabled them to bracket the enemy positions. The engineers were somewhat astounded when the Germans rose from their emplacements and surrendered en masse. This incident is remarkably similar to one recounted by S/Sgt George Oiye in *Fire For Effect* (see "Sources"), and may describe the same event. Lieutenant Al Binotti's forward observation party, which included Oiye, "directed artillery fire with such accuracy that 80 (German) grenadiers lay dead and another 54 surrendured."

During the campaign, the Battle of Bruyeres, the fighting took place in the Vosges Mountains. Incessant rains had turned the roads to a quagmire. To keep its trucks rolling, squads from the 232nd 'requisitioned' lumber from local sawmills to construct "corduroy roads" in order to get supplies through. Its trucks could negotiate the mud, but not its jeeps. Kaz has wondered since, he said, if the U.S. Army paid those small mills for the lumber. (Note: The forest in the combat zone would have little value subsequently, as the "air bursts" and other gun fire would leave metal shards in the trees, making them unsuitable for lumber - actually dangerous to mill). On one occasion near Bruyeres, Kaz's squad, taking supplies to the front, apparently passed beyond the American positions. Kaz mentioned that the forest in the Vosges Mountains was dark, gloomy, without roads and nearly inpenetrable. The squad leader, S/Sgt. Abe M. Fuji, directed Kaz to remain with the vehicles while he took a patrol forward to try and determine exactly where they were. A German machine gun emplacement opened up on the patrol, killing Fuji and Pvt. Takeo Yamamoto, an "eighteen year-old kid from Molokai," in Kaz's words. "The rest of the patrol inched back to our vehicles and we escaped." The two bodies were recovered when the 442nd took the area later. "Our squad was hit hard that morning and it really showed as the days passed. T/4 Edmund Ezuka...took over the squad, but I noticed combat fatigue was unknowingly beginning to show...(particularly with our) jeep drivers." Occupants of jeeps were exposed to tree bursts, that is, German artillery shells exploding in the trees overhead that rained shrapnel down on anyone unlucky enough to be below. The German artillery, with its tree bursts, "screaming meemies" and "88s," took a horrendous toll on men of the RCT.

Fortunately, Kaz remarked, the 232nd usually bivouacked to the rear each night, in contrast to the infantry, which remained in fox holes in the forest at the front. Kaz noted, however, that he spent "32 days in the same pair of pants." When German resistance slackened, the 442nd, excepting the 552nd Field Artillery Battalion, was withdrawn from this front. By Thanksgiving Day, the RCT bivouacked in the town of Sospel, France, along the French Riviera near Nice. There, elements of the unit patrolled the French-Italian border to keep spies and saboteurs in German-held Northern Italy from crossing into France. In early December, Kaz's squad laid S-mines in one area to prevent infiltrators from getting through. Kaz recalled, "I pulled the last pins (and proclaimed), nobody better give an order to clear this minefield." As it happened, however, Fujii had to take a run to Paris, which took about 9 days. Upon his return, he found to his horror that a company lieutenant had ordered the mine field cleared, which resulted in the deaths of Sgt. Theodore Uyeno and Felix Matsumoto. Kaz recalled that he was dissuaded by members of his squad from "going after the lieutenant." In addition to border patrols, other units had to conduct exercises to train replacements sent to replenish the losses suffered in the Battle of Bruyeres.

The 442nd's fighting days were not over. In mid-March, 1945, the RCT, with its equipment, boarded LSTs bound for Italy. Traversing the steep roads on the way to the ships, a couple of half-tracks, loaded with men, toppled off the steep road, crushing several soldiers. Thus, accidents took an additional toll. The LSTs took the RCT to a landing near Pisa, Italy, where the ships were unloaded. The 442nd became attached to the 92nd Division, Fifth Army. The units continued combat training and inspections until the first week of April, when the RCT went into action against the west end of the German's Gothic line. Though intended as a feint, the men of the 442nd advanced and captured German positions that had withstood repeated attacks for months. According to Kaz, the German defenders created a different type mine that caused problems for the engineers on the road from Massa to Carrara. 12-inch shells wired to a mine were buried deep in the road, which exploded when a dozer triggered the device. Kaz said the demolished dozer was buried on the spot. When Platoon Sgt. Ernie Kogawa told Kaz to help in the removal of several such mines, he responded willingly, despite the obvious danger. "I had seen what he and our other leaders had done, and I would do anything he asked me to do. He did the dangerous work in the hole, tying a cable to each shell, and I winched them out." The 232nd lost three dozers that day.

The engineers constructed a by-pass roadway across the Frigido River beyond which German artillery situated on Punta Bianca raised havoc with the 3rd Battalion near Carrara. Kaz remarked, again, concerning the German's effective use of artillery, which caused many casualties. Near Genoa, the 232nd was following the 3rd Battalion, and stopped for a moment. Kaz and T/5 Kenji Yaguchi were standing together next to the truck when a shell hit, sending shrapnel ripping into Yaguchi's shoulder. Kaz was not hit. By the end of April, 1945, German troops were surrenduring in droves. By May 2, the war in Italy had ended.

Men of the 232nd earned 103 Purple Hearts and 23 decorations for valor. Six of its nine officers earned a Purple Heart and three were decorated for bravery. The record does not indicate how many soldiers of the 232nd Combat Engineer Company were killed in action. By the end of the war, one-half of Kaz's squad had been killed or severely injured. His squad did not receive a single replacement. Kaz Fujii had served with the 442nd RCT through all of its campaigns in Italy and France; he earned four battle stars. Despite this record, he did not have enough points to come home immediately. The Army used men of the 442nd as guards for the thousands of German prisoners-of-war captured in the final days of the Po Valley Campaign. The Army planned to use the RCT in Japan. However, when Japan capitulated, the 442nd's job ended. Kaz Fujii received his honorable discharge in November, 1945.

His father, Bukichi Fujii, had resumed working the family's farm on Cherry Park Road in Troutdale. Kaz took the bus to Troutdale and trudged with his duffle bag over his shoulder up the hill to his home. Greeted by his mother and father, he told his mother, "I made it." Earlier, she had remonstrated with him, and told him he would not come back. However, he had returned. After spending his first night at home, he decided to walk to Troutdale in the morning. There, he saw signs posted in some business establishments: "No Japs Allowed" or "No Japs Wanted." Kaz Fujii resumed his life on the Fujii farm with his family (see "Bukichi Fujii/Yoshino Fujii," this volume). He had served his country for 4 years, 5 months, including nearly a year on the battlefields in Italy and France.

When Kaz talks of his war experiences, his voice breaks and the anguish he feels for the loss of his comrades etches his face and moistens his eyes. The author talked to Kaz almost exactly 60 years to the day when the 232nd fought in the Vosges Forest in France. His memories of the events there are so vivid to him, he remarked, that "it seems as if they happened yesterday." Kaz Fujii's efforts on behalf of his comrades in the 442nd have not ceased. When the drive to raise money to fund the World War II memorial in Washington, D.C., seemed to flag in Oregon and Washington, he became involved. Kaz Fujii raised approximately $275,000.00 for the monument. He was recognized by another veteran of the 442nd, 1st Lt. (now U.S. Senator) Daniel K. Inouye, 100th Battalion. (Lt. Inouye's Distinguished Service Cross award, after review, was upgraded to a Medal of Honor.) Kaz Fujii has certainly earned the recognition and honors bestowed upon the "greatest generation."

U.S. Senator Daniel K. Inouye and Mr. Kaz Fujii

Senator Daniel K. Inouye congratulates Kaz Fujii for his help in the fund raising effort to build the memorial in Washington, D.C., to honor World War II veterans. Both Pfc Fujii and 1st Lt. Inouye served with distinction in the 442nd Regimental Combat Team.

Photo courtesy of Kaz Fujii.

Menow M. and George Hara

Menow M. Hara, one of eleven children of Eichiro and Hamano Hara, grew up on a farm in Gresham, Oregon. Menow attended Gresham schools, graduating from Gresham High School in 1938. Nine of the Hara children survived childhood, two boys, Menow and George, and seven girls, Dorothy, Micheye, Fumi, Kimi, Carrie, Jean and Mary. Eichiro Hara rented the Powell place on Hogan Road between Stark and Division streets. The family raised berry and vegetable crops.

Drafted, Menow Hara was inducted into the Army on January 8, 1942, about one month after the attack at Pearl Harbor. The Army sent him to Camp Roberts, California, for basic training. Shortly after his arrival, the classification of Nisei soldiers changed to 4-C, "not acceptable because of ancestry," which created confusion for commanders and consternation among the Nisei affected. At this time, recruit Hara's commander transferred Menow to Fort Leonard Wood, Arkansas, to complete basic training. Hara remained at Fort Leonard Wood for approximately two years, serving as an orderly, a clerk and, finally, as an M.P. (military police).

Menow Hara, U.S. Army

Pvt. Menow Hara spent over two years at Fort Leonard Wood before the Army decided to make him an infrantryman.
Photo courtesy of Kazuko Hara.

In April, 1944, anticipating the need for infantry, the Army sent Hara to Fort McClellan, Alabama, for advanced infantry training. At McClellan, Hara trained as an ammunition bearer and heavy machine gun (50 caliber) operator. While there, Menow Hara bunked (in a hut) with Art Iwasaki, Jimmie Kokubu, and Shin Sato, all Oregonians.

In August, 1944, Menow Hara, together with Art Iwasaki, Shin Sato and other Nisei infantrymen traveled to Newport News, Virginia for deployment overseas. When the troopship passed Gibraltar, the troops knew they were destined for Italy. In September, 1944, the ship docked in Naples, Italy. From Naples, British troop transports took the replacements to Marseille, France. After a couple of days wait-

Pvt. Menow Hara at Fort Leonard Wood

The Army, uncertain just what to do with its Nisei soldiers, kept Menow Hara at Fort Leonard Wood for more than two years. He spent five months as an M.P.

Photo courtesy of Kazuko Hara.

ing for transportation, the replacements boarded a train headed north to Epinal, France, where they were to join the 442nd Regimental Combat Team, which was attached to the 36th Division, Seventh Army. Once there, Menow Hara was assigned to F Company, 2nd Battalion, 442nd Regimental Combat Team.

Pvt. Hara joined a light machine gun (30 caliber) squad just in time to take part in the Battle of Bruyeres. The 2nd Battalion's first objective, Hill "B," part of the mountainous terrain north of the town, became the focus of repeated attacks and counter attacks. It took the Americans about five days to overrun the German defensive positions and enter the town of Bruyeres. On October 21, F Company, 2nd Battalion and L Company, 3rd Battalion, became Task Force O'Conner, which was to move behind the German line to launch an attack on "Hill 505" from the enemy's rear. The plan worked as intended, breaking the German defenses with enemy infantry fleeing the field. For its part in this action, F Company received the Distinguished Unit Citation and Pfc. Hara a battlefield promotion to Sergeant. Bitter, intense combat followed as the 2nd Battalion, usually on the left flank, advanced through the Vosges Forest against an entrenched enemy. Until the 442nd was relieved in mid-November, 1944, its units slogged through the mud of the Vosges Forest, suffering horrendous casu-

Passing the Strait of Gibraltar

When their troopship passed the Rock of Gibraltar, Menow Hara and his shipmates knew for certain that they were headed for Italy.   *Photo courtesy of Kazuko Hara.*

Pfc. Menow Hara, 442 RCT

Pfc. Hara, wearing the "Go For Broke" shoulder patch of the 442nd Regimental Combat Team, sharpens his skills using a rifle   .Photo courtesy of Kazuko Hara.

alties, but taking a heavy toll on its German defenders. "Tree bursts," created by German artillery shells exploding in the trees above, caused many of the wounds and deaths the advancing Americans experienced. Sgt. Hara came through the ordeal unscathed.

After being relieved, the 442nd proceeded to Southern France where its units occupied defensive positions along the French-Italian border east of Nice. There, the men of the 2nd Battalion had an opportunity to relax, though the Germans across the border shelled the American positions twice daily. The welcome respite would soon end. General Mark Clark, Commander, Fifth Army, needed the help of the 442nd RCT in cracking the Gothic Line in Northern Italy. During March, 1945, the 442nd RCT (minus the 522nd Artillery Company) boarded landing craft that would take them back to Italy.

In Italy, the 442nd, attached to the 92nd Division, Fifth Army, had the task of creating a "diversion" toward the West End of the Gothic Line, the German defensive position designed to hold Northern Italy and the Po Valley. From

In France

Above: Menow Hara (left) and Jim Tsutsai enjoy a brief rest in the snow, probably in the Maritime Alps. Below: Nice, France, which the men of the Regimental Combat Team could experience on R and R.   *Photo courtesy of Kazuko Hara.*

April 5 to the 15th, the 2nd Battalion took the right flank in the action that broke the German defenses in the west. From April 15 to the 25th, the 2nd led the attack upon German defenders holding the high ground at Mt. Pizzaculo and Mt. Grugola. On April 25, the Battalion helped clear the town of Aulla. At this time, German resistance collapsed and enemy troops commenced surrendering

German Propaganda Leaflet

Eichiro Hara   Menow Hara and Kazuko Endo Wed

Above: German aircraft dropped thousands of this counterfeit dollar bill over Northern Italy, with this message: "The promises made by the Americans are always stated in vain and disappear like soap bubbles. Just like this banknote." Below left: Menow Hara's father, Eichiro Hara, who farmed in Gresham, Oregon, before the war. Below right: Menow Hara married Kazuko Endo in 1954. The Maid of Honor is Masako Hinatsu; the Best Man, Kazuo Fujii. War souvenir and photos courtesy of Kazuko Hara.

en masse. On April 28, the 2nd Battalion entered the Po Valley and the town of Asti, center of a grape-growing region. On May 2, 1945, the war in Italy ended with the official surrender of the Axis armies in Italy.

Sgt. Menow Hara remained in Italy as part of the Army of Occupation. The 442nd RCT's principal task was guarding German prisoners-of-war. His service record contained this citation: "[Sgt. Hara] was a member of a 30-caliber light machine gun crew in an infantry regiment in France and Italy. [He] advanced against enemy positions, laid fire upon enemy installations and guarded positions against enemy attack. [He] was a member of a task force given a special assignment to take [an] enemy position." For his involvement with this "task force (O'Conner)," Sgt. Hara received the Distinguished Unit Badge.

Menow Hara passed away in December, 1984, after returning from a visit to Japan. He is survived by his wife, Kazuko Hara, two children, Debra (Hara) Giltz and Macia Hara, and two grandchildren, Kelsie and Kyle Giltz (2006). His widow, Kazuko (Endo) Hara, grew up on a farm in Milwaukie, Oregon. In addition to the usual "truck garden" products, her parents used greenhouses to start plants for the farm and to sell.

During the latter part of the war, Sgt. Hara's brother, Pfc. George Hara, became a replacement in Fox Company, joining his brother in the 442nd. Sent to the Minidoka Relocation Center with most of his family, George received his draft notice in camp. He reported to Fort Douglas in Salt Lake City from which the Army posted him to Camp Blanding, Florida, for basic training. Because of the losses associated with the Battle of the Bulge and the concern that engendered, the Army called for infantry replacements. Consequently, in January, 1945, Pfc. George Hara was deployed overseas. He disembarked at LeHavre, France, then traveled by train and truck to Marseille. Upon his arrival there, the 442nd command assigned him to F Company, 2nd Battalion, the company in which his brother served. Pfc. Hara arrived in time to participate in the final campaign in Italy, the attack to break the German Gothic Line in Northern Italy. He earned the combat infantry badge and one battle star.

Pfc. Menow Hara Visits His Sister

While Menow Hara served his country, his sister, Micheye (Hara) Furukawa and her family at the "relocation center" in Tule Lake, California. From left, Micheye holds her son, Michael, her sister holds Micheye's daughter, Katie, and Menow stands to the right. Other members of the family were held at the Minidoka Relocation Center, Idaho. *Photo courtesy of Kazuko Hara.*

Pfc. George Hara served with the Army of Occupation during which one of his duties was escorting German prisoners-of-war to Munich, Germany, for processing, screening and release from captivity. He took three or four such trips during his service after the war. George Hara received his honorable discharge in September, 1946, after completing slightly more than two years in the Army.

Arthur Iwasaki

Arthur 'Art' Iwasaki, born in Hillsboro, Oregon, graduated from Hillsboro High School in 1938. His father, Billy Yasukichi Iwasaki, purchased a 50-acre farm in Hillsboro in 1912, which he and his family farmed, principally growing berries. Art had two brothers, George and Akira, and five sisters, Kate, Taka, Aya, Dorothy and Rose. In March, 1942, the local draft board sent Art "greetings" and he reported to the Presidio in Monterey, California, for induction. He took basic training at Fort McClellan, Alabama, after which the Army sent him to Fort Thomas, Kentucky. Art remained at Fort Thomas for approximately two years because of the uncertainty the Army displayed towards its Nisei soldiers after the government changed their draft classification to 4-C (not acceptable because of ancestry). When the War Department reversed the policy, the Army transferred Iwasaki back to Fort McClellan for basic and combat training.

In August, 1944, Art Iwasaki and other Nisei replacements traveled to Newport News, Virginia, for deployment overseas. In September, 1944, the

Yasukichi Iwasaki Family

Top, from left: Yasukichi, George and Akira Iwasaki. Front: Art, Taka, Ito (Baba) holding Aya, and Kate Iwasaki. The dwelling is the family's Hillsboro home.

Photo courtesy of Art Iwasaki.

Pfc. Art Iwasaki

Art Iwasaki, Company I, 3rd Battalion, 442nd Regimental Combat Team.
Photo courtesy of Art Iwasaki.

troopship landed in Naples, Italy, where Art joined the 442nd Regimental Combat Team. From Naples, a British troop transport took the regiment to Marseille, France. Upon his arrival in Marseille, Art Iwasaki was assigned to I Company, 3rd Battalion. After a couple of days waiting for transportation, I Company boarded a train headed north to Epinal, France, where they were to assemble, having been attached to the 36th Division, Seventh Army. During the final leg of the trip up the Rhone valley, Art witnessed the devastation visited upon German General Erwin Rommel's retreating armies by allied air power. Disabled Panzer tanks, horse-drawn equipment and hundreds of dead horses lined the route, victims of U.S. fighter aircraft strafing attacks.

Pvt. Art Iwasaki joined the Headquarters Platoon as a radioman. His job was to maintain communication between I Company and 3rd Battalion Headquarters. The village of Bruyeres, France had to be cleared of German troops, building by building. The German Army had occupied Bruyeres for some time and it was well defended. Once Bruyeres was cleared of the enemy, the 3rd Battalion advanced toward Biffontaine and Belmont. Art recalled, "I learned quickly how to dig a deep foxhole and to cover it with branches as German artillery fire, exploding in the trees overhead, rained shrapnel down on anyone unfortunate enough to be exposed below." On October 27, as I Company advanced to free the "Lost Battalion," a tree burst caught Art Iwasaki, sending shrapnel into his back. He reported to an aid station where his wounds were dressed. There, medics loaded him and two other wounded GIs into a Jeep to be transported to a field hospital in the rear. The medics strapped a badly injured GI to the Jeep's hood while Art and another wounded GI rode in the back seat. On the way, the Jeep hit a land mine, which blew it off the road. Art helped both of the injured GIs into a ditch for cover, for which act of courage he was awarded the Bronze Star. The GI who had been strapped to the hood succumbed to his additional injuries, but Art and the 2nd GI survived. Art remarked, "I never did find out what had happened to the Jeep driver. He just disappeared." In a short interval of time, Art Iwasaki had earned not only his 2nd Purple Heart for the additional

Modern Transportation, Italy

Art Iwasaki, right, and two buddies load supplies and their gear onto a captured mule as the war drew to a close in Italy.   *Photo courtesy of Art Iwasaki.*

injuries sustained when the Jeep hit a mine, but also a Bronze Star for heroism in moving the other two injured GIs to cover.

By the time Art had recovered sufficiently to rejoin I Company, the 442nd had been relieved and sent to the rear. The 442nd then received orders to proceed to Southern France where they occupied defensive positions along the French-Italian border east of Nice. There, the 2nd and 3rd Battalions often alternated on the front line, which permitted soldiers to sometimes relax and enjoy the French Riviera. The Germans, however, made certain that the American forces were aware of their presence, as they shelled American positions twice daily. Also, the men of the 442nd had to be alert to stop infiltrators and saboteurs trying to cross into Southern France. Though a welcome respite from the horrific combat experienced in the Vosges Mountains, the defensive duty in Southern France was destined to end; General Mark Clark, Commander, Fifth Army, needed the help of the 442nd RCT in cracking the Gothic Line in Northern Italy.

Consequently, the 442nd RCT (minus the 522nd Artillery Company) left France to land in Livorno, Italy, to prepare for its role in the Battle of the Po Valley. The German Commander had anchored the West End of the Gothic Line in the Apennine Mountains, which form a natural barrier between the coastal plain and the Po Valley. In early April, the 442nd, including I Company, assembled near the city of Lucca, Italy. I Company moved northward out of Azzano, given the task of flanking a German position on Mount Folgorita. Art

Pfc. Art Iwasaki

Pfc. Iwasaki received the Bronze Star for heroism and the Purple Heart with two oak leaf clusters for his battle wounds.
Photo courtesy of Art Iwasaki.

said, "We climbed the mountain side, no moon – it was pitch black. Sometimes a man would fall and a helmet would clatter down the slope. We had to touch the man ahead to maintain contact." However, the surprise attack worked perfectly: "We achieved total surprise and broke through."

Elements of the 3rd Battalion entered Carrara, Italy, on April 11, 1945. Partisans accompanied I Company and, according to Art Iwasaki, "were extremely helpful in identifying where enemy emplacements were located." He also recalled the shelling from the huge, long-range guns at Punta Bianca. "I don't understand why those guns were not taken out, but they weren't. They bombarded the area around Carrara regularly." It was in Carrara that Art Iwasaki received what he describes as his "million-dollar wound" (sufficient to earn 5 points toward going home). Shrapnel from a German 88 ripped into his left arm. When he rejoined I Company a couple of weeks later, he discovered that the shelling that had caught him had killed four of his comrades of the Headquarters Platoon as well as the Company Commander, Lt. James Wheatley. A shell hit the company command post, a cave near Fordinovo, Italy.

By the time Art Awasaki rejoined I Company, German troopers were surrendering bt units. He helped round up German prisoners, who were placed in a camp at Ghedi, Italy. In November, because he had sufficient points, Pfc. Arthur Iwasaki boarded a ship for home. He received his discharge at Fort Lewis on Thanksgiving Day, 1945.

Art Iwasaki returned to the family farm in Hillsboro to resume civilian pursuits. Because he had older brothers, and given the traditions adhered to by Issei parents, Art Iwasaki decided to purchase a farm near what is now Tanasbourne in Washington County. In 1949, he married Teri Yumibe of Portland. The couple have five children: Robert, Stephanie, Paul, Christi and Leslie. Because of the economics and hassles associated with berry farming, Art Awasaki completed a course in raising nursery stock using his GI Bill benefit. The well-known Gresham nurseryman, Frank Schmidt, was a classmate. Art Iwasaki started his own nursery business, which is now operated by his and Teri's oldest son, Robert. Teri and Art named the business after a neighbor's dog, Max, and the family's dog, Hildegaard. Thus Max and Hildy's Garden Store, located

Art and Teri Iwasaki Family

Left, Teri and Art Iwasaki. Right, the children, Rear, from L: Paul, Stephanie and Robert. Front, Leslie and Christi. *Photos courtesy of Teri Iwasaki.*

World War II Memorial, Washington, D.C.

Teri and Art Iwasaki visit the World War II Memorial in Wasgington, D.C. Art, a veteran of World War II, visited the Memorial to pay homage to his comrades in arms.
Photo courtesy of Teri Iwasaki.

on Cornell Road in Hillsboro, Oregon, got its name. Max and Hildy's continues to celebrate its founding with an annual dog show. Teri Iwasaki passed away in July, 2005.

Ike Iwasaki

Akira "Ike" Iwasaki, born in Hillsboro, Oregon, of Yasukichi and Ito Iwasaki, grew up on his family's 50-acre berry farm in Hillsboro. After receiving his draft notice, Iwasaki reported for duty on January 12, 1942, in Portland, Oregon. Inducted at Fort Lewis, Washington, the Army transferred him to Fort Knox, Kentucky, for basic training. After basic, according to Iwasaki, the "Caucasian trainees were sent elsewhere for advanced training," while the Army, which classified him 4-C (not acceptable because of ancestry), transferred him to Fort Thomas, Kentucky. There, assigned to the Quartermaster Corps, he helped process recruits coming to the post. While stationed at Fort Thomas, he attained the rank of T/5. In 1943, after the federal government changed its policy by permitting Nisei soldiers to fight for their country, the Army transferred Iwasaki to Fort McClellan, Alabama, for advanced infantry training.

After Ike Iwasaki completed training at McClellan, the Army sent him to Fort Meade, Maryland, for deployment overseas. A convoy departed the port of embarkation on August 24, 1944, and carried some 600 Nisei soldiers among its passengers. Because the 442nd RCT had suffered major casualties in the Rome-Arno Campaign, the Nisei on board were destined to be replacements for that unit. On September 7, 1944, the convoy reached Naples, Italy. Ike Iwasaki became a replacement in D Company of the 100th Battalion. Since D Company was a heavy (infantry) weapons unit, Iwasaki was assigned to one of its three 81-mm mortar squads. In addition to the mortar squads, the company also had

Ike Iwasaki, U.S. Army

Left, Ike Iwasaki, on furlough, visits his family at home before their internment. Right, While he was stationed at Fort Dawson, West Virginia, the Army quartered enlisted troops in tents. Officer quarters stand in the background. Photos courtesy of Ike Iwasaki.

Fort Thomas, Kentucky

Above: After completing basic training at Fort Knox, the Army transferred Ike Iwasaki to Fort Thomas, where, assigned to the Quartermaster Corps, he helped equip new recruits. Left: While stationed at Fort Thomas, Iwasaki (standing) found an acquaintance and fellow Oregonian (Hood River), Setsu Shitara, also stationed at the post. Photos courtesy of Ike Iwasaki.

three machine gun squads, equipped with the heavy, 50-caliber, air cooled, machine guns. The company used Jeeps to carry armaments, ammunition and personnel forward, and to evacuate casualties to aid stations. The replacements did not have long to become oriented to their new assignment. Near the end of September, the 442nd boarded assault boats that took them to waiting Navy ships, which were to transport them to Marseille, France.

In France, the RCT was attached to the 36th Division, 7th Army, and was under the direct command of Major General John Dahlquist. By mid-October, the 442nd, with the 100th and 2nd Battalions leading the way, launched an attack against "Hill B," directly north of Bruyeres, France. D Company's "heavy weapons" supported this attack. German artillery caused many casualties, particularly those shells that burst in the trees overhead. Ike Iwasaki recalled, "I heard

Ike Iwasaki, 81-mm Mortar Squad

Left, William Kishiyama prepares to load the weapon, Yasuhide Takushi kneels by the barrel, Atashi Iwai, standing left, and an unidentified soldier protect their ears anticipating the blast. Right, Ike Iwasaki hauls mortar ammunition by mule, sometimes used in the rugged country where the 442nd operated. Photo courtesy of Ike Iwasaki.

shrapnel 'singing' in the air." None of the "songs" hit him, however. The Americans secured Bruyeres after about a week of intense combat.

In the ongoing battle, 7th Army's 1st Battalion, 141st Infantry Regiment, had advanced beyond its support. Enemy forces surrounded the unit, which became known as the "Lost Battalion." General Dahlquist ordered the 442nd to rescue the surrounded men. The action started on October 17. Iwasaki's squad was to provide mortar barrages as the RCT advanced. To effect the rescue of some 220 men, the 442nd suffered about 800 casualties. After the rescue, when the RCT pulled back to a rest area, about 1800 of its wounded men were hospitalized in France. The regiment traveled by truck to Menton, France, near the French Riviera and the Maritime Alps, to await further orders.

There, the 442nd relieved the 19th Armored Infantry Division, taking over defensive positions along the French-Italian border. The 100th Battalion covered the right flank along the coast. The RCT maintained these defensive positions until Mid-March, 1945. Then the unit boarded landing craft that transported them back to Italy. In Italy, the 442nd, attached to the 92nd Division, assembled near Pisa, Italy. Once again under the command of General Mark

D Company in the Maritime Alps

Above left, Ike Iwasaki (left) and Leonard Yoshino rest for a moment with their 81-mm mortar. Above right, Ike Iwasaki stands before the squad's quarters near Menton, France. Below, from left, mortar squad members Tarao Okamoto, Leonard Yoshino and Ike Iwasaki examine a map during a training exercise in S.E. France.

Photos courtesy of Ike Iwasaki.

Clark, the soldiers of the 442nd faced the daunting task of defeating the Axis troops on the western-most extension of the Gothic line. Daunting because the defenders held the high ground and had thwarted every previous attempt to dislodge them.

On April 5, 1945, the 442nd, in an attack centered on Mount Folgorita, broke the Gothic line, a line that had stopped 5th Army's repeated assaults for

50-Caliber "Heavy" Machine Guns

50-Caliber heavy, air-cooled, machine guns, the type carried by the three machine gun squads of D Company. The men were trained, by repetition, to take apart and re-assemble the weapon blind-folded. Photo courtesy of George Mershon.

several months. The 100th Battalion advanced toward the town of Carrara, where resistance was intense. The mountainous terrain created problems for D Company's squads. Ike Iwasaki, promoted to Sergeant, recalled that "We marched mostly at night. Each man carried a heavy load, either the base plate, the tripod, the barrel, the radio or ammunition for the mortar, plus the usual field pack. In battle, wires ran everywhere. Each company laid communication wire and finding the proper wire was sometimes a puzzle. We communicated with our forward observers by [a crank-type] radio."

On April 30, German defenders began surrendering bt the thousands. The 5th Army cleared the Po Valley of German and Italian troops. On May 2, 1945, the war in Italy ended. Ike Iwasaki remained in Italy on occupation duty until November. He received his honorable discharge on December 15, 1945, having served approximately 3 years and 11 months in the U.S. Army.

Ike Iwasaki returned to the family farm in Hillsboro, which the family retained through the war despite the internment and the draft. In 1950, he married Mary Furusho, of Portland. The couple had three children, Roger, Rich and Ellen. Roger is a landscape architect, Rich a free-lance photographer and Ellen, a nurse at Oregon Health Sciences University. Ike and Mary Iwasaki, retired from farm life, now live in Hillsboro.

Yoshio Kinoshita

Yoshio "Yosh" Kinoshita, by all accounts, landed with the 442nd Regimental Combat Team at Naples, Italy, on May 29, 1944. However, since the ships carrying most of the 2nd Battalion stopped at the Algerian port of Oran to unload cargo, Kinoshita's arrival may have been delayed slightly. Because his service record has been misplaced, this account of his service has necessarily relied upon those who knew and served with him.

Yosh Kinoshita's parents owned a farm south of Powell Boulevard, west of what is now Towle and south of Johnson Creek, in Gresham, Oregon. He had an older brother, Kazuo, a sister, Mary, and a younger brother, Mas. The youngsters attended Gresham schools and Yosh graduated from Gresham High School. Likely because of Depression induced low market prices for farm produce, Yosh Kinoshita enrolled at the Oregon Institute of Technology to study mechanics. He completed the course of study and, in 1937, became a certified automotive mechanic.

When the Selective Service Law passed, Yosh Kinoshita registered for the draft and was inducted before the war started. Apparently because of his training as an auto mechanic, the Army sent him to Fort Riley, Kansas, where he was assigned to Troop D, 6th Training Squadron, Headquarters and Headquarters Detachment (a cavalry [tank] unit). After Pearl Harbor, as others have mentioned, the Army seemed puzzled as to what to do with its Nisei soldiers. Until the War Department's letter, dated January 22, 1943, the Nisei at many installations were in limbo. The directive, initiated by John J. McCloy, Assistant Secretary of War, provided for the establishment of a special unit in which these men would be permitted to serve their country. The Army selected Yosh Kinoshita to join the first cadre to report to Camp Shelby, Mississippi, for training

Yoshio Kinoshita, U.S. Army

Yosh Kinoshita, while stationed at Fort Riley, Kansas.   Photo courtesy of April Kinoshita.

with the 442nd Regimental Combat Team. The 442nd came into existence on February 1, 1943.

At Shelby, Kinoshita was assigned to H Company, 2nd Battalion, where he became a motor sergeant in the motor pool. H Company carried the heavy (infantry) weapons such as heavy machine guns and mortars as well as the vehicles (primarily Jeeps) assigned to the 2nd Battalion. Kinoshita and the other Nisei who had been selected or who had volunteered underwent extensive training over the following year. In April, 1944, the Army ordered all units of the 442nd, excepting the 1st Battalion, to be sent to Camp Patrick Henry, Virginia, for deployment overseas. Consequently, men of the 442nd entrained for transport to that port of embarkation for overseas duty. After the unit's equipment and material was loaded, on May 1, 1944, the men marched aboard Liberty ships that were bound overseas, destination unknown. When the convoy passed through the Strait of Gibraltar, the men surmised they were headed for Italy. However, ships carrying most of the 2nd Battalion put into Oran, Algeria, while the rest of the convoy proceeded on. This led to much speculation, but it turned out that the ships carried cargo for use in North Africa, and the stop was short-lived.

Sergeant Yosh Kinoshita, 442nd RCT

A stop at Palermo, Sicily, revealed the devastation visited upon that war-torn city. On May 29, 1944, the 442nd RCT (minus units of the 2nd Battalion) landed at Naples, Italy. On June 6, most units of the 442nd boarded landing craft bound for Anzio, Italy. The 2nd Battalion rejoined the RCT on June 17, after stopping in Naples to get everything in order. While in Naples, Yosh Kinoshita had to make certain that the 2nd Battalion's motor vehicles were in operating condition.

Sergeant Yosh Kinoshita participated in four major campaigns with the 442nd, earning four battle stars.
Photo courtesy of April Kinoshita.

June 24, 1944, the 442nd RCT, attached to the

2nd Battalion, 442nd RCT, Italy

2nd Battalion troopers take a rest in Aulla, Italy during the final days of World War II.
Photo courtesy of Tom Kuge.

34th Division, assembled near the town of Gravasanno to relieve elements of the 36th Division. On June 26th, the 2nd and 3rd Battalions launched an attack toward the town of Suverto, the two units first combat engagement. As Motor Sergeant, Kinoshita dispatched H Company's vehicles as needed to support the infantry movement forward. Enemy artillery fire created the greatest danger to "rear echelon" troops in a combat situation. However, H Company forward observers, near the front line, shared the danger faced by the 2nd Battalion's infantry. For the next month, the RCT participated in the 5th Army's drive north toward Livorno and Pisa, Italy, the latter on the Arno River.

Other campaigns followed for Sgt. Kinoshita: the Battle of Bruyeres, the rescue of the "Lost Battalion" in the Vosges Forest, the defensive "interlude" in S.E. France and the final battle in Italy. The 442nd RCT rejoined the 5th Army under General Mark Clark for the push into the Apennine Mountains and the Po Valley that helped secure the victory over the Axis armies in Italy. Yosh Kinoshita earned four battle stars for these campaigns. Twelve of H Company's complement were killed in action and 101 Purple Hearts were awarded to its men for battle wounds. Because of its weaponry, many of its men, including those assigned to the motor pool, fought on the flanks or behind the infantry companies. However, its forward observers, who provided targeting information by telephone, were on the line. H Company jeeps hauled weapons, personnel and ammunition forward and carried casualties to the rear. Of course, all elements of the Battalion came under fire in combat situations.

Those Nisei veterans with the highest points started their homeward journey on May 31, 1945. Though the war in Europe had ended, the conflict continued in the Pacific Theater. Given an opportunity, many men of the 442nd RCT volunteered for duty there. In August, the Army dispatched H Company to Naples to guard military installations. Presumably, Staff Sergeant Yosh Kinoshita ended his overseas service there, as the war ended on September 2, 1945.

Upon his return, Yosh Kinoshita returned to the farm in Gresham, where, with his older brother, Kazuo Konishita, the family resumed farming. He married Masako "April" Toyoshima. She and Yosh Kinoshita had two children, Nadine and Ted.

Toshiaki "Toshi" Kuge

Toshi Kuge had nearly completed his sophomore year at the University of Oregon's Medical School on the "hill," Portland, Oregon, when Civilian Exclusion Order Number 46, issued by the Western Defense Command, took effect. He and his family spent about three months confined in the Portland Assembly Center before being sent to the Tule Lake "Relocation" Camp in Northern California. Kuge remained there until the results of a "loyalty" program determined those internees either to be transferred elsewhere or to remain at Tule Lake. The government designated Tule Lake as the "camp" for those considered "troublemakers" or "disloyal."

After the 442nd Regimental Combat Team formed, Toshi Kuge decided to volunteer to join the unit. He left Tule Lake on June 28, 1943, bound for Camp Shelby, Mississippi, for basic training. After he completed basic, because of his background as a medical student, the Army assigned Kuge to the Medical Detachment, Headquarters Company, of the 442nd. All companies entered the next phase of the training regimen, unit training. After an inspection on March 4, 1944, which included Chief of Staff General George C. Marshall, the RCT prepared for deployment overseas.

Toshi Kuge, Medical Student

Toshi Kuge, who enrolled at the University of Oregon Medical School in 1940, completed nearly two years before being removed from the program in 1942, after the outbreak of war with Japan. Photo courtesy of Tom Kuge.

The troops traveled by train to Camp Patrick Henry, Virginia. A few days later, they boarded trains that took them to Hampton Roads, the Port of Embarkation The troopships carrying the 442nd left Chesapeake Bay on Mary 2, 1944, bound for an unknown destination. Once at sea, the men soon learned that their destination was Italy. The ships entered the Bay of Naples on May 29, 1944, and the troops disembarked. On June 10, the veteran 100th Battalion of Hawaii became part of the 442nd, in

The "Gang" From Camp Shelby

Sgt. Toshi Kuge is 3rd from the left, 2nd row. These are men of the Medical Detachment, Headquarters Company, 442nd Regimental Combat Team.

Photo courtesy of Tom Kuge.

place of the 1st Battalion (which had remained at Camp Shelby). The RCT then became attached to the 34th "Red Bull" Division for combat operations.

The 34th Division, with the 442nd, started combat operations on June 26, 1944. Sgt. Kuge, medic, was soon treating wounded men on the battlefield or getting them to an aid station or a hospital, for the more severely wounded. Because of his schooling and training at the medical school, he was highly qualified. The RCT gained high marks for its performance in completing its first combat assignment as participants in the Rome-Arno [River] Campaign.

After a rest, Army brass decided to attach the RCT to the Seventh Army in France. Consequently, on September 27, 1944, the 442nd boarded ships bound for Marseille. In France, Toshi Kuge participated in the Battle of Bruyeres during which units of the RCT rescued the "Lost Battalion" of Texans in the Vosges Forest. Though victorious, the 442nd suffered horrific casualties. Companies of 200 plus men had few fit for duty; I Company had only four riflemen and a light machine gun section in action, K Company had just 17 riflemen. The campaign ended for the RCT on November 17 at which time those not hospitalized or killed in action boarded trucks bound for Nice, France.

At Nice, Thomas Kuge, Toshi Kuge's younger brother, arrived as a replacement. He was assigned to K Company, 3rd Battalion, in which he started squad and unit training (see "Thomas Tomatsu Kuge, Gold Star Veterans," this volume). The Champagne Campaign in Southern France became one in which

In France

Above, from left: Cpl. Arthur Tsukayama, Sgt. Ralph Hayashi, Pvt. Ben Yamanaka, Sgt. Toshi Kuge, Pfc. Masahiko Onodera, Pfc. Masahiro Higa and Sgt. Minoru Masuda.

Hospital, Sospel, France

Toshi Kuge (left) and an unidentified soldier at the Regiment's hospital in Sospel, France. Photos courtesy of Tom Kuge.

the opposing forces maintained defensive positions. The 442nd guarded the border to prevent infiltrators or saboteurs from penetrating the line. However, the armies engaged in a daily series of artillery duels and fired mortar rounds for effect. This comparably peaceful interlude ended on March 29, 1945.

The 442nd, less the 522nd Field Artillery (which remained in France), returned to Italy to be attached to the 92nd Division, Fifth Army. The Army kept the presence of the RCT secret. The Fifth Army's commander, General Mark Clark, intended to use the 442nd to break the German Gothic Line. The attack commenced on April 5 and achieved a near total surprise because of the terrain where the 442nd hit the German line. The RCT assault broke through the German defensive positions, redoubts that had withstood allied attacks for about five months. It took about another month for

Italy, 1945

Above left: Abandoned equipment (and a dead horse) left by the retreating German army. Above right, Tom Nakahara and Masahiro Higa display a captured Nazi flag.
Photos courtesy of Tom Kuge.

Toshi Kuge, U.S. Army

After his brother received a draft notice, Toshi Kuge volunteered to serve in the newly established 442nd Regimental Combat Team.
Photo courtesy of Tom Kuge.

the Americans to defeat the German Army and enter the Po Valley.

Toshi Kuge received a battlefield promotion and commission to 2nd Lieutenant. The Army awarded him two Bronze Stars for heroic performance in combat, the Combat Medical Badge and four battle stars. Upon his return home, he resumed his studies at the University of Oregon Medical School and became a Medical Doctor. He also completed a training program for Army doctors at Fort Sam Houston Hospital in San Antonio. Dr. Kuge established a clinic for a private practice on Sandy Boulevard at N.E. 37th Avenue. He remained in the U.S. Army active reserve, serving on the medical staff at the Army hospital, Fort Vancouver, Washington. Toshi Kuge retired from the service in 1973, having attained the rank of Colonel.

Pvt. Richard Mishima in Italy

From left, PFC Yutaka Aono, Pvt. Richard Mishima and PFC Cherry Matsumoto, in Pisa, Italy. Soon, the 100th Battalion was in action, attached to the Fifth Army, in the war ending battle to clear the Po Valley, Northern Italy. Photo courtesy of Richard Mishima.

Richard Mishima

Soon after graduating from Ontario High School in 1944, Richard Mishima, displaced with his family from their farm near Troutdale, received his draft notice and on June 28, 1944, was inducted into the U.S. Army. The Army sent him to Camp Blanding, Florida, for 18 weeks of basic training. However, the Battle of the Bulge created a pressing need for infantry, and Private Mishima was soon on his way to a staging area in Maryland awaiting further orders. From there, he boarded the Queen Elizabeth for a quick trip to Southampton, England; thence by boat to Le Havre, France; thence by train to Marseille, France. There, a replacement, he was assigned to the famed 100th Battalion, 442nd Regimental Combat Team, which had just concluded a major battle, the Battle of Bruyers. During this battle, in southeast France, the 442nd RCT effected the rescue of the 3rd Battalion, 141st Infantry, the "lost battalion" of World War II fame. After a fierce struggle with many casualties, the German forces withdrew from the front in this particular sector, and the 442nd was relieved from its temporary attachment to the 36th Division and ordered to proceed to Nice, France, on the French Riviera. Private Richard Mishima joined the 442nd RCT there, a replacement in B Company of the famed 100th "Purple Heart" Battalion. However, duty there was not R & R, with constant patrolling of the border to find possible enemy agents, who attempted to cross from Italy into France for sabotage and espionage. In March, 1945, the 442nd boarded LST's bound for Livorno, Italy.

Once in Italy, the 442nd was assigned to the Peninsular Base Section staging area at Pisa, Italy. There, all units utilized what time was available for training, inasmuch as many of the new replacements (including Pvt. Mishima) had been rushed to Europe because of the Allied set back known as the Battle of the Bulge. Training exercises involved small unit problems with squads and platoons often working far into the night. The replacements, according to Mishima, were grateful for the opportunity to become better prepared for what was to come.

On April 5, 1945, the 442nd, attached to the 92nd Infantry Division, 5th (Fifth) Army, under General Mark Clark, went into action. The 100th Battalion prepared to launch a surprise attack on German positions on Mount Folgorita, which had been shelled and attacked over the previous 5-month period, without success. The 100th attacked at 0500 and by 0520 had secured its objective, the "Georgia" peak. It took the 442nd exactly thirty-two minutes to secure an area that had resisted the best efforts of Allied troops during the previous five months. In this battle, PFC Sadao S. Munemori, assistant squad leader, A Company, after his unit was pinned down, made a one-man frontal assault through direct fire against two machine-gun nests with grenades, destroying both. Withdrawing, he had nearly reached his squad when a grenade hit his helmet and bounced toward two of his men lying in a shell crater. Menemori dived for the grenade, smothering the blast with his body. For his heroic advance and action in saving his men, PFC Sadao S. Munemori was posthumously awarded the Medal of Honor, his country's highest decoration and the 442nd's first.

According to Pvt. Mishima, combat near the town of Carrara was extremely intense, and the 100th Battalion suffered many casualties. Ostensibly a feint to take the defenders by surprise, the 442nd took a position that had withstood attack for weeks. The units Presidential Unit Citation reads: "...In four days the attack (by the RCT) destroyed positions which had withstood the efforts of friendly troops for 5 months." By April 30, 1945, enemy resistance was collapsing and German troops gave up their arms. The Fifth Army soon cleared the Po Valley of the German and Italian forces defending the area. On May 2, 1945, the war ended in Italy. Thereafter, the 442nd engaged in occupation duties, which primarily meant, for the 442nd, guarding German prisoners-of-war.

The focus of the RCT became the war in the Pacific Theater, and the role the 442nd would have in that conflict. However, the capitulation of Japan ended that concern. Richard Mishima returned to the States and on November 7, 1945, received his Honorable Discharge. However, he chose to "re-up," and served in the Army until January 8, 1947, thus completing an approximate 2½ years in the Army.

Leke Nakashimada

Leke Nakashimada, born January 25, 1920, in Troutdale, grew up on the Bramhall place on Woodard Road, which his parents rented. He completed his elementary and secondary school years at Corbett, graduating from Columbian High School, Corbett, in 1939. When Japan bombed Pearl Harbor, people of Japanese ancestry were ordered to report to an assembly center. Leke was not among them as he had been drafted into the U.S. Army in July, 1941. However, since he was engaged in farm work, he received an extension until January, 1942.

Leke Nakashimada reported for basic training at Fort Warren, Wyoming, which took 12 weeks to complete. He also completed training to become a cook at the Baking and Cooking School there. He was then sent to Fort Riley, Kansas. He said, "The Army didn't seem quite sure of what to do with Japanese-Americans in the service." In February 1943, a Nisei unit, the 442nd Regimental Combat Team was formed at Camp Shelby, Mississippi. The Army transferred Leke to the 171st Replacement Unit, which had the responsibility of training elements of the RCT for combat. The Army soon sent the original unit, the 100th Battalion, overseas. The 100th landed in North Africa, attached to the 34th Division. In April, 1944, the Army dispatched the RCT overseas, and it landed in Italy. The 442nd, with the 100th re-attached, joined in the fighting in Italy and soon developed a reputation as a fighting unit. A cadre of the 1st Battalion was held back to train for replacement purposes, and Leke continued training replacement troops. He

Leke Nakashimada, U.S. Army

Leke Nakashimada, sent to Camp Shelby, Mississippi, trains for combat as a replacement in the 442nd. Photo courtesy of Leke Nakashimada.

remained in the States until March, 1945, when the Army, because the RCT needed replacements badly, ordered him and others to proceed to Maryland for overseas duty. The cadre landed at Naples, Italy, ready to join the 442nd about the time the war ended. In Italy, Leke was assigned to the Headquarters Company, 100th Battalion.

Since they had arrived late in the conflict, Leke's unit became part of the 3rd Occupational Army. The Army sent them to Ghedi, Italy, where they became guards at a prisoner of war camp, which involved watching and feeding 200,000 German prisoners. Next, the unit was sent to Lecco, Italy, where the Alps separating Italy and Switzerland loomed in the background, for a well-deserved period of rest and relaxation (R & R). Next it was sent to Livorno, Italy, where the unit performed occupational duties at another POW camp. Leke returned to the U.S. February 2, 1946, landing at Camp Kilburn, New Jersey. He was discharged from the Army in February 1946, having attained the rank of Staff (Mess) Sergeant. When discharged he had completed 49+ months in service to his country.

Leke Nakashimada In Italy

Leke tours Italy and (left) enjoys a visit to Leaning Tower of Pisa, 1945. Right, Leke and a buddy, Hajime Obata, look quite shaken as they return from a visit to the site in Milan where Italian partisans strung up the mutilated bodies of Benito Mussolini and his mistress by their ankles.   *Photos courtesy of Leke Nakashimada.*

Takey Nakashimada

Takey Nakashimada, born May 2, 1921, in Troutdale, grew up on the Bramhall place on Woodard Road, which his parents rented. He attended Corbett schools, but did not complete his senior year at CHS because people of Japanese ancestry were "evacuated" from the West Coast in the spring of 1942 after Japan bombed Pearl Harbor on December 7, 1941. Until that time, Takey worked for his father on the farm where the principal crop was cauliflower. When Japanese families arrived at the Portland Assembly Center on May 12, 1942, the Nakashimada family was among them. At the assembly center, the livestock area was partitioned, forming enclaves for families. Mattresses of straw were furnished and families used the former animal stalls as rooms. The Nakashimada family spent the summer of 1942 at the center. In September, 1942, the authorities sent the family to the Minidoka Relocation Center in Idaho. Takey Nakashimada earned his high school diploma at Hunt High School, Minidoka.

Takey Nakashimada, U.S. Army

Takey Nakashimada saw much action as Patton's 3rd Army advanced across France, Germany and into Austria.   Photo courtesy of Leke Nakashimada.

Takey Nakashimada enlisted in the Army in November, 1942. He completed basic training at Fort Hood, Texas. Apparently because of his slight build, the Army assigned Takey to advanced training as a tank gunner. After about 15 weeks training, he was sent to New Jersey for overseas duty. From there, the Army sent him to the European theater as a replacement, and he was assigned to General Patton's 3rd Army. Takey mentioned that George Scott did an excellent job portraying General Patton in the movie, "Just as he was, tough and shrewd." He also remarked that General Patton "Did his best to take care of his men and the equipment. He stressed the cost of items such as shells, apparently hoping we gunners would make every shell count."

Nakashimada said the Sherman M-4 tank was "lousy." When the 3rd Army first encountered German Panzers, it lost about 30 Shermans and more than 350 crew men. According to Takey, if a crew escaped from a tank that had been hit, they immediately took another tank (if they survived). The Sherman required a five-man crew: commander, driver, assistant driver, gunner and loader. Though the Sherman was easily repaired and dependable, its 75mm gun did not have sufficient muzzle velocity to penetrate a Panzer's armor, and its own armor was too thin, making it vulnerable to enemy tank and anti-tank weapons. It was soon labeled a "death trap." In the summer of 1944, an improved Sherman appeared with a 76mm gun with a higher muzzle velocity that helped some. Takey stated, "The only way we could stop a Panzer was to hit its tracks." With U.S. air support, the 3rd Army made satisfactory progress, however.

American ingenuity helped, also. When fall rains came, an innovation called "duck bills" could be added to extend the width of the track, which helped when the ground became muddy. An American also invented a 'hedge-row cutter" that enabled tanks and troops to penetrate the numerous hedgerows in Normandy. When the "breakout" occurred, the 3rd Army spearheaded the move. Soon its Divisions were attacking the ancient fort at Metz. When asked where he served in Europe, Takey Nakashimada stated that he "Went everywhere that Patton went."

Pvt. Takey Nakashimada in Germany

Takey Nakashimada (center) and a buddy pause for a moment in the drive across Germany to hand out candy to a young German girl who approached their tank.

Photo courtesy of Leke Nakashimada.

General Patton "went" places quickly, particularly after receiving the improved Sherman. By the end of August, 1944, the 3rd Army had crossed the Marne. Diverted North because of the Battle of the Bulge, the 3rd Army found itself in a "Fight for its life." Here, after a bitter struggle, Patton helped encircle the remnants of the German assault force attempting to retreat after its initial successes. On February 23, 1945, Patton's tanks crossed the Saar River, near the German border. About this time, the new Pershing Tank began arriving. The Pershing had a 90mm gun and four and one-half inch armor, which placed it on a par with the Panzers. By March 17, 1945, the 3rd approached Koblenz, on the Rhine, and a little over a week later, crossed the Rhine River. The 3rd Army took Frankfurt, Germany, on March 27, and then drove across Bavaria into Austria. Here, Patton's forces met the Russian Armies on the Enns River, which flows northward into the Danube River near Linz, Austria, Hitler's 'hometown.' According to Takey, his tank knocked out eight Panzers.

Takey Nakashimada received his honorable discharge in October, 1946. The 3rd Army was prepared to join the planned invasion of Japan, but the war in the Pacific theater ended before that came to pass. Takey obtained employment with the City of Portland's water bureau and became a supervisor for the Department. He retired from the water bureau in 1984. In 1948, Takey Nakashimada married Mavis Jacobson and the couple had two children, David and Tammy. Currently, Takey Nakashimada lives in North Portland (2003).

Sherman Tank

A Sherman tank of the type used by the 3rd Army in France, Germany and Austria. Takey Nakashimada served as a gunner in a similar tank. *U.S. Army photo.*

Kennie and Tom Namba

In January, 1943, the War Department decided that a Japanese-American combat unit should be formed. On February 1, 1943, the 442nd Regimental Combat Team (RCT) came into existence. The training cadre assembled at a site in Mississippi chosen as the base for the regiment, Camp Shelby. When the War Department reclassified Nisei, restoring both their rights and duties of citizenship, Tom Tomomi Namba immediately volunteered for the RCT, and the Army sent him directly to Camp Shelby. There, after he completed basic training, he was assigned to the 522nd Field Artillery Company. In the 522nd, Tom Namba learned, together with the other trainees, the intricacies of the battalion's principal pieces, the 57s and 105s. All personnel trained as forward observers and perfected techniques in directing fire against enemy positions. On May 1, 1944, the RCT left Camp Shelby for Hampton Roads, Virginia, for deployment overseas. There, they boarded Liberty ships that, unknown to the troops, were bound for Italy. The RCT reached Naples at the end of the month and debarked to a staging area where they prepared for combat operations.

Meanwhile Kennie Kenji Namba remained at Minidoka. He too, had wanted to volunteer, though he had not yet completed his senior year at Hunt. When the school agreed to grant him an early diploma, his father permitted Kennie to enlist. The Army sent him to Camp Blanding, Florida, for basic training, which lasted nine weeks. Then, transferred to Camp Shelby, he completed further basic training before being assigned to a replacement unit that trained riflemen. When the 442nd deployed in May, Kennie Namba remained at Camp Shelby to continue a more rigorous regimen of combat training. In August, 1944, his replacement unit received orders for overseas duty. In New York City, the unit boarded the Queen Mary. Its first stop was Glasgow, Scotland, where the men transferred to a troopship that took them to LeHavre, France. From the port, the replacement troops proceeded by train to a staging area near Bruyeres, France. There, the 442nd, attached to the 36th Division, Seventh Army, joined the assault against the German defensive positions..

At the staging area, the replacement troops were assigned to various infantry companies. The Army assigned Kennie Namba to the 3rd Platoon, L Company, 3rd Battalion. He reached the front in time to participate in the move to capture Biffontaine and Belmont. Continuing the attack, the 3rd Battalion took the center in a drive to rescue the "Lost Battalion," surrounded in the Vosges Mountains. German grenadiers had established a series of roadblocks which hampered the 3rd's advance. Finally, on October 30, 1944, men of I Company, 3rd Battalion, reached the surrounded troops, effecting the rescue of some 200 soldiers of the 141st Regiment, 36th Division. Because of its losses in the heavy

Kenji (Kennie) Namba, U.S. Army

Kennie Namba enlisted in January, 1944. He was wounded in April, 1945.

Photo courtesy of Kennie Namba.

fighting in the Vosges Forest, General John E. Dahlquist, 36th Division Commander, relieved the 442nd on November 18, 1944. The RCT boarded trucks to return to Nice for recuperation and reassignment.

The lull did not last long as the 3rd Battalion relieved the 79th Armored Infantry Battalion and moved into the town of Sospel, France. The RCT manned defensive positions in the mountains to the east to guard against any possible enemy move into Southern France, the Champagne Campaign. On December 21, the 3rd Battalion became the regimental reserve in L'Escarene, France, in time to celebrate Christmas. In late December, the Battalion returned to the line when the Battle of the Bulge raised concerns. The 2nd and 3rd Battalions sometimes alternated in occupying the defensive positions. Combat patrols continued and sporadic artillery fire revealed the continued presence of German forces. The intervals when the 3rd was not on the line were unusual for the infantry. Winter on the French Riviera was not all bad. Rest centers were open in Cannes and Nice, with night spots open. Holding a line with an occasional opportunity for R&R in Nice was quite a change from the Vosges Mountains. Kennie remarked, "The men in the lowlands had it made."

In mid-March, 1945, the 1st French Motorized Infantry relieved the RCT. The 522nd Field Artillery Company headed north to rejoin the Seventh Army for its push across the Rhine. The RCT assembled in Marseille, bound for a "top secret" destination, Italy. There, it was attached to The Fifth Army to be given the task of cracking the west end of the German Gothic line. Toward the end of March, 1945, the 442nd moved to a forward position near Lucca. During the first days of April, the 3rd Battalion assembled in Azzano, prepared to execute a daring plant to flank German positions. L Company had to ascend Mt. Folgorito, but the German emplacements on its summit rained fire and grenades on the advancing troops, who were exposed on the steep slope. At this point, "potato masher" grenades came bouncing down the slope. One exploded behind Kennie Namba, driving shrapnel into his back. Unconscious, he laid on the slope where medics could not reach him. He remained on the slope for

French Farm House, Sospel, France

The owner of this farm house invited Kennie Namba and his comrades to sleep in their unheated home. Kennie said it was more comfortable than the ground.

Photo courtesy of Kennie Namba.

Captured German Field Kitchen

Pfc. Genzo Toguchi and Sgt. Seisaburo Tada talk with a smiling German prisoner, left, while inspecting a field kitchen, which American troops recovered in the vicinity as the war ended. *Signal Corps photo courtesy of Kennie Namba.*

Pfc. Kennie Namba   Award Display

Left: Pfc. Namba at Fort Snelling to train for the MIS. When the war ended, he chose not to re-enlist for another two years. Right: Ruth and Kennie Namba diplay his awards. Top, the Bronze Star, awarded for heroism and the Purple Heart. Below, from L to R: Victory Medal, American Campaign Medal, European-African Campaign Medal (w/ three battle stars) and the Good Conduct Medal. Below: The Ruptured duck, Combat Infantry Badge and a Sharpshooter Medal.   Photos courtesy of Kennie Namba.

nearly an hour before help arrived. He had lost much blood, and was sent to a field hospital.

Kennie Namba remained in the hospital for about 1½ months. By the time he rejoined his unit, which had participated in breaching the Gothic Line, the 3rd Battalion had reached the town of Bologna, Italy, in the Po Valley. German resistance rapidly collapsed, and the war drew to a close. The 442nd helped collect the surrenduring German troops. The Americans, including the 3rd Battalion became engaged in guarding and feeding prisoners-of-war near Ghedi, Italy. Soon, Kennie Namba, ordered to headquarters, discovered that he, because he had attended a Japanese school, had been ordered to Fort Snelling, Minnesota, to attend its Military Intelligence School. This duty was "high priority," and the Army sent him to the United States by air. He reported to Fort Snelling to train for a role in the war in the Pacific. However, his situation changed with the surrender of the Japanese forces. Because of the "point" system, Kennie Namba was eligible for discharge, and, despite the entreaties of higher ups, he declined the honor. The Army then sent him to Fort Lewis, Washington, to be discharged (see "Etsuo/Shizuno Namba," this volume).

George Nishimura

George Nishimura, born in 1925, in Troutdale, Oregon, attended school in Troutdale and Gresham until his family, together with other local farming families, was "evacuated" from its Gresham farm on May 12, 1942. George had a younger brother, Richard "Dick" Nishimura and three surviving sisters, Haruko Ikebe, Kiku Watanabe and Tatsuko Kuribayashi. After spending an unpleasant summer at the Portland International Livestock Exposition Center, the Army sent the family, first to the Tulelake Relocation Center, then to the Minidoka Relocation Center near Twin Falls, Idaho. George and his father, Matsutaro Nishimura, were paroled from Minidoka to work on a farm near Nyssa, Oregon. George opted for farm work and did not complete high school at Minidoka.

On April 27, 1944, George Nishimura, age 18, was inducted into the U.S. Army. He reported to Fort Douglas, Utah, for processing and basic training. He then volunteered to serve with the 442nd Regimental Combat Team, and the Army sent him to Camp Shelby, Mississippi. There he trained with other Nisei in a replacement battalion. Because of the setback suffered by allied forces during the Battle of the Bulge, infantrymen were sorely needed and on January 6, 1945, George's replacement unit boarded a troopship bound for Italy. Upon his arrival there, he underwent further unit combat training, awaiting assignment. In March, the 442nd RCT assigned him to L Company, 3rd Battalion, as an infantry rifleman. The regiment remained confined to the Peninsular Base Section staging area near Pisa, Italy. There, units of the 442nd received badly needed equipment and supplies, obviously to prepare them for the next "push." The 442nd was attached to the 92nd Division, Fifth Army, which prepared to attack the western portion of the German Gothic line in Northern Italy.

George Nishimura, U.S. Army

Outpost in Northern Italy

Pvt. George Nishimura is the second from left; others not identified. George labeled the photo: "Piera Cara OP." Photos courtesy of Betty Nishimura.

Training intensified, as replacements, including George Nishimura, had no previous combat experience. On March 28, 1945, the 442nd left the staging area and moved to a position near the city of Lucca. On April 3rd, the 3rd Battalion marched to an assembly area near the town of Azzano. The next morning, I and L Companies moved northward from Azzano along the foothills of Mount Folgorita. L Company had the task of turning westward and attacking an enemy position on Mount Folgorita. The 442nd broke the enemy line, overrunning enemy positions that had withstood attacks for several months. The 3rd Battalion continued its advance on the left flank, occupying Montignoso on April 8th, then continuing northward toward Carrara. When the company entered Carrara on April 11, Italian partisans controlled the town. There, the 3rd Battalion remained in reserve for several days. The attack, intended as a diversion, had resulted in breaking the Gothic line in the west. For its success, accomplished over about ten days, the 442nd received the Distinguished Unit Citation.

On April 17, L Company resumed probing attacks toward the town of Fosdinovo and Mount Nebbione beyond. It was during these attacks, that Pvt. George Nishimura was awarded the Silver Star for gallantry in action. The citation reads:

"By direction of the President, under the provisions of Army Regulations 600-45, as amended, the Silver Star was awarded by the Theater

George's Platoon, Northern Italy

Above, the infantrymen of the 442nd had learned a hard lesson in the battles in the Vosges Forest of France: provide cover to protect against 'tree bursts.' Here, in the mountains of Northern Italy, the lesson was applied. Below, George's Platoon stands for review. *Photos courtesy of Betty Nishimura.*

Silver Star Medal

George Nishimura's Silver Star, received for "gallantry in action."
Photo courtesy of Betty Nishimura.

Commander to George Nishimura, Private, Infantry, L Company, 442nd Regimental Combat Team, for gallantry in action near Foce Il Cuccu, Italy, on 19 April 1945. When his platoon was pinned down by machine gun fire, Private Nishimura, on his own initiative, stood up with his automatic rifle and neutralized one machine gun by killing its crew, capturing three others and causing the rest to withdraw. Later, when it became necessary for the platoon to withdraw in [the] face of [a] superior enemy force, he sued upon (went after) the enemy again and covered his platoon's withdrawal. Private Nishimura's continuous desire to safe-guard his comrades, and his gallantry, is in keeping with the highest traditions of the Army of the United States. Entered service from Hunt, Idaho [The Minidoka Relocation Center]."

On April 23, the Germans started a hasty retreat as they were in danger of being cut off by the 34th 'Red Bull' Division. The 473rd Infantry entered Genoa, Italy on April 27. On the following day, L Company occupied the city. German resistance collapsed and units of the 442nd advanced 75 miles to Turin, Italy, located on the Po River. By May 2nd, entire German and Italian units had surrendered, and the war ended in Italy. George Nishimura remained in Europe until June, 1946. During that year, he had an opportunity to visit Switzerland, Germany and France. When Nishimura returned to the United States in July, he was stationed at Fort Belvoir, Virginia. Because of a non-service connected problem, the Army sent him to Fitzsimmons General Hospital, Lowry Field, Denver, Colorado, for treatment. On January 31, 1947, George Nishimura received his honorable discharge.

Upon George's return home, he and his parents, Matsutaro and Kijyu Nishimura, purchased the former Hoecker farm of 80 acres on the southern bank of the Sandy River, almost directly across from what is now the Springdale Job Corps complex. In fact, the farm acreage extended across the Sandy River to include the "Big Rock" area. On February 8, 1953, George Nishimura

Touring Italy and Back in the States

Left, Five L Company infantrymen tour Florence, Italy. Standing, from L: Bill Tomura (Purple Heart [PH], Combat Infantry Badge [CIB]), Kazue Nagasawa [CIB] and Akio Saito (CIB). Kneeling: Raymond Murata (Bronze Star, PH, Distinguished Unit Badge [DUB] with Oak Leaf Cluster, CIB) and George Nishimura (Silver Star, DUB and CIB). Right, T/Sgt. George Nishimura at Fort Belvoir, Virginia.

Photos courtesy of Betty Nishimura.

Nishimura Farm, Troutdale

Betty Nakashimada inspects the blackberry crop, Nishimura farm. Note cabbage hill across the Sandy River, background (very faint). *Photo courtesy of Leke Nakashimada.*

married Betty Hiuga, whom he had met at the Russellville Market where she worked. George and Betty have one son, Jerry. After the deaths of his parents, George and Betty Nishimura continued to farm. They raised blackberries, broccoli, cabbage, cucumbers, peppers, cauliflower and strawberries, but gradually, began to concentrate on growing cabbage and broccoli. George Nishimura passed away on April 9, 1999.

George and Betty Nishimura

George and Betty (Hiuga) Nishimura on their wedding day, February 8, 1953. Betty grew up on a farm in Kent, Washington. George grew up in Troutdale and Gresham.

Photo courtesy of Betty Nishimura.

Frank Okita

Frank Okita's family farmed at various locations in East Multnomah County for many years, finally moving, in 1932, to a farm off Palmblad Road near Gresham, when Frank was a junior in high school. He transferred from Columbian High School, Corbett, to Gresham High, from which he graduated in 1933. Thereafter, he continued to live on the farm, helping his older brother take care of the vegetable and berry crops the family raised. Frank's father had suffered a stroke in 1932, and as a result, George Okita, Frank's older brother, dropped out of high school to manage the family's farm operation. In January, 1942, shortly after the Empire of Japan bombed Pearl Harbor, Frank entered the service as a draftee. He was directed to report to Fort Warren, Wyoming, for basic training. According to his family, Frank recalled that first winter at Fort Warren as a chilly welcome, as the weather was severely cold. It was to be the first of several winters he spent at Fort Warren. By the time Frank had completed his basic training, his family had been forced from their Gresham farm and were housed at the Pacific Livestock Exposition Center in Portland. Frank felt the Army brass didn't quite know what to do with its Nisei soldiers, many of whom from the West Coast were stationed at Fort Warren. Later, after his family had been moved to the Minidoka Relocation Center in Idaho, Frank, granted a furlough, was able to visit them. Prior to their move, he could not visit his family since they were held in the Western Defense Command's Military Exclusion Zone 1.

Camp Warren, Wyoming

Frank Okita and Jim Sadaki Onchi at Camp Warren. Both entered the U.S. Army as draftees in January, 1942.

Photo courtesy of Mary (Tashima) Okita.

After Frank Okita returned from his visit to Minidoka, the Army assigned him to the Supply and Transportation Detachment #1. While many Nisei soldiers finally transferred to other units, Frank remained at Fort

Frank Okita, Convoy Training, Camp Warren

Above, Frank Okita training at Fort Warren for convoy duty. His poor eyesight may have kept him from an earlier deployment overseas. Left, Pvt. Okita at Fort Warren, where he remained for about three years before being deployed overseas. *Photos courtesy of Mary (Tashima) Okita.*

Warren, perhaps because of his poor eyesight, which required a thick, corrective lens for him to see clearly. He trained with Company 38, 3rd Training Regiment, as a truck driver, training in convoy and other techniques month after month. Finally, in the late fall of 1944, Frank Okita was transferred to the 442nd Regimental Combat Team, Fort Shelby, Mississippi, for overseas deployment. He was sent to Italy as a truck driver for the 442nd. Unfortunately, he had not undergone combat training, so this deficiency had to be corrected before he could be start taking supplies to the front. By the time he had completed combat training, the German resistance had collapsed, thus sparing Frank of actual combat duty.

Detachments of the 442nd were employed in guarding prisoners, but the Unit was preparing for deployment to the Pacific when Japan capitulated and the war ended. Frank Okita's detachment returned to the United States toward the end of the year, 1945, and he was discharged in January, 1946, completing four years service to his country during World War II. Shortly after his discharge, he married his betrothed, Mary Tashima, with whom he had been corresponding since they had become re-acquainted at Minidoka in 1942 (see "Shintaro Okita, Tatsu Okita," this volume).

Joe Masayuki Onchi

Joe Masayuki Onchi, born in Oregon in 1920, grew up on farms in rural Multnomah County. His father first rented a place in Montavilla, then moved his family to a rented farm in Gresham, Oregon. The family eked out a living growing berry and vegetable crops, a situation made more difficult by the death of Joe's father in 1932. With the help of her sons, Mizu Onchi held the family together through the Depression years until World War II started. Shortly thereafter, the United States government took action that drastically changed their lives.

After graduating from Gresham High School in 1939, Onchi helped harvest the family's berry crops on the farm. After the harvest, he found a job in California working at a produce shipping shed. That fall he started attending Multnomah College in Portland, Oregon, and completed a year of college. However, having turned 21, he registered for the draft and "drew a low number." In October, he received the expected "greetings," which ordered him to report on November 6, 1941, for a physical. Onchi passed the physical and was soon on his way to Fort Lewis, Washington. From Fort Lewis, the Army sent him to Camp Roberts, California, where, on November 15, he started basic training in an infantry battalion. While he was in basic training, the United States entered the war, declaring war on Japan, Germany and Italy.

After the declaration of war, Army brass seemed unsure of what to do with its Nisei soldiers. First they were told that they would be discharged. However, "higher ups" quashed that plan. On February 6, 1942, the Army transferred the Nisei soldiers stationed at Camp Roberts to Camp Joseph F. Robinson, Arkansas. (In some instances, local commanders became very protective and supportive, making every effort to keep a Nisei soldier in the unit. In most instances, however, the commanders transferred them to a designated base.) Joe Onchi reported to Camp Robinson. Assigned to a "landscaping detail," he trained for combat "by picking up cigarette butts and clearing brush." About three weeks later, for some unexplained reason, the Army placed him in the service command, where he became a film projectionist showing Army training films. On March 28, 1942, Pvt. Onchi received his first promotion, to Private First Class. He was able to visit his parents at the Tule Lake Camp in July, 1943. Onchi remained at Camp Robinson until October, 1944. In the interim, he had received two promotions. Consequently, when transferred, he had been promoted to Corporal.

In 1944, after reports circulated about the exploits of the 442nd Regimental Combat Team (RCT), Joe Onchi requested a transfer to that unit. The Army responded by sending him to Camp Shelby. There, his commander sent him to

Joe Onchi in "Training" at Camp Robinson

Left, Joe Onchi found himself "picking up cigarette butts and clearing brsh" when he first arrived at Camp Robinson. Next, he became a film projectionist running training films .Photos courtesy of Joe Onchi.

the non-commissioned officers' "refresher school." Because of the losses suffered in Italy and the Vosges Mountains in France, the RCT desperately need replacements. Six weeks after his arrival at Shelby, Onchi's replacement battalion traveled by train to Fort Meade, Maryland, for deployment to the European Theater. On November 23, 1944, the replacements marched onto the *Corporal Miles Standish*, which was bound for England. Joe Onchi was on his way overseas.

On December 20, 1944, the replacements left Southampton England, by a LCI. The landing craft reached LeHavre, France, the next day. On December 22, 1944, the replacements boarded trucks headed for Southern France, but they traveled by train (box cars) the final leg of their journey, which ended at Nice, France. The RCT had been pulled from the line after the successful campaign in the Vosges Mountains of Northeast France. Its new assignment involved defending the border in the Maritime Alps that separated three French provinces, Savoy, Dauphine and Provence, from Italy. The command dispatched L Company, 3rd Battalion, to which Joe Onchi had been assigned, to defensive concrete bunkers constructed by the Germans, who had formerly occupied

Joe Onchi, U.S. Army

In 1944, Joe Onchi volunteered to serve in the 442nd Regimental Combat Team. The Army transferred him to Camp Shelby, Mississippi, but he was soon on his way overseas.
Photos courtesy of Joe Onchi.

France. Onchi did undergo some limited combat training during the time he spent in France. The opposing armies, German and Allied, while holding defensive positions, continually fired on one another.

In March, 1945, a French infantry unit relieved the RCT from the defensive position it had occupied for a few weeks. The RCT assembled at Marseille, France. There, all units except the 552nd Field Artillery Battalion boarded ships bound for Italy. Once in Pisa, Italy, the RCT was attached to the 5th Army, whose commander, General Mark Clark, planned to launch an assault on the Gothic Line. All replacements received some combat training in the two weeks remaining before the attack was to be launched. For the assault, Joe Onchi became a Browning Automatic Rifleman (BAR) as did a friend, Roy Fujiwara.

On April 3, 1945, Companies of the 3rd Battalion assembled near the town of Azzano. On April 4, I and L Companies moved forward to attack German defensive positions on Mount Folgorita. According to Onchi, climbing Mount Folgorita was a difficult challenge, particularly since its German defenders held the high ground. In order to prevent the German defenders from learning of the planned assault, the attackers taped their dog tags, used no lights or radios, and were ordered not to talk as they climbed toward their objective at

U.S. Army Hospital, Italy

Above: After suffering his wound, Joe Onchi was first hospitalized at facilities in Italy, which the Army had taken over for its use. This is the 45th General Hospital.

Flown back to the states, the Army hospitalized Joe Onchi at Vaughn Medical Hospital, Hines, Illinois. A friend, Jean Hayashi, visited wounded veterans at Vaughn to boost their morale.

night. On the morning of April 5, as the 3rd Platoon, L Company's troopers crept forward, Onchi's Platoon Sergeant, Tom Sagimori, went down, hit by German sniper fire. Having previously been warned to keep down, Onchi immediately "hit the dirt,", which, he believes, caused the sniper's bullet fired at him to miss his head. However, the bullet hit his right leg, shattering it above the ankle. The sniper fire directed at them came from the area that the 1st Platoon was assaulting. Onchi's friend, Roy Fujiwara, also a BAR man, took a sniper's bullet moments later. The bullet entered his right cheek and exited at the back of his neck. Onchi recalled, "the Germans seemed to target BAR men." When the medics came running, Joe heard one remark that they had better get "this one" (Roy) to an aid station. They returned for Onchi later. He had positive comments to make about the medics: "They came immediately when someone was hit. We were under heavy enemy fire, but they ignored it." Though Sgt. Sagimori died, both Onchi and Fujiwara survived their wounds.

After being treated at two hospitals in Italy, first the 33rd, then the 45th General Hospital, on June 5, 1945, the Army flew Joe Onchi to the states for further treatment and to convalesce. He spent several months at Vaughn Medical Hospital in Hines, Illinois, before being transferred to Madigan Medical Hospital, Fort Lewis, Washington. He received his honorable discharge on May 18, 1946, having spent 4 years, 6 months and 12 days in the United States Army. Joe Onchi received the Bronze Star for bravery under fire and the Purple Heart for his wound. Because of the wound, his right leg is more than an inch shorter than his left.

Upon his return to civilian life, Joe Onchi resumed his studies at Multnomah College before enrolling at Pacific University to complete a program in optometry (see "Yukisaburo Onchi," this volume). Because he received his wound in action, he qualified for educational benefits under a special provision of the law, which provided payments beyond those provided by the GI Bill.

Roy Fujiwara

A sniper's bullet hit Roy Fujiwara, another BAR man in L Company, 3rd Battalion, just moments after Onchi was hit. The bullet hit Fujiwara in his right cheek and exited at the back of his neck. Fortunately, the wound, though serious, was not fatal.
Photo courtesy of Joe Onchi.

Jim Sadaki Onchi

Born in Montavilla, Oregon, in 1918, Jim Sadaki Onchi grew up on farms that his parents rented in a rural area of Multnomah County. When his father died in 1932, Onchi quit school in order to help his mother manage the farm. In 1939 after the crops were harvested, he, together with his brother, Joe Onchi, traveled to California to work in a produce shipping shed. Upon his return to Gresham, he obtained employment as a logger for the Long-Bell Lumber Company in Longview, Washington. There, he worked in a logging camp, but was able to return home on weekends. Jim Onchi purchased a new 1941 Chevrolet automobile, which he used for the commute. When the selective service act took effect, Jim Onchi registered for the draft. Unlike his brother, however, Onchi's number did not come up until January, 1942. He reported for a physical in Portland, passed it and then reported to Fort Lewis, Washington. Apparently, because the war had started, the Army sent Jim Onchi to Camp Robinson, Arkansas, which "camp" seemed to be one of those favored by the Army for its Nisei soldiers. Jim Onchi completed basic training at Camp Robinson. In February, 1943, a Nisei unit, the 442nd RCT, was formed at Camp Shelby, Mississippi. Jim Onchi volunteered and the Army soon transferred him to that post.

A Visit to Camp Jerome

Jim and Joe Onchi, stationed at Camp Robinson, visit family members interned at Camp Jerome, Arkansas. Rear, from left: Joe, Jim and George Onchi. Front: Sachi Onchi holding Mary Ann and Mizu Onchi holding Raymond.   *Photo courtesy of Joe Onchi.*

At Camp Shelby, Jim Onchi became a platoon sergeant, the NCO in charge of the training program for four squads with four corporals as squad leaders. Onchi remained at Shelby until April, 1945, training replacement soldiers for the 442nd RCT. During this interval, in October, 1944, Jim's brother, Joe Onchi, came to Camp Shelby. Joe, however, remained only a short time before being deployed overseas. When Joe left, Jim requested a transfer as a replacement for the 442nd, but his request was denied. His commanding officer indicated that his job training combat troops was too important and he could not be spared. However, when the need for replacements became critical, the Army relented. In April, 1945, Jim Onchi and other replacements boarded a train bound for Fort Meade, Maryland, for deployment overseas. While Onchi and the others waited at Fort Meade, Germany capitulated. The troops spent more time at Fort Meade until the Army decided what to do with them. Finally, the replacements boarded the *Queen Mary* bound for Germany and occupation duty. An interesting sidelight to the ocean trip was the presence of comedian Bob Hope on board. He and his troupe entertained the troops several times as the *Queen Mary* crossed the Atlantic Ocean to England. Once in England, the troops boarded a ship that took them to France. After landing in France, the soldiers traveled by train to a post near Nuremburg, Germany.

Jim Onchi spent approximately seven months serving with the Army of Occupation, Germany. He returned to the United States where, in February, 1946, after four years, eight days in the Army, he received his honorable discharge at Fort Lewis, Washington.

Camp Robinson, Arkansas

Nisei soldiers from Gresham and vicinity stationed at Camp Robinson. From left: Morey Okita, Menow Hara, Jim Onchi and Kaz Hinatsu.   *Photo courtesy of Joe Onchi.*

Frances (Kumazawa) Ota/John Ota

Frances Kumazawa, living with Carl and Mabel Southworth in Troutdale, Oregon, was in her junior year at Gresham High School when the war started with the bombing of Pearl Harbor by aircraft of the Empire of Japan. Because of the exclusion act promulgated by the Western Defense Command, she, together with an older sister, Grace, and older brother, Joe, was incarcerated in an "assembly center" in Portland, Oregon. At that time, her mother and four younger siblings lived in Japan. At the center, because of austere conditions, the three youngsters decided to volunteer to help farmers in Eastern Oregon with their crops. The three traveled by train to a labor camp located near Nyssa, Oregon. In September, 1942, Frances enrolled at Nyssa High School from which she graduated in 1943. That fall she enrolled in the U.S. Cadet Nurses program at Eastern Oregon College of Education in LaGrande, Oregon. She completed the "pre-clinical course," a prerequisite for further training at The Dalles Hospital, The Dalles, Oregon. However, because of the exclusion act, the War Relocation Authority refused to allow Frances Kumazawa to enter the "coastal zone."

Frances Kumazawa

This official photograph of Frances Kumazawa appeared on her "Certificate of Exemption," which allowed her to enter the zone restricted to "persons of Japanese ancestry." Unfortunately, she exemption came to late to permit her to complete a nursing program with her classmates.

Frustrated because she could not finish the course of study with her classmates, Frances wrote a letter to Eleanor Roosevelt explaining the situation. The letter worked, but it took six months for permission to be granted. During that time, the college had made arrangements for Frances to continue her studies at St. Marks Hospital in Salt Lake City, Utah. However, at St. Marks she encountered suspicion and prejudice, so she returned to Eastern Oregon College. While there, an Army recruiter approached her and suggested that she join the Army as a linguist. Frances Kumazawa accepted the offer and joined the Women's Army Corps as a volunteer on November 26, 1944.

The Army sent her to Fort Des Moines, Iowa for basic training then transferred her to Fort Snelling, Minnesota, where she was assigned to the Military Intelligence Service. She was among 14 Nisei women assigned to the intelligence school for training. After two months of doing clerical work, Frances requested a transfer to a medical unit, an assignment more in keeping with her interest and prior training. The Army assigned her to a hospital at Camp Crowder, Missouri, where she served as a medical technician. She remained at Camp Crowder until her honorable discharge on January 28, 1946. Because of her service, she received a certificate of appreciation from the Military Intelligence Service, a letter expressing President Harry Truman's "heartfelt thanks of a grateful Nation," signed by the President, and many GI benefits.

John Ota, an engineering graduate of the California Institute of Technology, became a draftee in the United States Army in the fall, 1941. Because he had a degree in engineering from the California Institute of Technology, the

Sgt. John Ota, U.S. Army

The Army yanked John Ota, graduate (engineer), Cal Tech, from OCS at Fort Belvoire, Virginia and sent him to Camp Grant, Illinois, to train as a medic. *Photo, Frances Ota.*

Army placed him in an Officer Candidate School at Camp Belvoire, Virginia. However, fate intervened, as the Empire of Japan bombed Pearl Harbor on December 7, 1941. Shortly, the Army yanked him from the program and assigned him to Camp Grant, Illinois, to be trained as a medic. Next, after a short stay at Fort Leavenworth, the Army transferred Ota to Camp Crowder, Missouri, where he became a surgical assistant. There, he first met Frances Kumazawa, who was destined to become his bride. When his unit received overseas orders, he had his shots and the customary preparation for deployment to the Pacific Theater. However, at the last minute, Ota's orders changed, and he remained at Crowder. During his service, the Army gave Ota an opportunity to join the MIS, but he did not

Surgical Staff, Camp Crowder, Missouri

Sgt. John Ota (firts left) trained as a surgical assistant at Camp Crowder, Missouri. He spent much of his 4 plus years in the Army at Crowder. Photos courtesy of Frances Ota.

Sgt. John Ota, U.S. Army

At Camp Crowder, John Ota met his future bride, Frances Kumazawa. The couple married shortly after the end of World War II.

choose to take advantage of the offer.

In 1945, the Army sent Sgt. John Ota to Camp Beckinridge, Kentucky, where, on December 2, 1945, he received his honorable discharge. The Army belatedly offered him a direct commission as an engineer, but Sgt. Ota refused the "honor."

Ray Shiiki

Ray Shiiki, born in 1927 of Roy and Asa Shiiki, Gresham, Oregon, completed grade school at Hillsview Grade, Clackamas County, Oregon. Hillsview, a two-room school, served a rural area near Gresham. He graduated from Hillsview in 1941, then attended Gresham High School. Toward the end of his freshman year, war broke out between the United States and the Empire of Japan, occasioned by the bombing by Japanese carrier aircraft of the United States Naval Base at Pearl Harbor, Oahu, Hawaiian Islands. The United States Government ordered the Shiiki family and other families of Japanese ancestry to assemble at the fairgrounds in Gresham, Oregon, for transport to to the Portland Assembly Center. Busses took the Nikkei families to the Pacific International Livestock Exposition Center in North Portland, Oregon, where most would spend the next four months. A few of Ray Shiiki's high school friends followed his bus to the center and he met them at the fence. However, they stood on the outside; Ray stood on the inside. He, a citizen, realized then that he had been imprisoned solely because his parents had immigrated to the United States from Japan ("rather than any other country on earth").

In September, 1942, the government sent many of the internees, including the Shiiki family, to the Minidoka Relocation Center, Idaho, near the city of Twin Falls. At the camp, Ray completed high school, graduating from Hunt High in 1945. Soon after graduation, he traveled to Indianapolis, Indiana, where he made arrangements to enroll at Miami University, Oxford, Ohio, for a summer session of college work. While attending the university, he received his draft notice. After completing the summer session, Ray returned to Minidoka. In August, 1945, he reported to Fort Douglas, Utah, for induction into the U.S. Army.

The Army sent him to Camp Hood, Texas, for basic training, which he completed in about 10 weeks. Shortly after his arrival at Hood, hostilities ended with the surrender of Japan. After Ray completed basic training, the Army assigned him to an anti-tank outfit. Always eager to play baseball, Ray became a member of his company team, which took the regimental baseball championship during his time at the base. For some reason, early in 1946, the Army decided that all Nisei soldiers stationed at Camp Hood should be sent to the Military Intelligence Service (MIS) Language School at Fort Snelling, Minnesota.

Consequently, Ray reported to Fort Snelling, where, through the intervention of a friend, he became the supply sergeant for F Company, MIS Language School. Apparently, because the war had ended, the need for Japanese language interpreters declined. The Army decided to move the Language School

Kisae and Ray Shiiki   Ray Shiiki, U.S. Army

Left: Ray Shiiki, on furlough, visited his sister, Kisae, at Grandview, Idaho. Right: T/5 Ray Shiiki, Supply Sergeant, attached to F Company, Military Intelligence Service Language School, Fort Snelling, Minnesota.   *Photos courtesy of Ray Shiiki.*

Fort Snelling, Minnesota

The building at Fort Snelling in which Ray Shiiki stayed during his stay at Fort Snelling. The barracks housed F Company, Military Intelligence Service Language School.

from Fort Snelling to the Presidio at Monterey, California. In effect, this combined the two "schools" at one location, the Presidio. Ray Shiiki completed his military obligation there. He received his honorable discharge at Fort Ord, California, on November 18, 1946.

After Shiiki's discharge, he returned to Oregon, joining his family in a rental unit at Vanport, Oregon (for details about how the Shiiki family lost their farm, see "Roy Rikizo Shiiki," this volume). Ray and his brother, Tom Shiiki, with help from Al Hoffmeister, a family friend, found a farm on Hogan Road that the brothers rented. Thus after six years, the Shiiki family resumed a life on a farm; a life that had been interrupted by events some six years previously. Ray Shiiki, always enthused about baseball, joined a baseball team of Nisei veterans, which enjoyed some success at the sport.

The team, not organized initially, started playing baseball for enjoyment. A few "old-timers," John Murakami, Ted Tsuboi and Art Somekawa, then organized a team to play other teams in the Portland area and beyond. Games were scheduled on Sunday afternoons, and the team played at Benson High School, Cleveland High School, Lents Park and at other venues. Soon, the veterans were playing against "vet" teams in Spokane, Seattle, Fife [Tacoma], Portland and Hood River (for the Northwest Tourney, played on the Fourth of July).

Nisei Veterans' Baseball Team

Back, from left: Art Somekawa, Mutt Furukawa, Roy Sumino, Shigeru Takeuchi, George Sakurai, George Muramatsu, Bill Wakayama, Tom Shiiki and John Murakami. Front: Tom Fujii, John Tanaka, Joe Kato, Shiro Takeuchi, Hood Shiogi, Ko Yada, Jack Kato and Ted Tsuboi. *Photo courtesy of Ray Shiiki.*

Shigeru Takeuchi

Shigeru Takeuchi grew up on a farm on the 'hill,' located on Wand Road. The Takeuchi home was north of Jasper Mershon's home, and across the road from Ig and Alice Wand. In July 1941, he was drafted into the U.S. Army. Sent to Camp Grant, Illinois for basic training, he was assigned to the medical corps upon completion of basic. He received his training as a medic at Camp Robinson, Arkansas. Granted leave in the spring of 1942, he could not visit his family as a person of Japanese ancestry could not enter western Washington, Oregon or California.

Though trained as a medic, the army decided that it needed infantry. Therefore, the Army transferred Shigeru to Fort McClellan, Alabama, for advanced infantry training. After completing training, he volunteered to serve in the 442nd Regimental Combat Team (RCT), a "Nisei" unit slated to serve in the European theater. In 1944, the 442nd arrived in Italy and became attached to the 34th Infantry Division. On June 26th, the 34th relieved the 36th Division, and the RCT commenced its involvement in the Rome-Arno Campaign, which took the 442nd from Grossetto to beyond the Arno River. Despite fierce resistance from its German defenders and vicious fighting, by September 1 the Americans had crossed the Arno. The RCT was relieved during the first week of September and sent to a bivouac area. On September 18, 672 replacements joined the 442nd, which required further training to prepare the replacements for the next "push." News from France promised an early end to the war, and men of the 442nd were pleased to hear that they were to be assigned to the Seventh Army, in France.

Shigeru Takeuchi, U.S. Army

Shigeru Takeuchi fought in Italy and France with the 442nd Regimental Combat Team, a unit formed of Nisei Americans. He came through the war unscathed. *Photo courtesy of Shiro Takeuchi.*

On September 27, 1944, the RCT embarked for Marseille. However, the 442nd soon discovered that the optimistic reports from France were in error; the German units fought tenaciously, viciously and effectively. The Seventh Army had met stiff resistance and had suffered many casualties. The RCT was attached to the 36th Division, which had as its initial objective, freeing the French village, Bruyeres. On October 15, the RCT became engaged in the attack aimed toward that town. On the 18th, Takeuchi's I Company together with L Company, 3rd Battalion, participated in the attack on the town. After a severe battle, Bruyeres was in American hands by 6:30 p.m. The RCT captured 134 prisoners during the engagement that day. On the 19th, the attack resumed to the east toward Belmont and Biffontaine, where Companies I and K found themselves in the middle of a mine field. Here, the RCT mounted one of its most celebrated actions of the war, the rescue of the 1st Battalion, 141st Infantry. The "Lost Battalion" had advanced beyond its support and could not fight its way out. The 100th and 3rd Battalions were ordered to break through to the surrounded troops, with the help of some attached units as well as the 522nd Field Artillery and the 133rd Field Artillery. Despite a counter-attack by the Germans, the units reached a point less than one-half mile from the beleagured troops. In the ensuing advance, an I Company patrol reached the outer defenses of the "Lost Battalion," and the surrounded troops were extricated. For his part in this action, Takeuchi received the Bronze Star for valor under fire.

Shigeru remarked that he was one of the few men in the unit to serve without suffering more than a few scratches and bruises in combat. After I Company helped extricate the "Lost Battalion," its strength was reduced to only 8 men. Takeuchi's closest call came when a mortar round landed in his foxhole and exploded as he headed for it to take cover. The 442nd had the highest casualty rate, 314%, of any American fighting unit in World War II. According to data collected by its veterans, soldiers in I Company, 3rd Battalion, received the following decorations:

1 Medal of Honor;   1 Distinguished Service Cross;

20 Silver Stars;   453 Bronze Stars;

391 Purple Heart Medals.

Forty-seven of the company were killed in action. After the Battle of Bruyeres, only eight men (four riflemen, including Shigeru Takeuchi) answered roll call.

Shigeru came home in 1945. He helped his brother, Masao, farm the home place upon his return. He rented the Bates place, which he farmed for a few years. In 1948, he married Lucy Kubo, of Fresno, California, whom he had met while he was stationed at Camp Robinson. Lucy's family had been interned at the Jerome Relocation Camp, Arkansas. Takeuchi met his future bride at the camp, which often hosted Nisei soldiers for entertainment and refreshments. In 1953, Shigeru and Lucy moved to Fresno, Lucy's home town. He continued to live in Fresno until his death in 2005.

Shiro Takeuchi

Shiro Takeuchi, too, grew up on his parent's farm on Wand Road. The family cleared the land and had farmed the place for many years. Shiro graduated from CHS in 1936. He continued to work on the farm for a couple of years, then went to work for his brother, Hiro, in Hiro's grocery store. Shiro was drafted into the U.S. Army on October 13, 1941, and sent to Camp Grant in Illinois for basic training. He applied for clerical school, for which he had to take a typing test. Although he had not touched a typewriter since taking typing from Miss Genevieve Rosen at CHS, he passed the test easily. While he was attending the school, Japan bombed Pearl Harbor. All soldiers of Japanese extraction were told to report to the recreation building. Shiro's buddies told him, "If anyone lays a hand on you, let us know. We'll take care of them." Given leave, he used the time to visit Chicago as he was not permitted to return to the West Coast. Later, the Nisei (American-born citizens of Japanese ancestry) were all transferred to Kelly Field, Texas, and from there, dispersed to other bases. Shiro was sent to Harlingen Army Air Force Base in Southern Texas to train as a medic.

Shiro Takeuchi, U.S. Army

Drafted in 1941, Shiro first trained as a medic. However, the Army needed more infantrymen and sent Shiro to the European theater as a replacement destined for General George Patton's 3rd Army.
Photo courtesy of Shiro Takeuchi.

Later that year, the Army sent Shiro to the station hospital, Camp Wolters, Texas. In 1944, he was sent to Camp Barkley for advanced medical training, but demand for more infantry caused the Army to interrupt his training as a medic. Instead, Shiro was sent to Camp Livingston, Louisiana, for advanced infantry training. After completing the training, Shiro embarked on a troopship bound for the European theater. On April 13, 1945, the ship landed at Le Havre, France. As his outfit disembarked, they heard taps being played. Somewhat mystified by this introduction to combat, they soon discovered that President Franklin D. Roosevelt had died, and taps was being played in his honor.

Shiro was assigned to the 14th Infantry, 71st Division, 3rd Army, under General George Patton. By this time Patton's tanks were moving so rapidly across Germany and Austria that Shiro and the other replacements had difficulty reaching the front. War materiel, particularly gasoline, had a higher priority than replacement troops. They did reach the front, however, and joined the 3rd Army before it halted on the west bank of the Enns River, where it met Russian troops who had advanced from the east. The Enns River flows northward to the Danube just east of Linz, Austria.

Since Shiro had just arrived, he did not have enough "points" accumulated to get a 'ticket' home. Therefore, he spent an additional year in Germany with the Army of Occupation before being sent home in March, 1946. He attained the rank of Master Sergeant, which, he says, "was one of his proudest moments."

On March 13, 1946, Shiro Takeuchi was discharged from the U.S. Army. He had spent four years and five months in the service. Shiro recalled, "If the war had not ended when it did, I would have fought with the 3rd Army in Japan." On January 15, 1950, he married Misawo Uyeoka, of Fresno, California. Shiro and Misawo had two children, Margaret "Peggy" and Susan. After the war, Shiro went into the grocery business. He and Misawo raised their family in S.E. Portland, and live there still.

Air Support for the 3rd Army

Unbeknown to Takey Nakashimada and Shiro Takeuchi, another graduate of CHS, Virgil Kirkham, was providing air support for the 3rd Army during its advance across France and Germany. Virgil was shot down (kia) while attacking a German convoy on April 30, 1945, eight days before the war ended.   Photo courtesy of Marion Kirkham.

George and Fred Toya

George Toya's father came to the United States from Canada near the turn of the century. He obtained employment as a gardener for the Mountain View Floral Company on the bluff above the Sandy River near Troudale, Oregon. The company provided his father, Kaguma Toya, with a small cabin in which he lived. In 1916, Kaguma married Yone Ito. The couple had four children, three of whom survived childhood. George Toya was born on March 22, 1919, during the period the family lived in the cabin on Stark Street. George started elementary school at the historic one-room Cedar School on Troutdale Road. In 1929, Kaguma Toya moved his family to an 18-acre farm located on Lucas Road about one-half mile north of Springdale, Oregon. George attended Springdale Grade School from which he graduated in 1933. He then enrolled at Columbian High School (CHS) in Corbett and completed his first three high school years there. He worked for his father on the farm while the family resided in Springdale.

George Toya, U.S. Army

In the fall of 1936, Kaguma Toya moved his family to a farm in Powell Valley east of Gresham, Oregon. George Toya completed his senior year at Gresham High School and graduated in 1937. After graduation, he worked for his father on the farm. Because of the onset of war in Europe, farm prices had improved to a level that made attending college a possibility. Since Fred had also completed high school, the brothers formulated a plan so both could attend college yet continue to help their father on the farm. Their plan had George enrolling first, attending for a year, then Fred would take his turn for a year. George visited Oregon State College with plans to enroll that fall. He found a private home that would rent to Nisei students (the college would not

George Toya, U.S. Army

From left, George Toya, stationed at Fort Leonard Wood; center, training as a medic; and right, at the Army's intelligence school, Fort Snelling, Minnesota.

Photos courtesy of George Toya.

accommodate Nisei students in its dormitories). However, upon his return home, he found the draft board had reclassified him from 4A (agricultural deferment) to 1A (draft eligible). George called the board and offered to go in with the next group and "get his one-year obligation over with." Consequently, on July 1, 1941, he joined the U.S. Army. Shigeru Takeuchi and Art Blanc, former schoolmates at CHS, were in the same group.

The Army sent George to Camp Grant near Rockford, Illinois, for basic training, which took about three months. Next he was sent to Fort Leonard Wood, Missouri, to train as an engineer. While George was stationed at Fort Leonard Wood, the Empire of Japan attacked the United States at Pearl Harbor. He remained at Fort Leonard Wood, but the Army decided to train him as a medic. After completing the training, he was transferred to Camp Chaffee, Fort Smith, Arkansas, attached to the medical detachment of the 6th Armored Division. George remarked that the Army seemed ambivalent about the suitability of having Nisei soldiers in some combat units. Therefore, he was sent to Camp Shelby, Mississippi, and assigned to the 442nd Regimental Combat Team, a unit composed of soldiers of Japanese ancestry. During his stay a Camp Shelby, George was interviewed by a cadre from Army intelligence who found that he could speak and understand Japanese.

From Shelby, the Army sent George to Fort Snelling, Minnesota, to attend the Army Intelligence School. After about 4½ months, he received a furlough to visit his parents at the Minidoka Relocation Center in Idaho, where his family was confined. While there, he met and dated Sonoya Hirata of Ontario,

General McArthur's Headquarters, Tokyo

During his service with the MIS, Army of Occupation, George Toya worked from the ground floor of the Daichi Building, used by General Douglas MacArthur as his headquarters as Military Governor of Japan.   Photo courtesy of Scott Cunningham.

Oregon. After he returned to Fort Snelling, he corresponded with Sonoya. With another break in the offing, he proposed to Sonoya, who joined him at Fort Snelling. On February 19, 1945, the couple wed.

Soon thereafter, George found himself on a troopship bound for the Philippines via Einewetok, Marshall Islands. At Einewetok, sent ashore to interrogate enemy prisoners, he encountered problems on rejoining his ship. Clambering aboard, he found a different O.D. (Officer of the Day) on duty, who refused to allow him to board. After he protested, he was asked four or five questions, such as "Who won the world series," which he answered correctly. Fortunately, the O.D. who had been on duty when he left was still on the ship. He was able to confirm George's story and George was allowed to re-board. The troopship then continued on its voyage to the Philippine Islands, George's assigned duty station. There, George Toya served at General MacArthur's Headquarters as an interrogator and interpreter in the Allied Translation and Interrogation Section. He remained in the Philippines until the war ended. He was supposed to be at the treaty signing on the USS Missouri in Tokyo Bay, but his plane was delayed at Okinawa by a typhoon. However, he soon landed in Tokyo and became a part of the Army of Occupation.

George Toya's job in Japan was to inform local authorities of their responsibilities under the occupation. His office was on the first floor of the Daichi Building in Tokyo; General MacArthur's office was on the fourth floor. George remained in Japan until early in 1946. The troopship on which he returned was bound for Seattle, but docked in Portland instead due to weather conditions farther north. On February 6, 1946, S/Sgt. George Toya received his honorable discharge at Fort Lewis. His "one-year" obligation had become a tour of five years, seven months and five days. He was among a number of Nisei soldiers who served in roles similar to his in the Pacific Theater during World War II. After receiving his discharge, he promptly took a bus to Ontario, Oregon, to join his wife, Sonoya (see Kaguma Toya, this volume).

George Toya's brother, Fred Toya, also served in the U.S. Army during World War II. He was sent to Fort Meade, Maryland, for basic training. Upon completion of basic, he was assigned to Fort Snelling in Minnesota. He may well have followed George's path if the war had not ended before he had completed training. Upon learning that his aging parents were having difficulties after returning to the farm in Powell Valley, Fred Toya applied for and received a hardship discharge to help his parents re-establish themselves on the farm. Thanks to a friend, Rudy Salquist, who took care of the farm during the war, the Toya family had been able to return to their Gresham home.

Fred Toya

Left, Fred Toya, at the Nyssa labor camp, 1942; right, Fred Toya (left) stationed at Fort Snelling, visits a friend, Joe Onichi, who was being treated for wounds at the nearby Vaughn General Hospital (Illinois). Photo courtesy of Joe Onchi.

Nisei "Gold Star" Veterans

Thomas Tamotsu Kuge

On January 22, 1943, government authorities announced that draft-age Nisei men would henceforth be subject to the Selective Service Act. Consequently, Thomas Tamotsu Kuge, imprisoned with his family at Camp Minidoka in Idaho, soon received his notice to report for induction. He reported to Fort Douglas, Utah, passed his physical examination and became a recruit in the United States Army. The Army sent him to Fort Blanding, Florida, for basic training. After completing basic, he underwent a period of advanced infantry training.

Grave, Pvt. Thomas Kuge

Killed in action April 22, 1945, Pvt. Thomas Kuge was interred in this U.S. military cemetery at Castel Florentino, Italy. His brother, Lieutenant Toshi Kuge, medical detachment, 442nd visited his brother's grave and took this photograph
.Photo courtesy of his nephew, Tom Kuge.

The 442nd Regimental Combat Team had suffered the loss of about one-half its infantry soldiers, killed or wounded in the Battle of Bruyeres in Northwest France. Its infantry battalions sorely needed replacements to bring the unit back to fighting strength. Because a large contingent of Nisei soldiers trained at Fort Blanding, the Army relied upon this cadre to fill the ranks. Thus, the Army soon had Pvt. Thomas Kuge on his way by train to a port of embarkation.

Kuge arrived in LeHavre, France in December, 1944. The Army transported the replacements by truck and train to Nice, France. There, they joined the 442nd, which had been relieved after the engagements in the Vosges Forest. The Army assigned Pvt. Kuge to K Company, 3rd Battalion, which had experienced the loss of about 90% of its infantry strength, killed or wounded, in the battle. The replacements immediately started undergoing squad and unit training.

In March, 1944, landing craft took the 442nd to Italy, where it rejoined the

Fifth Army under General Mark Clark. Training continued for about two weeks to help prepare the replacements for what was to come. On April 5, 1944, Pvt. Kuge went into Combat with the 3rd Battalion, which took the right flank in the effort to reduce German defensive positions on Mount Folgorita and Mount Cerretta. The attack successfully broke through the German defenses, though K Company suffered heavy casualties when subjected to a mortar barrage. On the advance north toward Carrara, the 3rd Battalion took the left flank and occupied Montignoso, which opened the highway to Massa. In the attack toward the Frigido River, K Company acquitted itself well, capturing much equipment and about 50 prisoners. While L Company occupied Carrara, K Company bypassed the city and advanced into the mountains north of the town. On August 16, the unit broke the line at Mount Tomaggiora. On April 22nd, K Company launched an attack on Tendola, which led to an engagement that lasted all that day. In this firefight, Pvt. Thomas Kuge was killed in action. The following day, the German defenders pulled out, starting a retreat that ended when the German Commander surrendered on May 2, 1945. The war in Italy ended just 10 days after Pvt. Thomas Kuge died in combat (see "Gisaburo Kuge," this volume).

Minidoka Relocation Center Honor Roll

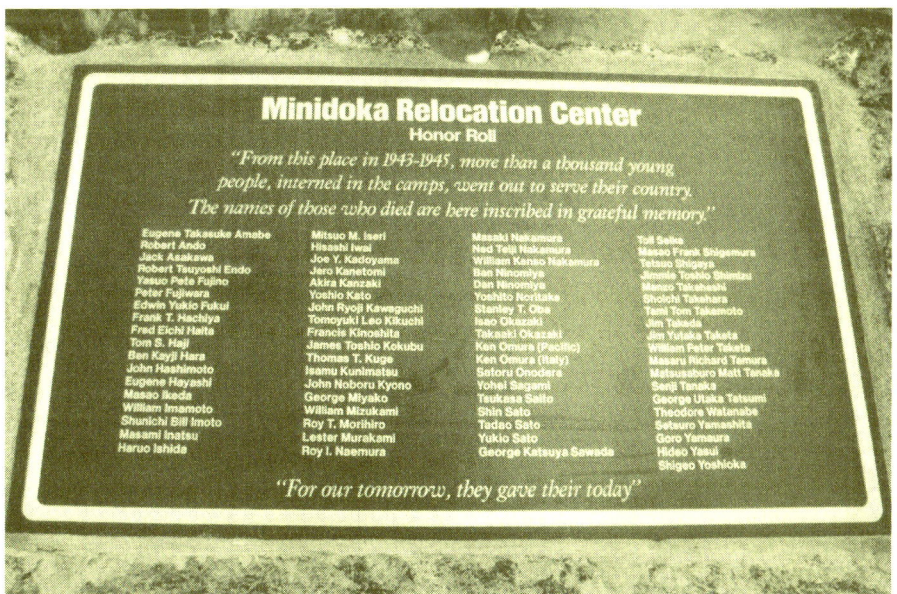

The inscription reads: "From this place in 1943-45, more than a thousand young people, interned in the camps, went out to serve their country. The names of those who died are here inscribed in grateful memory...For our tomorrow, they gave their today."

Photo courtesy of James Toyooka.

Roy Tatsuo Morihiro

Roy Tatsuo Morihiro, the eldest son of Fudesuke and Ayako Morihiro, was born in Independence, Oregon. His family had settled on a farm in Troutdale, which is where they resided when the attack at Pearl Harbor occurred. Roy had completed two years at the University of Washington prior to the "evacuation." The Western Defense Command ordered Nikkei families in the Troutdale area to report to the Pacific International Exposition Center in Portland. After spending the summer months of 1942 at the center, the War Relocation Authority sent most of the internees, including the Morihiro family, to the Minidoka Relocation Center, Idaho. Because of Roy Morihiro's reputation as a model airplane hobbyist and designer, he left the camp to take advantage of an opportunity to work for the Cleveland Model Airplane Company in Cleveland, Ohio.

Morihiro remained with the company until he enlisted in the Army. After completing basic training, he was sent overseas when the situation on the western front looked perilous with the German attack in Northwest France that became known as the Battle of the Bulge. The 442nd command assigned Roy Morihiro to G Company, 2nd Battalion, as a Browning Automatic Rifle (BAR) man.

Pfc. Roy Morihiro, U.S. Army

Roy Morihiro, together with his family, lived in Troutdale before the outbreak of Worl War II. On April 14, 1945, he was killed in action in Italy.
Photo courtesy of Frances Toyooka.

Unfortunately, as mentioned earlier (see "Joe Masayuki Onchi, Nisei Veterans," this volume), German snipers often targeted BAR infantrymen because of the firepower they brought to bear in a firefight. On April 14, 1945, Roy Morihiro died in action as a result of a sniper bullet near the town of Castelpoggio, Italy, during an engagement in which G Company and other elements of the 442nd RCT attacked Fort Bastione, a German held stronghold in the Apennine Mountains of northern Italy. While Roy Morihiro fought in Italy, his family remained in the Minidoka Relocation Center, Idaho, as internees.

A grateful nation awarded Pfc. Roy Morihiro the Bronze Star, the Purple Heart, the Combat Infantryman Badge and the Distinguished Unit Badge. He is interred at the Arlington National Cemetery, Virginia.

Roy Naemura

Roy Naemura, son of Sakaju and Seki Naemura, formerly of Fairview, Oregon, received his draft notice after graduating from Nyssa High School, Nyssa, Oregon, during the summer of 1944. He reported to Fort Douglas, Salt Lake City, for induction. Because his family lost his service records in the Vanport flood, 1948, this account has depended upon those with whom he served to reconstruct his record of service. The draft took a former Hunt classmate, Richard Mishima, at about the same time. Since the Army sent Mishima to Camp Blanding, Florida, for basic training, that is likely the post to which Naemura was sent.

The "Battle of the Bulge" caused nervous commanders to worry about the situation on the western front. A desperate call for reinforcements and replacements went forth, and those troops in basic or advanced infantry training were sorely needed. Consequently, the Army likely shortened Naemura's training regimen by sending him overseas early in 1945, similar to what happened to Mishima.

Once in France, the Army assigned Pvt. Naemura to B Company, 100th Battalion, 442nd Regimental Combat Team. At the time of his deployment, the RCT defended the border in the Maritime Alps, which separated France and Italy. Both the Allied and Axis armies maintained defensive positions, with no effort to dislodge the foe by either of the antagonists. However, artillery and other fire occurred daily. In order to help the replacements become an integral part of the company, small unit problems with squads and platoons took place on a sustained basis, both in France and when the RCT returned to Italy in March, 1945.

Roy Naemura U.S. Army

After graduating from Nyssa (Oregon) High School, Roy Naemura received notice to report to Fort Douglas, Utah, for induction. He was mortally wounded on April 14, 1945, during the Po Valley Campaign. Photo, Setsuko Okino.

Explorer Boy Scout Troop 635

Left to right, kneeling: Roy Seiler, Jay Chiodo, Roy Naemura and Chuck Butler. Standing: Gordon Schneider, Don Surface, Bob Davidson, Richard Barnes and Bill Stanley.
Photo courtesy of Richard Barnes.

On April 4, 1945, the RCT assembled near the town of Vallechio, Italy, preparatory to launching a surprise attack on German positions in the nearby mountains. That night, the 100th Battalion clambered up a steep slope, hoping to catch the German defenders by surprise. Precautions were taken to keep the movement undetected, for example, dog tags taped, no radio contact, no talking and other precautions. The 100th Battalion caught the defenders, many still asleep, in their foxholes and caves. Still, the battalion had to deal with an entrenched enemy. By April 6, the 100th had gained the crest of Mount Cerretta. The assault broke the western end of the Gothic Line, which had withstood nearly five months of repeated attacks by the Fifth Army. The Germans counter attacked, but the Americans held, securing an important objective for the drive northward. After intense fighting, the 442nd placed the 100th in reserve, near Altagnana.

On April 11, the 100th Battalion marched over mountainous terrain to seize Colonnatta. In the advance toward Ortonovo, the 1st Battalion of the defending 361st Panzer Grenadier Regiment ambushed leading elements of B Company. For his heroic actions in the ensuing skirmish, the Army posthumously awarded Pvt. Roy Naemura the Silver Star. Severely wounded on April 14th, he died of his injuries on April 15, 1945 (see "Sakaju Naemura, Seki (Katayama) Naemura," this volume).

Shin Sato

Shin Sato, son of Yoshinosuke and Asano Sato of Beaverton, Oregon, received his draft notice shortly after the bombing of Pearl Harbor on December 7, 1941. He had starred in football at Beaverton High School, from which he graduated in 1938. He attended Pacific University in Forest Grove, Oregon, where he also played football. Inducted at Fort Lewis, the Army sent Sato to Camp Roberts, California for basic training. When the government changed the classification to its Nisei soldiers to 4-C, the command at Camp Roberts sent Sato to Camp Riley, Kansas. He was also stationed at Camp Hale, Colorado before a transfer took him to Camp Shelby, Mississippi. At Shelby, the 442nd Regimental Combat Team (RCT) assigned him to G Company, a heavy weapons company. When a contigent left Shelby for Fort McClellan, Alabama, for advanced infantry training, Sato was among them.

Pvt. Shin Sato, U.S. Army

Pvt. Shin Sato was killed in action on November 1, 1944, after the 442nd had reached the "Lost [Texas] Battalion."   *Photo, Teru Sato.*

In August, 1944, the Army sent Shin Sato and other Nisei replacements to Newport News, Virginia, for deployment overseas. In September, 1944, their troopship landed in Naples, Italy, where Sato rejoined the 442nd RCT. From Naples, a British troop transport took the replacements to Marseille, France. Upon his arrival in Marseille, Shin Sato was assigned to E Company, 2nd Battalion as a machine gunner (light). After a couple of days in Marseille, the replacements boarded a train headed north to Epinal, France, where they were to assemble, having been attached to the 36th Division, Seventh Army. During the train ride north, Sato saw the devastation American fighters had caused to retreating German armies. Destroyed tanks, disabled equipment and dead horses lined the route, victims of U.S. strafing attacks.

The Sato Family

Pvt. Sato joined E Company in mid-October, 1944, about the time the 442nd launched an assault on the road center of Bruyeres, France, in the mountainous, forest-covered region known as the Vosges Forest. The 2nd Battalion's objective was Hill "B," north of Bruyeres. Fierce fighting engaged all elements of the RCT in the next several days. On October 26, General John E. Dalquist ordered the 442nd to join in the effort to rescue to 1st Battalion, 141st Infantry, which had advanced beyond its support. Four days later, an I Company patrol reached the besieged troops and, shortly, a B Company platoon. On October 31, the 442nd had established defensive positions in the area. Pvt. Shin Sata was killed in action on November 1, 1944, after the RCT had completed the rescue of the "Lost Battalion." During this engagement, the 442nd RCT suffered more than 800 casualties. Pvt. Shin Sato received the Purple Heart and the Combat Infantry Badge.

Pvt. Shin Sato's brother, Roy Sato, though younger, had been with M Company (heavy infantry weapons), 3rd Battalion, since the 442nd RCT first arrived in Italy. Pfc. Roy Sato received the Purple Heart and the Combat Infantry Badge.

Upper left: Pfc Roy Sato served in Company M, 3rd Battalion, 442nd RCT. Middle left: From left, Asano, Shin, Marie and Lois Sato. Bottom left: Yoshinosuke, Lois and Asano Sato.

Photos courtesy of Teru Shin.

Other Nisei Soldiers Killed In Action

Tom Tami Takemoto worked at a store in Portland, Oregon before he was drafted. Originally from Clatskanie, Oregon, his family had settled in Troutdale, Oregon before the war. He was inducted into the Army in February, 1942. In May, 1942, the Western Defense Command ordered his family to report to the Portland Assembly Center to be interned. Later, the WRA moved the family to the Minidoka Relocation Center, Idaho. 1st/Sgt.Tom Takemoto was among the first volunteers to serve with the 442nd RCT. He arrived in Naples with the first contigent of the regiment on May 29, 1944. The 100th Battalion became part of the 442nd RCT, and training commenced. The 442nd RCT moved into the line on June 26. 1st/Sgt. Tom Takemoto, K Company, was killed in action on June 27, 1944, the second day after the RCT was committed. He received the Purple Heart and the Combat Infantry Badge. Tom Takemoto is interred at Lincoln Memorial Park, Portland, Oregon.

George T. Yamaguchi of Portland, Oregon, had graduated from the University of Washington before the Western Defense Command caused he and his family to be interned at the Portland Assembly Center in May 1942. Later, the family moved to the Minidoka Relocation Center, Hunt, Idaho. In 1944, Yamaguchi was drafted into the Army. Because of his proficiency in the Japanese language, the Army sent him to the Japanese language school at Fort Snelling, Minnesota. In June, 1945, the Military Intelligence Service sent T/4 Yamaguchi to the Pacific Theater. George Yamaguchi was killed in the crash of an Army transport plane taking off of an airfield on Okinawa on August 13th, shortly before the war ended. George Yamaguchi is interred at Arlington National Cemetery, Virginia.

Nisei Soldiers Killed in the Line of Duty

Tsukasa Saito was inducted into the U.S. Army during January, 1942. He was in the service when The Western Defense Command ordered his family to report to the Portland Assembly Center on May 12, 1942. In September, the WRA moved his family by train to the Minidoka Relocation Center near Twin Falls, Idaho. During his training at Fort Snelling, Minnesota, T/5 Saito lived in a tent heated by a coal-fired heater. Apparently the heater was not properly ventilated, and Saito succumbed to carbon monoxide poisoning on February 4, 1945.

Sources

Crost, Lyn, *Honor by Fire*, Presideo Press, Novato, CA., 1994.

Duus, Masayo Umezawa, *Unlikely Liberators, The Men of the 100th and 442nd*, University of Hawaii Press, Honolulu, Hawaii, 1987.

Girdner, Audrie and Loftis, Anne, *The Great Betrayal*, The MacMillan Company, New York City, New York, 1972.

Hosokawa, Bill, *Nisei, The Quiet Americans*, William Morrow and Company, Inc., New York City, New York, 1969.

Northwest Association, MIS Newsletter, "American Courage Award Presented to WWII Army Military Intelligence Service," Seattle, WA., October 9, 2004.

Ibid, "Richard Sakakida, CIC Special Agent, Rescues 500 Filipinos Held Prisoner by Japanese," *Spy Catchers of the U.S. Army in the War with Japan*, Seattle, WA.

Onishi, Ryoko, "A Nisei Woman and Women's Army Corps," Nikkei Monthly Magazine, Los Angeles, October 2004, November 2004, December, 2004.

Shirey, Orville C., Americans, *The Story of the 442nd Combat Team*, Washington Infantry Journal Press, December, 1946.

Yamashita, Jim, Data regarding Nisei killed in action, World War II, Americans of Japanese Ancestry, WWII Memorial Alliance, LaHabra California, not published.

Various, *Fire For Effect, A Unit History of the 522 Field Artillery Battalion*, Fisher Printing Company, Inc., Honolulu, Hawaii, 1998.

Various, *Minidoka Interlude*, published by residents of the Minidoka Relocation Center, 1944.

Western Defense Command, *Japanese Evacuation From The West Coast*, 1942 (Report). United States Government Printing Office, Washington, D.C., 1943.

Special Note

About the same time that the men of the 36th 'Texas' Division declared all members of the 442nd Regimental Combat Team (RCT) "Honorary Texans" after soldiers of the RCT rescued the remnants of its 141st Regiment (the famed "Lost Battalion" of World War II), the Hood River American Legion Post removed all names of Nisei service men from its posted honor roll. In East Multnomah County, the roll of service men and women maintained by a local church excluded the names of service men of Japanese ancestry. The author discovered this fact when writing a history of East County men and women who served during World Wars I and II. These deletions and omissions together with the personal accounts of Leke Nakashimada, Lily (Sakurai) Kajiwara and Shio Uyetake led the author to complete this account.

Index

Symbols

141st Infantry 188
   3rd Battalion, the "Lost Battalion" 188
19th Armored Infantry Division 178
34th 'Red Bull' Division 143, 183, 202202
   100th Battalion 141
36th Division 188
3rd Army 146, 194
   71st Division
      14th Infantry 223
442nd Regimental Combat Team
   143, 159, 188, 190, 199, 220
   100th Battalion 159, 160
      B Company 231
   1st Infantry Battalion 159
   206th Army Band 159
   232nd Combat Engineer Company 159
   232nd Engineering Company 159
   2nd Infantry Battalion 159
   3rd Infantry Battalion 159, 199, 208
      I Company 172
      L Company 199, 208
   552nd Field Artillery Battalion 159
442nd Regimental Combat Team, Insignia 143
5th (Fifth) Army 189, 199, 209
   34th 'Red Bull' Division
      442nd Regimental Combat Team 182
   92nd Division 178, 189, 199
      442nd Regimental Combat Team 178, 183, 199
7th (Seventh) Army 161
   36th Division 161

A

Adam, Given name unknown 111
Akiyama, Coach Tak 140
Althaus, A.C. 55
   Althaus, Lenore 55, 57
Althaus dairy farm 55
Amache Relocation Center, Colorado 126
Ando, Bob Minoru 144, 151
   Ando, Sakae (Fujii) 153
      Ando, Diane 153
      Ando, Roberta 139, 151, 152, 153, 154
      Ando, Sandi 153
Ando, Suematso 'Pops' 139
Ando, Suematsu 151
   Ando, Masaki (Yokote) 151

Ando, Bob 151
Ando, Denny 151
Ando, Frank 151
Ando, Mae 151
Ando, Tom 151
Aoki, Bob 140
Aono, PFC Yutaka 188
Aoyama, George 140
Arai, Mr. 10
Asai, Maria 97
Asai, Taro 99
   Asai, Maria (Namba) 99
      Asai, Janelle 99
      Asai, Kevin 99
      Asai, Marta 99
      Asai, Tara 99
Asakawa, Nogi 59
   Asakawa, Mary (Kinoshita) 59
      Asakawa, Julie 59
      Asakawa, Landon 59
      Asakawa, Maxine 59
Asakawa, Roy Iemon 55
   Asakawa, Kiku 55
      Asakawa, Ben 55, 62
      Asakawa, Jack 55, 144, 155, 156
      Asakawa, Katherine 55, 57
      Asakawa, Nogi 55
      Asakawa, Toyoko 'Toyo' 55
      Asakawa, Walter 55, 57, 62
Asakawa, Walter
   Asakawa, Carol (Murahashi) 55, 60, 62, 82
      Asakawa, Linda 62
      Asakawa, Peggy 62
      Asakawa, Scott 62
      Asakawa, Walter 'Butch' 62
Awakuni, Private Masao 143
Azumano, George 128

B

Barnes, Richard 232
Bass, Mr. Leslie (Principal) 57
Bates, Floyd 2
Bates, Harley 14
Bates, Rod 27
Battle of Bruyeres 161
Battle of the Po Valley 173
Bednar, Doug 111
Benfield, Francis 26
Berney, Gene 45
Berney, Louis 51
Bettendorf, Lorall 57

Bjornsted, Bill 111
Bjornsted, Bob 111
Bjornsted, Jim 111
Bjornsted, Ken 111
Blanc, Art 225
Boyd, Mr. 67
Brown, Meredyth 26
Burgoyne, Reverend Sherman 99, 100
Burkholder, Dean 27
Burlingame, Iris 65
Burnacci, Doris 57, 65
Burnacci, Edward 57, 65
Burness, Alfred 27
Burness, M. 27
Burnett, Ron 3
Butler, Chuck 232

C

Camp Joseph F. Robinson 207
Canzler, Alfred 27
Canzler, Henry 45
Capon, O. 26
Cereghino, Anna 57, 65
Chamberlain, Earnest 26
Chiodo, Jay 232
Clark, General Mark
   167, 173, 186, 189, 209
Clinton, President William 'Bill' 74, 75
Collins, Elaine 2
Cone, F. 27
Conforth Ranch 91
Corporal Miles Standish 208
Cunningham, Andrew 129
   Cunningham, Charlotte 64, 69, 129
      Cunningham, Charlotte 66
      Cunningham, Scott 57, 65, 66, 129

D

Dabney, Mr. 18
Dabney State Park 18
Dahlquist, General John E. 178, 196
Dahlquist, Major General John 177
Dahlquist, Major General John E. 144
Daichi Building, Tokyo 227
Damonte, Frank 28
Daty, Henry 119
   Daty, Lillian (Tamura) 119
      Daty, Michael 119
Davidson, Bob 232
Davis, Estelle 26
Davis, Norah 50
Derrick, Bob 111
Deverell, Hazel 27

Deverell, Shirley 27
DeWitt, Lieutenant General J.L. 121
Donald, Florence E. 95
Dorches, Glenn 65
Dorches, Guy 65
Dunlop, Vance
   Dunlop, Arlene (Uyetake) 53
   Dunlop, Beth 54
   Dunlop, Tara 54

E

Eastside Farmers' Market 2
Ellis, Clifford 27
Ellis, L. 27
Emerson, Mr. Leslie M. 27
Empey, Mr. 97
Endicott, F. 27
Endo, Mr. and Mrs. 10
Espenel, Al 69
   Espenel, Anita 69
Espenel, Donald 57, 65
Espenel, Wayne 65
Evans, Lois 26
Exclusion Order, Western Defense Command 121
Executive Order No. 9066 121
Ezuka, T/4 Edmund 162

F

Faught, Lewis 26
Federal Bureau of Investigation
   visit from, Fujii farm, number 1 67
   visit from, Fujii farm, number 2 67
Fehrenbacher, George 26
Fehrenbacher, Jerome 27
Fehrenbacher, Mrs. Helen (teacher) 65
Fernandez, Fred 117
Filer Orchard 91
Fitzsimons, E.M. 137
Forsyth, Hap 111
Frommelt, Dorothy 27
Frommelt, Lucille 27
Fuji, S/Sgt. Abe M. 162
Fujii, Bukichi 63
   Fujii, Umi (Arima) 63
      Fujii, Toshio 63
      Fujii, Yoshino (Yamakado)
         63, 78, 129, 163
      Fujii, Akiye 63
      Fujii, Harumi 'Edward' 63, 157
      Fujii, Kazuo 'Kaz' 63, 159, 163
      Fujii, Kimiko 63
      Fujii, Kiyoshi 'Jack' 63, 157

Fujii, Mamoru 'James' 63, 65, 157
Fujii, Tadato 63, 69
Fujii, Tomio 'Thomas' 63
Fujii, Edward
   Fujii, Aya (Iwasaki) 66, 68
   Fujii, Becki 69
   Fujii, Scott 69
   Fujii, Tami 69
Fujii, James 'Jim' 158, 159
   Fujii, Suzie 'Jinx' 69
     Fujii, Cheryl 69, 158
     Fujii, Jill 69
     Fujii, Patty 69
     Fujii, Ray 69, 159
     Fujii, Ron 69
Fujii, Kazuo 'Kaz' vi, 139, 144, 169
   Fujii, May (Nakata) 68
   Fujii, Karen 68
   Fujii, Tim 68
Fujii Produce 69
Fujii, Raymond 159
Fujii, Tom 219
Fujii, Thomas Tomio 69
   Fujii, Mary (Nakata) 69
     Fujii, Gerald 69
     Fujii, Lisa 69
     Fujii, Mark 69
     Fujii, Shari 69
Fujimoto, Miyeko 111
Fujiwara, Roy 209, 210, 211
Fukuda, Mr. 50
Fukutomi, Bob 140
Furukawa, Micheye (Hara) 170
   Furakawa, Michael 170
   Furulawa. Katie 170
Furumasu, Bill
   Furumasu, Fujie (Uyetake) 54
     Furumasu, Russell 54
     Furumasu, Stacey 54
Furukawa, Matt 219

G

Gandy, Clarence 57, 65
General MacArthur's Headquarters 226
German, Marion 58
Giancone, Billy 57, 65
Giese, Grace 76
Gifford, Doris 113
Gifford, Jack 113
Gifford, Verda 113
Gilstrap, Beulah 57
Groce, Art 4

H

Hamada, Noburo 16
   Hamada, Mary (Matsubu) 12, 13, 14, 15, 16
Hara, Eichiro 165, 169
   Hara, Hamano 165
   Hara, Carrie 165
   Hara, Dorothy 165
   Hara, Fumi 165
   Hara, George 165
   Hara, Jean 165
   Hara, Kimi 165
   Hara, Mary 165
   Hara, Menow 165
   Hara, Micheye 165
Hara, Kazuko (Endo) 126, 165, 166, 168, 170
Hara, Menow M. 144, 165, 169, 213
   Hara, Kazuko (Endo) 169
Hara, Pfc. George 170
Harder, Ric
   Harder, Diane (Ando)
     Harder, Kaylin 154
     Harder, Mariko 154
     Harder, Robert 154
Hasegawa, Mr. and Mrs. 99
Hayashi, Jean 210
Hayashi, Sgt. Ralph 186
Hayashi, Tom 140
Herman, Babe 17
Herman Frasch 84
Heyamoto, Sjusie 140
Heyamoto, Toshi 140
Heyerdahl, T. 137
Higa, Pfc. Masahiro 186, 187
Higurashi, Mary 140
Hinatsu, Dan 97
Hinatsu, Kaz 213
Hinatsu, Masako 169
Hirago, Tom 9
Hodgson, Beatrice 26
Hoffmeister, Al 'Shorty' 111, 113, 219
Hoffmeister, Bob 111, 112
Hongo, George
   Hongo, Margaret (Nakashimada) 23
Honorary Texans - Special Note
   442nd made honorary Texans 236
Hope, Bob 213
Houseman, August 108
Hunt, Miss Ecco (Minidoka teacher) 138

I

Ikeda, Don 82
  Ikeda, Martha (Murahashi) 82
    Ikeda, Amy 82
    Ikeda, Karen 82
    Ikeda, Lucy 82
    Ikeda, Robert 82
Imhoff, Eddie 111
Inamine, Edward
  Inamine, Mabel (Matsubu) 16
Inouye, 1st Lt. Daniel K. (also U.S. Senator) 164
Inouye, Josephine 76
Internment Centers 124
Inukai, Kazuo 99
  Inukai, Ishino 99
    Inukai, Richard 99
    Inukai, Shige 'Ruth' 99
    Inukai, Takako 99
Ishi, Mr. 10
Ishida, Eichi
  Ishida, Rosemary (Nakashimada) 21
Ishida, George 153
Ishida, Jack
  Ishida, Joyce (Matsubu) 16
    Ishida, Jason 16
    Ishida, Jennifer 16
Ishihara, Chickie 140
Itami, Charles 29
  Itami, Chieko (Okita) 29
Iwai, Atashi 178
Iwami, S. 137
Iwasaki, Akira 'Ike' 144, 176
  Iwasaki, Mary (Furusho) 180
    Iwasaki, Ellen 180
    Iwasaki, Rich 180
    Iwasaki, Roger 180
Iwasaki, Arthur 'Art'
    144, 165, 171, 174, 175
  Iwasaki, Teri (Yumibe) 174, 175
    Iwasaki, Christi 174, 175
    Iwasaki, Leslie 174, 175
    Iwasaki, Paul 174, 175
    Iwasaki, Robert 174, 175
    Iwasaki, Stephanie 174, 175
Iwasaki, Billy Yasukichi 171
  Iwasaki, Ito (Baba)
    Iwasaki, Akira 171
    Iwasaki, Aya 171
    Iwasaki, Dorothy 171
    Iwasaki, George 171
    Iwasaki, Kate 171
    Iwasaki, Rose 171
    Iwasaki, Taka 171

J

Jackson, Frank 27
Jackson, Walter 26
Japanese School 50
Japanese 'Z Plan.' 150
Johnson, M. 137
Johnson, Margaret 27
Joquith, Frank 9

K

Kagawa, Tsuneki 26
  Kagawa. Kinu (Okita) 26
    Kagawa, John 26
    Kagawa, Mabel 26
Kajiwara, George 143, 144, 145
Kajiwara, Lily (Sakurai) 128
Kajiwara, Pfc. George 33
Kamata, Ruth 140
Kasubuchi, Ben 27
  Kasubuchi, Mary (Okita) 27
    Kasubuchi, Alan 29
    Kasubuchi, Ben 27
    Kasubuchi, Dennis 29
Kato, Jack 219
Kato, Joe 219
Kato, Kazuo 111
Kazuko Hara 170
Keeton, Mildred 27
Kendall, Albert D. 18
Kerslake, Fred 2
Kerslake, Grace 3
Kido, Edward 57
Kido, Tom 57
Kikkawa, Emik 97
Kikkawa, Kazuo 94
  Kikkawa, Emiko (Namba) 94
    Kikkawa, Elaine 99
    Kikkawa, Gail 99
    Kikkawa, Joyce 99
    Kikkawa, Marcia 99
Kimura, Hisa 140
Kimura, Yutako 140
King, Shirley 57
Kinoshita, April 181, 182
Kinoshita, Charles 140
Kinoshita, Frank 103, 104
Kinoshita, Kazuo 181
Kinoshita, Mary 181
Kinoshita, Mas 181
Kinoshita, Mrs. 103
Kinoshita, Tom 103
Kinoshita, Yoshio 'Yosh' 144, 181

Kinoshita, Masako 'April' 183
   Kinoshita, Nadine 183
   Kinoshita, Ted 183
Kirkham, Marion 222
Kirkham, Virgil 222
Kishiyama, William 178
Kleinkopf, E. 137
Klinski, Ed 39
Knarr, Jean 57, 65
Knieriem, Eva 50
Knieriem, Goldie 26
Kobayashi, Lily 140
Kokubu, Jimmie 165
Kondo, Henry
   Kondo, Alice (Adachi) 6
Kondo, John 150
   Kondo, Nori (Kido) 6
Kondo, Oscar
   Kondo, Lois (Itano) 6
Kondo, Roy
   Kondo, Dorinne 5
   Kondo, Jeffrey 5
   Kondo, Midori (Tamiyasu) 5
Kondo, Roy Ken 1
   Kondo, June (Takashima) 1
     Kondo, Helen 4
     Kondo, Henry 2
     Kondo, John 2
     Kondo, Mary 1
     Kondo, Oscar 2
     Kondo, Roy 1
Konishita, Kazuo 183
Kubo, Sgt. Hoichi 148
Kuga, Jim 140
Kuge, Gisaburo 7
   Kuge, Takaye 7
     Kuge, Chosei 7
     Kuge, Kingo 7
     Kuge, Kiyoko 7
     Kuge, Mitsuru 'Henry' 7
     Kuge, Seiji 7
     Kuge, Tom Tamotsu 7, 144, 185, 228
     Kuge, Toshiaki 'Toshi' 7, 9, 144, 183, 184
     Kuge, Yutaka 7
Kuge, Sgt. Toshi 186
Kuge, Tom
   9, 10, 183, 185, 186, 187, 229
Kuge, Yutaka 9
   Kuge, Addie (Shinozaki) 9
Kumazawa, Frances 124, 150, 214, 215
Kumazawa, George 76
Kumazawa, Grace 150, 214

Kumazawa, Joe 76, 214
Kuroki, Sgt. Ben 146, 147
Kuwabara, Joe 53
Kuwabara, Yoshiko 53

L

Lambert, R. 137
Larson, Jeanne 26
Larson, Mildred 26
Larson, Robert 'Bob' 36, 37
Larson, Robert 'Tood' 20, 128
Lee, Ronald 57
Lessert, Sandi (Ando)
   Lessert, James 154
Lestiko, David 113
Lewis, Esther 57
Libby McNeil and Libby 3
Lost Battalion 172, 178, 185
Lovell, Neil 57
Lucas, Clarence W. 2
Lusby, Mr. George 30

M

MacArthur, General Douglas 149
   Military Governor of Japan 226
Madigan Medical Hospital, Washington 211
Marshall, General George C.
   Chairman, Joint Chiefs of Staff 184
Martin, Quay 36, 37
Martin, Virginia 57
Masuda, Sgt. Minoru 186
Masumoto, Gladys 76
Matsubu, Henry 'Hank' 16, 140
   Matsubu, Edna (Hirabayashi) 16
     Matsubu, Jody 16
     Matsubu, Kiyoko 16
Matsubu, John 16
   Matsubu, Mary (Brunnette) 16
     Matsubu, Kiyomi 16
     Matsubu, Paul 16
Matsubu, Shigehachi 11
   Matsubu, Yone 'Mama san' 11, 12
     Matsubu, Asako 12
     Matsubu, Tetsuo 12
     Matsubu, Tsurue 12
     Matsubu, Yoshiaki 12
Matsubu, Shigeko 11
   Matsubu, Kiyomi 11
     Matsubu, Akio 'Henry' 13, 16
     Matsubu, Ayako 'Mabel' 11, 13
     Matsubu, Hiroko 'Joyce' 16
     Matsubu, Hisashi 'Thomas' 13
     Matsubu, Mary Umeko 11
     Matsubu, Mitsuru 'John' 13

Matsubu, Thomas 16
   Matsubu, Helen (Takemoto) 16
     Matsubu, Benjamin 16
     Matsubu, Francine 16
     Matsubu, Jeff 16
     Matsubu, Kirk 16
     Matsubu, Tracey 16
Matsuda, Katie 140
Matsumoto, Felix 162
Matsumoto, PFC Cherry 188
Matsumoto, Roy 149
Matsushita, Ray 85
   Matsushita, Amy (Naemura) 85
   Matsushita, Carrie 85
   Matsushita, Lennie 85
Max and Hildy's Garden Store 174
McCleary family 39
McCloy, John J. 181
McConnell, Frank
   McConnell, Donna (Uyetake) 54
   McConnell, Mark 54
McGinnis, Shirley 57, 65
McKay, M.B. 46
McKercher, Gary 57
McLoughlin, Mr. 111
McLoughlin's Cannery 108
Merrill, Brigadier General Frank D. 146, 149
Merrill's Marauders 149
Mershon, Clarence 50
Mershon, George 50, 180
Mershon, George Jr. 6
Mershon, George 'Jum' 45, 50
Mershon, Laura Isabelle 50
Migaki, Mas 118
   Migaki, Yoneko (Tamura) 118
Military Intelligence Service (MIS) 141
Minidoka Relocation Center, Idaho 133, 134, 217
Mishima family 106
Mishima, Henry 79
   Mishima, Julia (Quan) 79
     Mishima, Henry Jr. 79
     Mishima, Kathy 79
     Mishima, Thomas 79
Mishima, Katumi 77
   Mishima, Sakae (Nagata) 77
     Mishima, Harry 77, 79
     Mishima, Henry 77
     Mishima, Richard 77
     Mishima, Yoshio 77

Mishima, Pvt Richard 188
Mishima, Richard 144, 188
   Mishima, Kumiko (Ike) 79
     Mishima, Eric 79
     Mishima, James 79
Mishima, Yoshio 79
   Mishima, Aster (Takao) 79
Mitsudo, Ray 140
Miyasaki, T/Sgt. Herbert 146
Mori, Mickey 22
Morihiro, Fudesuke 230
   Morihiro, Ayako 230
   Morihiro, Roy Tatsuo 230
Morihiro, Pfc. Roy Tatsuo 144, 230
Morton, A. 137
Munemori, PFC Sadao S. 189
   Medal of Honor awarded 189
Murahashi, Hikosaku 80
   Murahashi, Suga (Hayashi) 80
   Murahashi, Ichiki 80
   Murahashi, Misue 80
   Murahashi, Shizue 80
   Murahashi, Sueki 80
   Murahashi, Toyoki 80
Murahashi, Ichiki 80
   Murahashi, Ayako (Hayashi) 80
   Murahashi, Carol 80
   Murahashi, Hikoki 80
   Murahashi, Martha 80
   Murahashi, Miyoko 80
Murahashi, Toyoki 81
   Murahashi, Kazue (Yokote) 81
   Murahashi, Larry 81
   Murahashi, Oscar 81
   Murahashi, Roy 81
Murakami, B 137
Murakami, John 219
Murakami, M. 137
Muramatsu, George 219
Murata, Raymond 203

N

Naemura, Dr. Joe 119
   Naemura, Miyeko (Tamura) 119
     Naemura, Jeanine 120
     Naemura, Joseph 120
     Naemura, Lori 120
     Naemura, Tracey 120
     Naemura, William 120
Naemura, Helen Seki 88
Naemura, Pfc. Roy 231
Naemura, Sakaju 83, 231

Naemura, Seki (Katayama) 83, 231
   Naemura, Emiko 'Amy' 83
   Naemura, Roy 83, 144, 232, 232
   Naemura, Setsuko 83
   Naemura, Shigeru 'Joe' 83
Naemura, Shigeru 'Joe'
   Naemura, Miyeko (Tamura) 84
   Naemura, David 85
   Naemura, Ted 85
Nagasaki, Japan, bombing of 82
Nagasawa, Kazue 203
Naismyth, Walter 65
Nakahara, Sab 140
Nakahara, Tom 187
Nakamura, Seiichi 64
   Nakamura, Akiye (Fujii) 64
   Nakamura, Alan 68
   Nakamura, Dennis 68
   Nakamura, Hisae 68
   Nakamura, Richard 68
   Nakamura, Vicki 68
Nakashimada, Leke
   128, 142, 144, 190, 192, 193, 203
   Nakashimada, Mary (Hirata) 21
   Nakashimada, Debbie 21
   Nakashimada, Diane 21
   Nakashimada, John 21
   Nakashimada, Lisa 21
Nakashimada, Sgt. Leke 142
Nakashimada, Takey 146, 192, 222
   Nakashimada, Mavis (Jacobson) 23, 194
   Nakashimada, David 194
   Nakashimada, Tammy 194
Nakashimada, Tatsuzo 18
   Nakashimada, Kisano (Seki) 18
   Nakashimada, Betty 18, 203
   Nakashimada, Elsie 18
   Nakashimada, George 18
   Nakashimada, Leke 18
   Nakashimada, Margaret 18
   Nakashimada, Mary 18
   Nakashimada, Rosemary 18
   Nakashimada, Shigeo 18
   Nakashimada, Takey 18
   Nakashimada, Thomas 18
Nakata, Albert "Al" 92
   Nakata, May (Fujita) 92
   Nakata, Gail 92
   Nakata, Nancy 92
Nakata, Frank 92
   Nakata, Ruth (Watanabe) 92
   Nakata, David 92
   Nakata, Janyce 92

   Nakata, Julie 92
Nakata, Harry 92
   Nakata, Kyoko (Kamada) 92
   Nakata, Dennis 92
   Nakata, Steven 92
Nakata, Joe Josuke 89, 122, 139
   Nakata, Tsutano (Kato) 89, 139
   Nakata, Albert Takeshi 89
   Nakata, Alfred Yutaka 89
   Nakata, Frank Wataru 89
   Nakata, Harry Akira 89
Nakata, Mr. 50
Nakata, Thomas
   Nakata, Elsie (Nakashimada) 21
Namba, Aki 140
Namba, Akio 'Art' 101
   Namba, Jan 101
   Namba, Randy 101
Namba et al v. McCourt and Neuner 96
Namba, Etsuo 93, 99
   Namba, Shizuno (Nakayama) 93
   Namba, Akio 'Art' 93
   Namba, Emiko 93
   Namba, Kenji 'Kennie' 93
   Namba, Maria 93
   Namba, Tomomi 'Tom' 93
Namba, Kennie Kenji 99, 144, 195
   Namba, Shige 'Ruth' (Inukai) 100
   Namba, Diane 101
   Namba, Teresa 101
Namba, Maria 99
Namba, Teresa 101
   Namba, Kaeti 101
Namba, Tom Tomomi 99, 144, 195
   Namba, May (Date) 99
   Namba, Dean 99
   Namba, Gary 99
   Namba, Jimmy 99
   Namba, Larry 99
   Namba, Ralph 99
Nazaki, John 97
Niiya, Sumi 140
Nishimura, Betty (Hiuga)
   200, 201, 202, 203
Nishimura, George 199, 203
   Nishimura, Betty (Hiuga) 150, 204
   Nishimura, Jerry 204
Nishimura, Matsutaro 199
   Nishimura, Kijyu 202
   Nishimura, Haruko 199
   Nishimura, Kiku 199
   Nishimura, Richard 'Dick' 199
   Nishimura, Tatsuko 199

Nishino, Bob 97
Nispel, I. 137
Northway, Mary 27

O

Obata, Hajime 191
Ochiai, N. 137
Oda, Toshio 85
    Oda, Amy (Naemura) 85
    Oda, Keith 85
O'Dell, Melvin 57
Ogawa, Kiyo
    Ogawa, June (Uyetake) 54
    Ogawa, Steve 54
Oja, Mike 119
    Oja, Pamela (Tamura) 119, 120
    Oja, Teresa 119
    Oja, Valerie 119
Oka, Terumasa 140
Okada, Tosh
    Okada, Mitzi (Uyetake) 54
    Okada, Dale 54
    Okada, Kerrie 54
Okai, Thomas 6
    Okai, Helen (Kondo) 6
Okamoto, Tarao 179
Okazaki, Mino 97
Okino Farm, Gresham 87
Okino, Toshio 'Tosh' 85, 139
    Okino, Setsuko (Naemura) 85, 231
    Okino, Eugene 88
    Okino, Gary 86
    Okino, Karen 88
    Okino, Richard 86
Okita, Frank Morio 26, 28, 144, 205
    Okita, Mary (Tashima) 27, 28, 29, 159, 205, 206
    Okita, Cheryl 29
    Okita, Gayle 29
Okita, George 26, 205
    Okita, Chiyo (Okita) 27
    Okita, Bette Ann 27, 28
    Okita, Carolyn 27, 28
    Okita, Marion 27, 28
Okita, James
    Okita, Paul 26
Okita, Mary 27
Okita, Mary (Tashima) 29, 159, 206
Okita, Morey 213
Okita, Morio 'Frank'
    Okita, Mary (Tashima) 27, 206
    Okita, Cheryl 29
    Okita, Gayle 29
Okita, Shintaro
    Okita, Tatsu 25
    Okita, Chieko 25
    Okita, George 25
    Okita, James 25
    Okita, Kinu 25
    Okita, Mary 25
    Okita, Morio 'Frank' 25
    Okita, Todd 25
    Okita, Yoshito 25
Okita, Ted 140
Okita, Todd 29, 146
    Okita, Dorothy (Kaihara) 29
Okita, Yoshito 29
    Okita, Ann Margaret 29
    Okita, Richard 29
Olson, Mariam 111
Omoki, 1st/Sgt. 144
Onchi, George 104, 105, 212
    Onchi, Sachi (Mishimo) 104, 105, 212
    Onchi, Georgene 106
    Onchi, Mary Ann 105, 212
    Onchi, Norene 106
    Onchi, Raymond 105, 212
    Onchi, Ronald 106
    Onchi, Vicki 106
Onchi, Hidekichi 102
Onchi, Ikisaburo 102
Onchi, Ikisaburo
    Onchi, Mizu (Takeshita) 102
    Onchi, George Shigeru 102
    Onchi, Jim Sadaki 102
    Onchi, Joe Masayuki 102
    Onchi, Mitsue 102
Onchi, Jim Sadaki 107, 146, 205, 212, 213
    Onchi, Fumi Yumibe 107
    Onchi, Curtis 107
    Onchi, Dwight 107
    Onchi, Gary 107
    Onchi, Harvey 107
    Onchi, Kelvin 107
Onchi, Joe Masayuki 107, 144, 212, 213, 227
    Onchi, Toby (Ninomiya) 107
    Onchi, Douglas 107
    Onchi, Gregory 107
    Onchi, Valerie 107
Onchi, Lt. Curtis 107
Onchi, Yukisaburo 207
    Onchi, Mizu (Takeshita) 207
Onishi, Don 114
    Onishi, Arie 'Addie' (Shiiki) 114

Onodera, Pfc. Masahiko 186
Ota, Frances 76
Ota, John 146
Ota, Sgt. John 215
Otsuka, Mr. 10
Owens, Dick 57
Owens, Fred 57
Owens, Jimmy 65

P

Pack, C. 27
Patton, General George 41, 146, 194
Peet, Azalia E. 76
Perot, Ross 48
Perry, George VI 35, 129
Peterson, Mary Jean (teacher) 111
Poor, Miss Sarah 26
Porter, Amos 45
Portland International Livestock Exposition Center 129
Powers, Mabel 57
Pulliam, Charles 26

Q

Queen Mary 213

R

Rathman, Stan 57, 65
Rathman, Vern 57, 65
Reed, Donald 26
Riggs, Bill 111
Riggs, Thurma 111
Rogers, Jesse 'Mike' 51
Rogers, Margaret 27
Rommel, General Erwin (Germany) 172
Roosevelt, Eleanor 124, 214
Roosevelt, President Franklin D. 121
Rose, Steve 113
Rose, Trey 113
Rosen, Miss Genevieve 43, 222

S

Saito, Akio 203
Saito, Eric 'Rick' 88
    Saito, Karen (Okino) 88
Saito, Tosh 140
Saito, Tsukasa 235
Sakakibara, Sho 140
Sakakida, Richard 149
Sakurai, Masaru 30, 136
    Sakurai, Chiyoko (Takeuchi) 30, 137

Sakurai, Betty 30, 129, 136
Sakurai, Edward 30, 137
Sakurai, George 15, 30, 137, 219
Sakurai, Judith 30, 137
Sakurai, Lily v, 15, 30, 137, 139
Sakurai, Richard 'Dick' 15, 30, 129, 136, 138
Salizar, Paul 91
Salquist, Rudy 227
Salthe, Robert 65
Sasaki, Mr. 10
Sasaki, Mr. T. 10
Sata, Lindy 140
Sato, Mr. 10
Sato, Roy 234
Sato, Pvt. Shin 165, 233
Sato, Teru 233
Sato, Yoshinosuke 233
    Sato, Asano 233, 234
        Sato, Lois 234
        Sato, Marie 234
        Sato, Roy 234
        Sato, Shin 234
Saverude, Mr. (Gresham HS Principal) 107
Saverude, Mr. (Principal, Gresham High) 64, 107
Schedeen, Poly 114
Schmidt, Frank 174
Schmidt, M. 137
Schneider, Ed 57
Schneider, Gordon 232
Schneider, Lawrence 57
Schneider, Marvin 57
Seiler, Roy 232
Shelley, Harold 2
Shelley, Vivienne 27
Shepperd, George 26
Sherman, Miss Maude 30
Shiiki, June 113
Shiiki, Sgt. Ray 148
Shiiki, Ray 114, 140
    Shiiki, Mary (Muramatsu) 114
        Shiiki, Gail 114
        Shiiki, Lon 114
        Shiiki, Rik 114
Shiiki, Roy Rikizo 108, 217
    Shiiki, Asa (Shiraishi) 108, 217
        Shiiki, Addie Arie 108
        Shiiki, Kisae 108, 218
        Shiiki, Ray 108, 217
        Shiiki, Sumie 108
        Shiiki, Tom Tan 108

Shiiki, Tom Tan 219
Shimoyama, Alice 150
Shimoyama, Mitori 150
Shimoyama, Neba 150
Shimoyama, Nellie 150
Shimoyama, Siego 150
Shin, Teru 234
Shinozaki, Mr. and Mrs. 10
Shiogi, Hiro 140
Shiogi, Hood 219
Shitara, Setsu 177
Sinner, Al 57
Smith, R. 137
Snell, Donald 65
Snell, Lloyd 65
Somekawa, Art 219
Southworth, Carl 76, 214
    Southworth, Mabel 74, 76, 214
Springdale Grade School 47
Stanley, Bill 232
sticker (planting cabbage) 4
Stimson, Henry L.
    Secretary of War 147
Stolin, Marie 26
Stolin, Walter 26
Strachan, Lillian Mrs. (teacher) 2, 4
Stull, C. 137
Sugimoto, Reverend 10
Sugiyama, Mary 76
Sumino, Roy 219
Sunderland, Jim 57
Surface, Don 232

T

Tada, Sgt. Seisaburo 197
Tadaki, Mr. 10
Takemoto, Tom Tami 235
Takenaga, Masami 97
Taketa, Jimmy 152
Takeuchi, Erika 41
Takeuchi, Hiro 37
    Takeuchi, Mary (Yabuki) 40
        Takeuchi, Jerry 40
        Takeuchi, Lynn 40
Takeuchi, Jared 41
Takeuchi, Masao
    Takeuchi, Masumi (Ninomura) 37
        Takeuchi, Donald 39, 40
        Takeuchi, Kathy 40
        Takeuchi, Mel 40
        Takeuchi, Nancy 40
        Takeuchi, Robert 40

Takeuchi, Sakajiro 36
    Takeuchi, Yaye (Sumihiro) 36
    Takeuchi, Hiro 36
    Takeuchi, Masao 36
    Takeuchi, Shigeru 36
    Takeuchi, Shiro 36
    Takeuchi, Tadashi 150
    Takeuchi, Tadashi 'Tad' 36
Takeuchi, Shigeru 144, 219, 220, 225
    Takeuchi, Lucy (Kubo) 41, 221
    Takeuchi, Brian 41
    Takeuchi, JoAnn 41
    Takeuchi, Keri 41
Takeuchi, Shiro 146, 219, 222
    Takeuchi, Misawo (Uyeoka) 43, 223
    Takeuchi, Margaret 'Peggy' 43, 223
    Takeuchi, Susan 43, 223
Takushi, Yasuhide 178
Tambara, George 97
Tamura farm 116
Tamura, George 115
    Tamura, Toyoko (Aoki) 115
    Tamura, Kazuma 'Kaz' 115
    Tamura, Lillian Yayoi 57, 115
    Tamura, Miyeko 115
    Tamura, Takashi 115
Tamura, Kazuma 'Kaz' 56, 117
    Tamura, Helen (Taniguchi) 118
    Tamura, Pamela 119
    Tamura, Paul 119
Tamura, Kuniji 115, 118
    Tamura, Mitsuru (Fujimura) 116, 118
        Tamura, Carol 116
        Tamura, Darlene 116
        Tamura, Richard 116
        Tamura, Terri 116
Tamura, Minekichi 115
    Tamura, Sute 115
        Tamura, George Genchiro 115
        Tamura, Kuniji 115
        Tamura, Mary Yoneko 115
        Tamura, Seiko 115
Tamura, Paul
    Tamura, Laura (Hada) 119
    Tamura, Kimberly 119
Tanaka, John 219
Taraka, Mara 9
Taylor, Jack 111
Timberlake, Colonel Edward 'Ted' 146
Toguchi, Pfc. Genzo 197
Tomori, Mr. and Mrs. 99
Tomura, Bill 203
Townsend, Bonnie 57

Toya, Fred 2, 150, 227
  Toya, Kimi (Tainaka) 49
    Toya, Daniel 49
    Toya, Rollin 49
Toya, George 150, 224
  Toya, Sonoya (Hirata) 47, 225
    Toya, Evelyn 47
    Toya, Georgene 47, 49
Toya, Kaguma 45, 224
  Toya, Yone (Ito) 45, 224
    Toya, Fred 45
    Toya, George 45, 224
    Toya, Josephine 45
Toyooka, Frances 230
Toyooka, James 229
Truman, President Harry 215
Tsnunemitsu, Joe 140
Tsuboi, Ted 219
Tsukayama, Cpl. Arthur 186
Tsutsai, Jim 168
Tule Lake Center 126

U

Uyeda, Charles 'Chuck' 48
  Uyeda, Josephine (Toya) 48
    Uyeda, Janice 48
    Uyeda, Jerry 48
    Uyeda, JoAnne 48
    Uyeda, John 48
    Uyeda. Sherri 48
Uyeno, Sgt. Theodore 162
Uyetake, Harry 14
Uyetake, Juichi 'Harry' 50
  Uyetake, Chise 50
    Uyetake, Fujie 50
    Uyetake, June 50
    Uyetake, Kor 50
    Uyetake, Mitzi 50
    Uyetake, Shio 50
Uyetake, Kor
  Uyetake, Mary (Hishinuma) 54
    Uyetake, John 54
    Uyetake, Sidney 54
  Uyetake, Lyle 54
    Uyetake, Sue (Ireland) 54
Uyetake, Shio v, 26, 52, 128, 139
  Uyetake, Nobuko (Mukai) 52
    Uyetake, Arlene 52
    Uyetake, Donna 52
    Uyetake, Lyle 52
    Uyetake, Vern 52

V

Vaughn Medical Hospital, Illinois 211

W

Wakabayashi, Fred
  Wakabayashi, Mary (Kondo) 5
Wakayama, Bill 219
Walker, Willy 57
Walrad, Les 104, 107
Wand, George 27
Wand, Ig 31, 39
War Relocation Authority 137
Welsick, Rocky 101
Welsick, Ross 101
  Welsick, Diane (Namba) 101
    Welsick, Bryana 101
    Welsick, Wesley 101
Wheadon, Pete 57
Wheatley, Lt. James 174
Williams, Emmett B. 55
Wilson, Bob 114
Wilson, Charles 27
Wilson, Ray 46
Winters, Elmer 27
Winters, Howard 21
Woodle, June 26
Woodle, Mabel 27
World War II Memorial 175

Y

Yada, Ko 219
Yaguchi, T/5 Kenji 163
Yamada, Dr. Roy 68
  Yamada, Kimiko (Fujii) 68
    Yamada, Randall 68
    Yamada, Rodney 68
    Yamada, Russell 68
Yamaguchi, George T. 235
Yamaguchi, Kaz 97
Yamamoto, Admiral Isoroku 150
Yamamoto, Pvt. Takeo 162
Yamamoto, Tetusaburo 58
  Yamamoto, Toyo (Asakawa) 58
    Yamamoto, Colleen 58
    Yamamoto, Janet 58
    Yamamoto, Marlene 58
    Yamamoto, Roy 58
    Yamamoto, Susan 58
Yamanaka, Pvt. Ben 186
Yamashita, Corporal George 60
  Yamashita, Katherine (Asakawa) 60

Yamashita, E. 137
Yamashita, George 60, 136
   Yamashita, Katherine (Asakawa) 60, 144
      Yamashita, Byron 61
      Yamashita, Diane 61
      Yamashita, Donna 61
      Yamashita, Perry 61
      Yamashita, Roger 61
      Yamashita, Wayne 61
Yamashita, Lauretta
   57, 58, 60, 136, 141, 154, 157
Yamihiro, Ben 66
Yoneyama, Tosh 104
Yoshimura, T/Sgt. Akiji 146
Yoshino, Leonard 179
Youngblood, Charles 3